With thanks to:
My Mother and Father (G. R. T. S.)
Brothers Irvine (G. R. H. S.) and Philip
My faithful staff, Beryl, Dot and Michael

Dedicated to:
My wife Anne

Children:
"Our" Lisa, Nathan, Simon and "Little" Lisa

Grandchildren:
Isaac (G. R. H.S.), Rafael, Samuel, Max, Harry and Louie

A least one third of the purchase price of this book will be donated to Tommy's the Baby Charity to carryout essential research into preventing still born babies, premature births and miscarriages.

And with thanks to David Barnes, Richard Abbey and RMC for their patience and guidance.

First published in the UK by RMC Books in 2013
Tel: 0114 250 6300
www.rmcbooks.co.uk

RMC Books is a division of the Regional Magazine Company Ltd
6 Broadfield Court, Broadfield Business Park, Sheffield, S8 0XF
www.regionalmagazine.co.uk

Edited by: Richard Abbey
Designed by: Richard Abbey & Steven Levers

Typeset in Bembo 12pt
Printed and bound in the UK by Buxton Press Ltd
Palace Road, Buxton, Derbyshire, SK17 6AE
www.buxtonpress.com

ISBN 978-1-907998-13-3

Contents

1

These things happen to me!

For more than 50 years I was a junk dealer. I suppose if I had lived in China this would have meant I sold boats; or in the United States, traded drugs. Here in the United Kingdom I bought and sold. Anything.

To say it is in my blood is an understatement. Both my parents and grandparents were also junk dealers. On many occasions I have told stories of my working experiences to friends who all said I should write a book. Now, at long last, here it is. And here are just a few anecdotes to whet your appetite.

One day in Sheffield Market, my first customer asked how much a Chesterfield three-piece suite was. I told the lady it was £175. She examined it and then enquired how she would get it home. I asked where she lived and she replied, "Halfway", a village near Sheffield. I explained we could deliver but there would be a charge of £10.

She was happy with this but said she had just finished her shopping and was on her way to catch the bus home and only had a fiver left. I suggested that she could leave this as a deposit and pay the rest on delivery. In fact, the boys could take her home right away with the suite and she could pay them.

She agreed and just as she was leaving said, 'by the way, do you mind if I pay you in fives?'

I said I didn't have a problem with that, and off they went. An hour and a half later the boys returned. I said, 'Any problems?'

'No,' was the reply.

'Where's the money then?'

'In the van,' the driver said.

'You mean to say you've left £180 in the van?'

'Yes.'

I quickly made my way to the van, cursing the boys as I went. The driver unlocked it and pointed to a pile of bags. One hundred and eighty pounds... all in five pence pieces!

Yes, things happen to me that just don't happen to others.

In the nineties we began to attend the Newark Antique Fair, the largest antique fair in Europe, I'm told. This meant arriving at Newark for 2pm on Sunday, waiting in a queue until the doors opened at 6pm, never getting to your actual pitch until after 6.30pm, and then erecting your tents and unloading two vans full of junk. We would arrive back in Sheffield around 10.30pm or later and have to be up again at 4am the next day to open for business at 6am. Not an easy life. The second day, Tuesday, was easier as the fair didn't open until 8am.

One Tuesday, Anne, my wife, decided to take our dog with us. As Anne and my brother Philip were much more capable than I of getting rid of the junk that was left, I thought I'd take him (the dog) for a walk around the perimeter of the fair. It took an hour, which gives you some idea how big the Newark showground is. On my return Philip said, 'Pleased you're back, how much are these paper bags?'

'Stop taking the Mickey, Philip,' I told him. 'We give them away with any small goods.' They were small Outspan brown paper bags.

'Look,' replied Philip. 'I've got a customer who's bought quite a bit of paper and he wants to know how much they are.' We referred to any postcards, comics or leaflets as 'paper.' In desperation I said, '50 pence each or three for a pound.'

Philip came back with £2. 'He's had six,' he said smiling. Laurence the Irishman became a regular customer from that day but he never bought any more paper bags. Philip did ask him at the next fair if he wanted any more and he replied in his very broad Irish accent, 'No, they don't sell very well.'

Yes, these things happen to me.

On another occasion at Newark all three of us were serving with quite a crowd around examining our junk when a lady asked, 'Why has this cup not got a handle?' There was silence until Anne replied, 'perhaps it's because it's a sugar basin.'

Yes, you meet all types as a junk dealer.

2

The first Patnick arrives in Sheffield

The road to Newark Antique Fair was long and eventful for me and my family, spanning several generations. It began in Eastern Europe in the late 19th century and involved economic hardship, persecution, bravery, tragedy, perseverance, luck, a little skulduggery, strange coincidences and damn hard work.

I was born at 745 Gleadless Road, Sheffield on the 19th June 1936, the fourth son of Bessie and Aaron Patnick. Later I discovered their first-born son, Norman, had died at the age of five having never walked or talked. This terrible tragedy probably changed my life and those of my parents and my two older brothers even though I wasn't born until some seven years after his death.

Mum and dad spoke little of their eldest son and really it was only after my father's death in 1979 that everything seemed to fit into place, but more on that subject later.

My father Aaron was born in Sheffield in October 1897, the day after Yom Kippur (the Day of Atonement). There followed 12 more children, nine of which survived. His father, Harry, was born in Estonia in 1877, and arrived in Sheffield in the 1880s.

Harry came with his father, Nathan La Patnick, to escape the Russian persecution of the Jewish people, as depicted in the stage musical and film *Fiddler on the Roof*. Thousands of Russian Jewish people arrived in England. Many of them were en-route to America, but this proved a journey too far for the majority: they ran out of money and settled here.

Nathan, my great grandfather, had acquired a job at a Sheffield synagogue as a Hebrew teacher. It was in North Church Street and was the first purpose-built synagogue in the city. They had advertised in a newspaper that was printed in Yiddish – a mix of many mid-European languages, plus Hebrew – and widely distributed among Jewish people throughout the Baltic States.

He replied to the ad and got the job. With it went a small house next to his work place where he lived until his death at the astonishing age of 111. He was a very religious, pious man. Mother always said he could foretell the future, and even cure illnesses with his prayers. Her actual words were 'he was a seer and healer.' I recently met a Rabbi from New York whose father was also a Rabbi (born in Sheffield) and apparently used that same expression as my mother.

My great grandfather's grave can be found at the Jewish cemetery at Walkley, Sheffield. Just before he died it was stated in the local newspaper that he was the oldest person in the country.

זקן המדינה
ה'ה הרבני המופלג אי"א באמת כש"ת
מוה"רר נחום לאפאטניק נ"י, בשעפפיעלד.

Reputed to be 111 years old, the Rev. Nathan Lapatnick, of Sheffield, is said to be the oldest man alive in England.

Grandfather Abey, or Harry, as he was known, had to find work quickly to provide for the family – no easy task since he was unable to read, write or speak English very well. After days of fruitless search his perseverance paid off when he heard that there was work available at Neumann's Glaziers.

He met Mr. J. N. Neumann who at first was unhelpful, but after seeing grandad's disappointment said he could help him set up his own business by offering him glass, putty and a glasscutter, together with a backpack. He would have to travel around the streets of Sheffield knocking on doors asking if they had any broken windows and, if so, put new ones in for them. Much of this was done in sign language! However, he persevered and managed, with hard work, to make a living. When his stock was low, he would return to Neumann's to pay for his original glass and purchase more materials.

Harry thought nothing of walking from Sheffield to Leeds knocking on doors and putting in windows as required. He also found customers would ask how to get rid of unwanted items. These, he would either take away for free, or buy, and carry them to the next house to sell. If he was unsuccessful he would take the unwanted goods back to his home and leave them in the backyard. At that time he was still living with his parents. After a while the synagogue authorities became none too pleased at having their yard filled with junk.

To try to shift some of the unwanted items he took a stall in Sheffield Market, affectionately known as the 'Rag and Tag Market'. Grandad still worked most days as a glazier traipsing around Sheffield but devoted Tuesdays to the market. He spent Saturday, the Sabbath, in the synagogue with his family. Most Fridays in summer he would set off on foot early on a long journey to Leeds installing windows on the way. He made sure to arrive in the city before nightfall for this was the beginning of the Sabbath. He stayed overnight with relations and returned to Sheffield on the Sunday.

On one of these outings he met Esther Taylor, whom he eventually married and they started their lives together in Sheffield. Their first home was a shop in Duke Street, next to Gallons the grocers. Grandma Esther looked after the shop while Harry carried on his glazing business and of course his stall in the Rag Market.

Saleable goods were hard to find. People would only sell or give away goods they obviously didn't want and were thus hard to shift. This led Harry to the local auction rooms around the Jewish quarter of the city, the Campo Lane area of town. Here he would buy goods, pay cash, and carry them to his shop. Later he graduated to a homemade trolley and later a horse and cart and finally to a van.

Grandad didn't really understand vans. He was more used to a horse and cart. But getting up Chapeltown Hill with a full load en-route to Barnsley Market was always a challenge for the poor horse. They frequently had to stop and walk with grandad coaxing the animal with the whip. When the van stopped on the hill one day grandma said, 'Are you going to whip the van like you do the horse?' It turned out he'd forgotten to fill the tank with petrol.

Gradually business prospered and my father, Aaron, was born in that shop in Duke Street. But his birth wasn't straightforward. Grandma Esther had fasted the day before, it being Yom Kippur, the holiest day in the Jewish calendar (which I believe even Rabbis would advise pregnant women not to do). Father wasn't breathing at birth. Everyone was shocked and assumed nothing could be done, but a large lady, presumably the midwife, picked up the "dead" baby and held him to her breast. Thankfully (or I would not be here) the baby began to breathe.

This was quite a beginning to my father's eventful and interesting life, which spanned 60 years of work as a junk dealer. Dad grew up in the Park district of Sheffield. From the age of five, he went to Park School, which is still going today. His life revolved around the shop and of course the synagogue, which was in the same area as the auction rooms.

Dad was very bright and by the time he was eight had taught his father to write his name in English. This of course gave grandad new opportunities that had previously seemed impossible. With his son's assistance, Grandad Harry opened a bank account and transformed his small enterprise into a legitimate business. Thus, with the help of his eldest son, he was able to pay for goods by cheque, keep accounts and pay taxes and rates. Harry believed in supporting his adopted country. His word was his bond and he was 'as honest as the day is long'.

My father soon found that he could run from school at lunch breaks and spend time with his father at auctions. Always armed with an apple or a banana and a bar of Cadbury's Dairy Milk chocolate, he would help him pay his bills or just stand and watch the goods being sold. At the age of ten he knew that by nodding his head or waving his hand, he could even bid himself.

He bought books – the one thing grandad (who was unable to read English) had no interest in whatsoever. They became dad's great love, providing knowledge and money. After reading them he would take them to his father's stall in the Rag Market and sell them.

Keeping an eye on his son, grandad would enquire how much the books had cost and what he was taking and demand rent of sixpence or more for the stall, depending on father's profit. Immersed in the auction room activity and the market, dad's business skills improved by the day.

After leaving school, he was articled as a trainee pharmacist at Newsome Chemist, on the corner of Aldine Court and High Street. However, this proved too close to his beloved auction rooms. Many times he would be sent on errands only to be waylaid by an auction. Finally he, or his employer, decided that the pharmacy wasn't for him. One can only assume his passion for buying and selling bric-a-brac overcame his ambition to be a chemist. So began his full-time occupation as a market man.

But, like thousands of young men throughout Europe, his career was punctuated by the First World War. On his 18th birthday dad was called up to join His Majesty's forces and after a short training period with the Northumberland Regiment he was posted to the frontline in France.

Six months before the end of the war he was wounded and invalided out of the combat zone, one of the fortunate ones to escape with his life. He was awarded a pension for life, a small weekly amount, but the War Office advised him to take a lump sum, which he did. This turned out to be four guineas. But it led to his return to the Sheffield Rag Market and the meeting between him and my mother...

Dad in uniform

3

The Levines of Lithuania

My mother, Bella Razel, was born in Slobodka, Lithuania in 1901. She arrived three weeks before Pesach (Passover) on a Monday and like our own Monarch, adopted an official birthday as the 16th April, because she couldn't work out her English birthday. Her father, Morris Levin, was studying to be a Chazzan (Cantor) at a Yeshiva (a Jewish University) but like his son, grandson and great grandson, was never to finish his education.

He married Sarah Rachel in Lithuania when he was young and left his studies and a pregnant wife to seek his fortune in the world. Morris decided this would be in America, 'the land of milk and honey', and he would get there through fair means or foul. Once, he took the ship ticket of his stepbrother, who was a juvenile and had been bought a child's ticket by his father. This of course proved impossible and he was turned away trying to use it.

After many other devious attempts to obtain the necessary money (in my mother's words 'beg, borrow or steal') grandfather Levin managed to obtain a position on a cattle ship taking Russian horses to Doncaster in England. To him this was the first step in his quest to achieve his dream of a new life in America. The job paid his fare and food on board from Hamburg to Hull. The contract included attending to the horses on the ship and then walking them all the way to the Doncaster sales.

Luckily for grandfather, there was a Jewish community and synagogue in the town so he was able to mix and speak with people in Yiddish. He had a conversation with a Jewish gentleman who had met a person in England from Morris's hometown, Covina in Lithuania.

Grandfather was very interested to know more and when he heard he was a tailor called Selznick he realised this could be his cousin who had left Covina for

America some months previously. The gentleman provided him with an address, in Meadow Street, Sheffield.

Thus Morris began his journey to Sheffield armed with a piece of paper with 'Selznick, Meadow Street, Sheffield,' written on it. He, of course, couldn't speak English and walked from Doncaster showing his piece of paper to anyone and everyone hoping they would point him in the right direction. Days later he arrived at his cousin's shop. He was welcomed with open arms and stayed there as a stopgap to America. Many days were spent in this quest but to no avail. Most of the Jewish congregation had started out on this same dream and were certainly not going to finance anyone else.

Selznick encouraged Morris to think about his wife in Lithuania and find a way to bring her to join him in Sheffield. This meant my grandfather needed to obtain the money for her fare and needed a job, not an easy task for someone who couldn't speak English and with no trade. For months it was a fruitless search until someone suggested that Neumann's of West Bar had jobs. Yes, that same man who gave my paternal grandfather Harry his break. Quite a coincidence!

Like Harry, Morris was given glass, putty, a glasscutter and a backpack to carry his wares around Sheffield to repair broken windows. This he did, learning his trade and the language as he walked around the city. The first year was hard, but productive, and grandfather managed to send money to his wife to purchase a ticket for the boat trip from Hamburg to Hull.

My mother was born six months after her father left Lithuania. According to mother, as she made her way to Hamburg to board the ship to Hull, her mother carried her in her arms and, at times, kicked her bundle of worldly possessions in front.

At each village she would be stopped by police or Cossacks who would ask where they were going, grandma repeating the same story over again, 'I'm taking my sick daughter to see a doctor in the village.'

Luckily they were always allowed to continue and finally arrived in Hamburg, boarded the ship and arrived in England. They were met off the boat by Morris who escorted them to their new home, a small rented house in Brownhill Street.

It is remarkable how both my grandfathers took similar routes to becoming traders. Like Harry, Morris had taken a stall in the Rag Market because he also found people were offering to sell him goods they didn't want and he was always prepared to take them off their hands for very little or no expense. Their backyard had all types of goods for sale, day or night, to cater for desperate customers in need of a teacup, plate or spoon to entertain unexpected visitors. The problem, however, was that grandma couldn't speak a word of English, which meant she either had to use sign language or there would be no sale.

Grandfather Levin carried on with his glazing and buying around the streets of Sheffield, but on Tuesdays he would sell his wares in the market. Unfortunately he developed a taste for drink and for playing cards. Gambling, drink and business just do not mix. Whiskey was his favourite right up until his death in 1961.

Grandpa Morris
and Sara Levin

He was as strong as an ox. I remember him in the fifties, picking up a tea chest full of heavy pots, a feat that I wouldn't have attempted and I was only half his age; he would often be given a heavy wringer machine which he would carry home single-handedly.

Grandma discovered her husband couldn't be trusted to return home with the takings from the market. Her only solution was to go to the market herself and since she only spoke Yiddish, her three-year-old daughter was required to assist in translating the customers' questions. So at the age of three my mother effectively became a sales girl in the market. She became known as Betsy, the little girl who could sell you anything. She always said that the people in her area drank out of jam jars before she arrived.

She spoke to her mother in Yiddish and to the customers in English, which proved helpful right though her life whenever she needed to speak to a member of her family without customers knowing their conversation, or the price of an article before mother had completed her sales pitch.

Betsy enjoyed selling anything and this became an art. The next two years were probably the shaping of mother's life and career. She knew how important she was to her mother and the rest of the family in providing money for the essentials because they never knew if their father would return with money.

Betsy's life turned upside down when she was five. In her words, 'The woman next door grabbed hold of me and took me to Netherthorpe School.' Mother stood this for one week and hated every minute. Not to be in the market on Tuesday was the last straw. Mother demanded to see the headmistress and told her she was unable to attend school on Tuesdays, as it was a Jewish holiday. After the first Tuesday, she never did. How on earth she got away with it is a mystery because her best friend, Sadie, who also sat next to her in class, was Jewish and attended every Tuesday along with all the other Jewish children.

Mother carried on working in the market and serving people who arrived at the door of their home, while Morris continued his glazing business and his occasional visits to the auction rooms for goods, in between his visit to the pubs and card games. Many games of cards would continue all weekend from the end of the Sabbath (Saturday night) to Monday morning. This was Betsy's life, only interrupted by having to go to school which she detested.

Grandfather Levin was a colourful character, a man whose aim in life was his own enjoyment, which work often interfered with. If he was ever short of money, which was often, he always managed to find someone who needed a new window. He wasn't averse to paying young boys to throw stones at windows so that he could appear at the back door asking if they needed any glazing doing. If the answer was no he would ask them to check and, lo and behold, they would discover a broken window.

Grandfather Levin had what I would call an unconscious sense of humour which was enhanced by his broken English. Unlike grandfather Patnick, he never became naturalised which meant he never received an old age pension. This could prove to be a disappointment to most but not to him. On one occasion I decided to ask him if he would like to go to the cinema to see "The Ten Commandments". I had seen it and believed he would enjoy it. One afternoon a week the Odeon had concessions for old age pensioners. I took Grandfather Levin to the cinema and waited while he received his concession ticket. The other people in the queue produced their old age pension books which he didn't possess. The lady cashier asked for his to which he replied, "don't I look like an old age pensioner", and proceeded into the film. I returned to pick him up after the show ended and ushered him to my car. I asked if he had enjoyed the film and received a reply I wasn't expecting. "It wasn't as good as de book".

On another occasion we all went to a family Bar Mitzvah in Leicester. My elder brother Irvine spent most of the evening dancing and talking with a local girl. Grandfather decided he wanted to know more about Irvine's friend. He enquired about what she did. Irvine replied she was a vet. Grandfather then said, 'what does she do, vet de bed'. Irvine wasn't amused but we all were. From then onwards grandfather referred to Irvine as, "Dem Lord". This was long before Irvine's political career took off and remained a family name for him, but not to his face.

My grandfathers were two completely different characters. Harry, my paternal grandfather, enjoyed a game of cards but didn't drink. He was hard-working and believed in paying his way; his word was his bond. They were business opponents, both as glaziers and second-hand dealers, but co-existed without any arguments, even helping one another.

My brother Philip remembers the pair replacing a window in a shop. They placed the glass on the floor and walked on it in stocking feet, deciding where and how to cut it, which they did without measuring it. It fitted perfectly, just using a piece of string for the size.

Morris carried on with his glazing business right through the Second World War, still from his house in Brownhill Street, but Harry eventually finished in the market. A friend encouraged him to go into the demolition business, knocking down buildings and selling everything on the site that was of value.

He pulled down such places as St. Paul's Church in Sheffield city centre in the 1930s. The Peace Gardens, next to Sheffield Town Hall, now stand on that site. Peter Harvey, a reporter, wrote in the Sheffield Star in 1997, that they'd failed to uncover any of the church foundations. I explained to Peter, who was a customer of mine, that when a Patnick is asked to clear everything they do just that.

4

Love at first sight

My father, Aaron, met Betsy Levin in the Rag Market during his demob leave and you could say it was love at first sight. Mother was 18 and it wasn't long before dad proposed and they got engaged. He vowed to buy an engagement ring with whatever money he took on his stall that particular day. Mother swore blind that dad took more money that day than he'd ever done.

Aaron and Betsy

Langset Road 1929

A watercolour of Langsett Road by D.A. Dakin

Grandfather Patnick argued this was far too much to spend on a ring and suggested his son spend only half and keep the rest to assist in his new life with Betsy.

They bought an old pub, the Prince of Wales, on the corner of Channing Street and Langsett Road, and converted it into a junk shop. The shop had the pub name in the glass on the door right up to the time it was demolished in 1969 (although you could only see it from the inside of the shop).

Aaron and Betsy's wedding took place on the 23rd June 1920 at the Campo Lane synagogue, almost next door to Ellis, Willis and Becket's Auction Rooms. Mother joked the only reason dad arrived on time was that the auctioneer was invited and finished his sale early to attend. All the dealers were outside to see the bride arrive. In fact there was quite a crowd. Harry was quick to inform Betsy that the crowd were not there to see her, but to witness him in a collar and tie, an unusual sight indeed, for Harry always wore a muffler. Dad was the eldest of nine children, all of whom grandfather saw married except for Bernard, the youngest, who married a few years after his death. Grandmother Esther Patnick didn't like my mother's name, Betsy, so she decided to change it to Bessie, and she was known as Bessie for the rest of her life.

**Mum and dad's wedding day 1920. Seated (L–R) is Aunt Esther (America),
Aunt Leah, Aunt Minnie and Aunt Hetty**

Dad and mum opened their junk shop the day after their wedding with a stock of wine decanters. Grandfather Harry had given them two bottles of whiskey, with instructions to reward everyone who bought a decanter with a tot. It was the beginning of a long and successful business, dad buying goods in the salerooms, mother selling them in the shop. Dad was still standing in the market on a Tuesday but his first love was the auction rooms and buying anything he believed was cheap. His second love was books. Mother used to say, 'Your father handles a book like a mother does a child.'

In those early days dad would try anything to avoid paying for goods until he had sold them. One ruse was at the end of a sale to give his chequebook to the clerk who was preparing the bills, asking him to fill it in while dad loaded the van. Of course, dad would conveniently forget to sign the cheque. He would arrive back at the shop then phone the auction room and ask if he had left his chequebook behind. He would thank them and say he would pop in the next day and collect it. This gave mother the chance to sell the goods before dad paid for them the next day.

Mother had her first child, Norman, in 1927. He was perfect in every feature;

blond hair, blue eyes, but sadly died at the age of five having never uttered a word or taken any steps. Mum and dad had taken Norman to every specialist they could, including Europe, but with no success. No one seemed able to help or give advice as to his illness or treatment. Dad was always convinced that the Reverend who performed the circumcision on Norman was drunk at the time and botched it up and this caused his problems.

I remember giving a talk to a ladies' group the day before my mother's death and a woman came up to me saying, 'I held your eldest brother in my arms and he was beautiful, too beautiful to live.' This to me was an odd phrase and I remember thinking I must tell mother about the lady and her recollection of Norman, but unfortunately I never managed to speak with her on the subject before her death.

Things were never the same after Norman's death. Dad had a nervous breakdown and spent quite a while in Blackpool. My brother Irvine was born in 1929, a couple of years before Norman's death, and Philip in 1934. They were both born at Langsett Road.

Dad had a bungalow built in a five-acre field nearly opposite his father's smallholding in Gleadless. The bungalow was erected using materials from Harry's demolition of St Paul's Church. It was designed to accommodate Norman. He and mum didn't want anyone to be able to see him from the road, so it was not overlooked in any way and there wasn't a step anywhere on the entire site. Unfortunately Norman never had the opportunity of enjoying it. I was the only son born there. Dad was never really happy there and spent a considerable time at the shop, which they used as a second home up to the time they moved to Wadsley Grove.

Dad's stories of his business life are worthy of repeating. So here goes - I will try to put into words some of his deals and tell you something of mother's considerable talents as a salesperson. She was rarely wrong. How she knew how much to charge for any single item is a mystery. One thinks of second-hand car dealers who have a price guide to assist them, but mother had nothing but her own instinct. To make it doubly difficult, dad hardly ever communicated to her how much he had paid for the goods.

Nevertheless they managed to make a living, a miracle by any standards. Somehow things worked out for them. For instance, on one occasion dad bought all the carpets in a theatre and much to his surprise, and everyone else's, found there were three carpets underneath the one he had viewed. Aaron always had an eye for a bargain but four for the price of one was too good to be true. However, he had quite clearly purchased the carpets throughout the building so the bonus was gratefully accepted.

Another time, he was called to Sheffield University to buy unwanted furniture.

Mother with her three sons (left to right), Philip (age 3), Irvine (age 8) and myself (age 6 months)

He was asked to make an offer for the contents of the entire room. The deal was that he would take away everything that was moveable – good, bad, or just rubbish. To his surprise, he discovered a large number of tea chests he hadn't seen when he made his offer. Tea chests always came in handy, so he decided to make the load up with them. But lifting the first one he realised they were full, not empty as he had first thought.

He pondered for a few minutes and remembered he'd promised to move everything in the room, so whatever was in the boxes was his. He couldn't wait to get back to the shop and find out what was in them. Quickly prising open the lid, he found, much to his disappointment, that the boxes were full of bones. Thinking they were useless he and Alec (his one workman) began filling the dustbins with the contents of the boxes.

The bins were soon full, so the rest of the chests were left on the van and taken to market. Customers always used to help unload the van looking for an early bargain but no one had informed them that the chests had to stay on the van. Dad straight away said, 'They're no good, just put them under the stall,' and carried on chatting with anyone who fancied a natter.

Later in the morning, with my father still holding court, as mother called dad's chats with his friends and acquaintances (some of whom were customers), a young man came up with a bone from one of the tea chests. 'How much is this?' he asked.

'That's no good,' dad replied, 'Go to the meat and fish market - you may get one with some meat on it.' He was certainly no salesman. The young man asked again.

'Okay, threepence,' dad finally told him.

To his surprise and delight this exchange started an avalanche of young people asking the price of bones. Each time dad put the price up by a penny, but no one refused to buy and the price per bone soon reached shillings.

Dad had of course put dozens into the waste bins. He then called to Alec, 'Watch the stall I will be back in a minute.' (Why Alec had to watch the stall I don't know because dad never did. He would spend his time talking to acquaintances about everything under the sun, only to be interrupted by people asking for a price for an article on the stall. He never actually stood at his own stall but sat at Mr. Woolf's opposite, who sold stockings.)

With bones in mind, dad ran to the phone box to speak to his wife.

'Bessie where are you?'

'I was in the shop serving.'

'Get rid of the customers and go in the yard and guard the bins. They're worth a fortune. I'm sending Alec back to collect them.'

When Alec returned with the bins, dad said, 'Just tip them out onto the stall.' This was promptly done; the bones and everything else, tea leaves, potato peelings and all the usual rubbish were all emptied out. It was a bit of a mess, but by this time dad was overwhelmed with young men eager to purchase the bones. He sold them all that day at an inflated price compared with the first young customer.

On his return to the shop he found a policeman waiting to interview him on how he came to be in possession of human bones. It turned out that he'd been selling skeletons that were used by medical students at Sheffield University!

Another time dad bought a lot of iron and brass bedsteads. They consisted of the head and foot, plus side rails and metal slats, which attached to the side rails, and enabled a mattress to be put on them. The head and foot were mainly iron, painted black in a gloss finish, with brass knobs on the four corners. Mother was selling these for £7.10 shillings without the mattress.

They certainly didn't fly out, but anyone showing any interest certainly received the full weight of mother's sales patter. One lady asked the price.

'Yes love, aren't they lovely, they don't need black leading, the brass never needs cleaning and they really are comfortable; you only need a mattress and you will sleep like a log. I've got one and I have never slept so well in my life.'

'How much are they Mrs Patnick?'

'Come with me, I'll show you mine, it's upstairs. Lie down on it, see how comfortable it is.' Once again the lady asked the price. 'Come downstairs and pick which one you like.'

'Yes, but how much are they?' came the reply.

'I tell you what, since it's you I'll let you have this one; it's mine, better than the rest, for seven pounds and ten shillings.'

The lady said she would ask her husband. Mother knew she'd lost a customer. No woman ever has to ask her husband when she really wants something, but perhaps this was the exception that proved the rule, because…

A couple of weeks later mother hurt her back, probably trying to sell the iron bedsteads; moving them around the shop, putting them up to show prospective customers and taking them down again. The doctor advised bed rest. This meant dad looking after the shop.

Dad's idea of looking after the shop was to sit in the room behind in a Captain's chair with his feet up on the fireguard (which went all the way round the Yorkshire range); occasionally stoking the raging fire and smoking his pipe which used umpteen boxes of matches to one pipe of tobacco, throwing the matches towards the fire and very occasionally hitting the target, the rug receiving most of the discarded matches, some still alight, and burning holes.

Anyone arriving would be greeted by him shouting, 'Yes what do you want?' Whatever the answer dad would reply, 'Help yourself, and bring the money in here,' never moving from his favourite chair, or the fire.

On one occasion a lady replied, 'I've come for my bed.'

'Help yourself – head and foot, plus the side rails and the slats and bring me your £7.10 shillings.' The lady then said, 'No, my bed is upstairs.'

'All the beds are in the shop, we don't have any upstairs.'

The lady, still speaking from the shop, replied, 'Mrs Patnick said I could have the one upstairs.'

Dad didn't understand so he asked the lady to come into the back room. 'Now dear what are you talking about, the beds are in the shop – help yourself – £7.10 shillings complete,' never leaving his chair or moving his feet from the fireguard.

'Mrs. Patnick said the one upstairs is a better one, so I've decided to have that one.'

Dad didn't understand at all. 'Alec, just tell this lady where all the bedsteads are.'

'In the shop,' was the reply.

The lady then said again to Alec and dad, 'Mrs. Patnick said she has a better one upstairs and that's the one I want.'

'My wife's in bed. She's not ill, only a bad back. Come upstairs and you can speak to her, but she will only confirm we don't have any beds upstairs.' Dad finally got to his feet and took the lady upstairs. 'Bessie, this lady wants a bed.'

'Hello love, have you come back for your bed?'

'Yes please Mrs. Patnick.'

'That's fine, is it this one?'

'Yes please.'

'Aaron, get Alec to find two or three lads to give him a hand.'

So mother was placed on the floor and the customer had her bed. She had made her sale. Dad left her on the floor until she'd recovered, hoping it would teach her a lesson, but it never did. I suppose she never sold another bed of her own but she sold many other things from our household.

We (my brothers and I) would often come home for lunch or tea and find there were no dining table or chairs. We would look questioningly at mother to receive her usual answer. 'A man needed a table and he liked ours.'

Dad did make a rule in 1953, after buying Wadsley Grove (by auction of course), that nothing from that house could be sold unless it was surplus to requirements and first taken to the shop, or if it was being replaced anyway.

One day, dad was offered some cutlery at the shop. He was shown a sample and told that there would be two crates the following Tuesday and he could collect them anytime after 4pm. He agreed a price and said he would pick them up the following week. Much to his surprise on arriving at the appointed time and place he was told the goods weren't there but they would be the following week.

When he returned, sure enough the cutlery was there. Dad had a quick look, paid and had them loaded on the van and left for the shop quite pleased with his purchases. A couple of days later the police arrived with the news that he was selling stolen goods.

Dad couldn't believe this, insisting he had bought the goods in good faith. They informed him that two crates had been stolen two days before off the back of a van. He explained the entire deal to the police – how he was shown a sample, then a week later going to collect them only to be informed that they hadn't arrived but would be there the following week. The man who had sold the goods to dad was arrested and he was cleared of handling stolen goods. The full story was then relayed to him. The people who had sold him the sample were testing the market to see if he would purchase them.

A week later the van pulled up at its usual stop for lunch. While the driver was away the men took the two boxes from the van down a passage and after a short time returned them to the van. They were checking if anyone was watching them. The next week they carried out the robbery. The police agreed that dad couldn't possibly have known the goods were stolen because technically they were bought before the robbery took place.

Yes, dad never knowingly broke the law but he did have close shaves. Whether buying or selling his motto was, 'I am not 24 carats but I am not 9 carats either.' He also instilled in me never buy goods brought to the shop or to the market stall. If you go to the home or shop it is a good chance they are legitimate, and you knew where they came from if anything went wrong. This stood me in good stead for over 40 years.

Dad had other brushes with the law. He was once accused of being in cahoots with an auctioneer. He would bid for anything if he thought there was a potential profit. Ball, an auctioneer, was also a bailiff who sold goods he'd seized from debtors. Dad never missed one of his sales and since he never specialised he would bid for every lot, buying more than many of the other dealers.

One dealer in particular decided Patnick seemed to be buying everything. Ball also could take a dislike to people from whom he seized goods. In some cases he would knock down goods quickly because he was getting near the totals required. Since dad bid for everything he often had things knocked down after his first bid. One of his competitors reported him to the authorities. The trial was stopped by the judge who said the wrong person was in the dock and maybe the police should investigate his competitor who'd made the allegations. Dad never spoke to this competitor again, finding every opportunity to park his van outside the man's shop or as close as possible. The van had a large sign that read, 'A. Patnick. We Buy and Sell Almost Anything.'

Pre-1940: Uncle Sonny (left), Aunt Leah (in front), Aunt Esther (Scottish) and Mother

In the mid-thirties, dad bought loads of cutlery from a firm called Chrysteel. I presume they were going out of business and were clearing all the stock before new owners took over. Father bought the entire batch, finished and unfinished, and began selling it in the market and at Langsett Road. On the unfinished goods he had some Little Mesters finish with his own name engraved, 'A.Patnick, Langsett Road, Sheffield, England.'

The new owners were furious that a junk dealer was selling their goods and tried to stop him from selling the cutlery, even though dad had bought all his stock legitimately. He had visits from the police who of course were satisfied it was all above board. The new owners then decided to take matters into their own hands. They arrived at Langsett Road telling father he had no right to sell their goods with his name on it. Dad listened to them politely and then told them he would see them in court. Then one of the partners pleaded with him to stop selling the cutlery so cheap. He never spoke to this gentleman again, after asking him to leave his premises. This gentleman, who was Jewish, turned up to offer his condolences after dad's death. Mother was none too pleased.

Another time when dad returned from an auction mother's first question was as usual, 'Do you want a cup of tea, Aaron?'

'No,' he replied, 'Put your hat and coat on and come with me.'

'Don't be silly, Aaron,' she told him, 'The lads will be back from school soon and I'm busy trying to sell the things you bought this morning.'

'Don't worry about that – your sister Leah can look after the kids and close the shop.'

'Why do I have come with you now? Can't it wait till later or tomorrow?'

'I want to show you some houses.'

'What do I want to look at property for? I've got the shop and the bungalow, that's enough for me.'

'I bought them this afternoon.'

'Aaron! You did say houses didn't you?'

'Yes,' came the reply.

'What do they look like?'

'I've not seen them.'

'You haven't seen them! How can you buy something you haven't seen and how many are there?'

Dad sheepishly said, '90.'

'WHAT? You've bought 90 houses and you haven't even seen them?'

'Well Cyril Lockwood was selling property when I arrived at the sale room and they sounded cheap… though he did say there could be a compulsory purchase order on them at any time.'

Dad had bought 90 houses in Little London Road and Little London Place without even seeing them. He paid £300 for the lot. That was dad – an eye for a bargain and also faith in the auctioneer. The war delayed any compulsory purchase and dad rented them out. However, they were in a grim state and most of the income went on repairs. The compulsory purchase order eventually went through 30 years later, dad being paid £12,000 in compensation.

Cutlery. Houses. Dad bought anything. Even footwear. He was asked by an auctioneer if he would be interested in a shop full of shoes in Haymarket Sheffield, as they didn't seem the sort of thing that would sell by auction.

Dad of course was interested and bought the entire stock that day. As he was leaving the premises a sign was being erected, 'Shop to rent.' Right away he figured that if he could rent the shop the shoes could be sold from there.

He managed to rent it for a week by convincing the agents that it would be better for them to have the shop occupied while they found a customer. A week was all mother needed to sell the entire stock. This also saved dad the trouble of moving everything out and it also gave the estate agent the benefit of having prospective customers view the premises in full flow. A win-win situation for all.

Dad was attracted to anything and everything in the salerooms. Once, Eadon Lockwood had a motorboat for sale, which dad spent quite a time examining. Mr. Lockwood himself came over. 'Now Patnick. What are you up to?'

'I just thought this would be nice for Bessie, the kids and me for our holidays.'

'Do you know, Patnick, it costs £25 just for petrol?'

'That's not a problem. I can afford that, but how much is it likely to fetch?'

'Don't be silly Patnick. That's what it cost just to turn the engine over. Think of how much petrol it cost to actually run it on the water. And don't forget petrol's still on ration!'

I'm sure dad would have bought the boat but Mr. Lockwood's intervention put him off and he wisely declined to bid.

Dad would go anywhere in search of a bargain. In York one day he bought, of all things, a vanload of brass hand bells, the type teachers used in the playground. Needless to say, these didn't go very well. But mother as usual came to the rescue. It was the start of the football season and the shop was near Hillsborough, the home of Sheffield Wednesday. In those days most fans walked to the match and I was ordered to stand outside the shop with a friend ringing the bells and calling out, 'Come on Wednesday, up the Owls.' It worked a treat.

Philip also remembers going with mother to the Regent Cinema to ring the bells to attract a crowd when they were trying to get Sunday opening for cinemas. Their reward was free admission to the film. How times have changed!

5

The 1930s: Pre-War Sheffield

The years leading up to the Second World War were eventful for the Patnick/Levine family. As I mentioned earlier, grandfather Patnick graduated into the demolition business, giving up his shop and moving to live at Springfield House, a smallholding in Gleadless. With dad's sisters Hetty and Minnie, and my Aunt Kate all living nearby, the area became a family enclave.

Sadly grandma Levine suffered a stroke and could do nothing for herself. Her daughter, my Aunt Leah, took on the responsibility of looking after her mum and dad. Leah always said this was the reason she never married and even changed her surname to Levine. Of grandma's other children, mother of course was married and running her business, Esther had emigrated to America and Bernard travelled the country selling 'Bony Shine,' an all-purpose cleaner.

In later life, Aunt Leah complained that because her two sisters escaped the family home she became the dutiful daughter whose life was devoted to looking after her parents. She also spent much of her time looking after us, "her three boys", as she called us.

Uncle Bernard was known as 'Sonny,' but when he joined the Forces he discovered that the name on his birth certificate (and therefore his official name) was Bennet because of his mother's inability to speak English. A neighbour registered his birth and believed that Bennet was what grandma wished to call him.

Uncle Sonny met his Scottish wife Esther on one of his many trips to sell his Bony Shine and brought her back to visit his family in Sheffield, which meant a visit to the bungalow. Aunt Esther loved the bungalow and asked if she could marry Sonny in the grounds (it is a Jewish custom to marry outdoors if at all possible). They were lucky enough to be able to do so and after they were married they lived in Glasgow.

Aunt Esther was a true Scot and when Sonny was called up to join the Forces mother said she looked forward to seeing her brother in a kilt, but Scottish Aunt Esther, as she was known, in order to distinguish her from mother's sister in America, was quick to point out that 'they wouldn't put a bloody Englishman in a kilt.'

Uncle Sonny was a chip off the old block. He loved a drink and to gamble, but we, his nephews, idolised him. To us he was a very smart man-about-town with a great sense of humour. His suits were hand-made by Barney Goodman (the local tailor) who would make him a suit and allow Sonny to take it and pay for it when he had the money. This was on the condition that he asked everyone whether or not they liked his new suit and (if they approved of it) told them it was tailored by Barney Goodman. Sonny used this arrangement for years, only paying for his suit when he needed another but he proved to be a good clothes hanger and a good walking advert for Barney.

Esther and Sonny

As grandma Levine's health deteriorated she was taken into the City General Hospital, now the Northern General, which mother referred to as 'the workhouse.' It was a difficult hospital to get to and for that matter still is, but during the Sheffield blitz the journey was frightening. If you got there, you never knew if you would get back. Grandma died in the middle of the blitz in 1941.

In the late thirties dad bought a piece of land near the top of Channing Street and had two houses built on it. One he let to Alec, his one and only official workman, who by now was married. Sadly, Alec went into the army but never returned.

It was hard trying to find goods to sell and customers to buy, but we got by. The compulsory purchase orders on the various properties dad had bought had been delayed due to the war and he had rented them out. The money helped the family make ends meet, although the repairs on the properties frequently outweighed the receipts. There was no way around this as the people living in the Little London properties were always bringing in the inspectors. The five shillings or seven and sixpence a week rent for these back-to-back houses was soon gobbled up.

Dad also acquired small houses on either side of the shop, plus a couple of workshops in a yard at the side of the Wycliffe Church, as well as another workshop, across the road in Channing Street, which also had a building used by spiritualists. He very shrewdly bought property as and when the opportunity arose, some in March Street, and, for mother, three houses in the Newlands Estate (which, compared with the rest, were quite modern). He also acquired a large number of ground rents near his shop or within walking distance.

Around this time he was offered the chance to buy the Barracks just down from the shop on Langsett Road on the opposite side of the road. It was a large stone building with land all around it, which for £10,000 was a steal. However, his bank, the Yorkshire Penny Bank, refused to lend him the money.

Dad did his usual thing – took to his bed and mother was left to try to raise the money, but to no avail. Had they been able to secure the loan it certainly would have changed our lives. The site became Burdalls, the gravy salt buildings; they made a fortune during the war years by letting the soldiers' quarters as flats. Again, but for the war they would have been condemned. After the war they were turned into small industrial units, and now house Morrison's supermarket and other chain stores.

This wasn't dad's last trouble with banks. He later fell out with the Midland when the manager decided there were too many Patnicks with bank accounts at the Hillsborough Corner branch. Bearing in mind that dad had two accounts and his wife and three sons one each (not to mention my wife's which was added in 1966) he may have had a point. But how did he manage with the many Smiths and Joneses in the area? Dad took the hint and moved to the National Westminster Bank and was satisfied with them up to his death in 1979.

Aunt Leah had a job working at the Stoker Drill factory, to help the war effort. It was very close to mum and dad's shop so when she finished work or at lunchtime she would pop in and help my mother with my two brothers and me.

During my childhood, which was divided between the shop and the bungalow, I have a vivid memory of a three-wheeler van arriving regularly at Langsett Road, parking in the yard at the side and being unloaded with all sorts of goods. The driver was a man called Gibson, whom everyone called 'Gibby.'

I remember unpacking cases filled with pots and the straw all over the yard. They were plates and dishes imported from Bavaria with various fruit designs printed on them. Dad had been on holiday there with mother and visited a factory. As usual he had asked how much it would cost for him to buy in bulk but decided they were far too expensive; he enquired about seconds, but they also proved dear. The salesman suggested he might be interested in their 'lump' sales which couldn't be classified even as seconds. This was anything that they couldn't sell and needed to get rid of.

A price was agreed and so started my dad's long association with Bavarian pottery, which was of course exciting because no one knew what was in the crates as they were unpacked. I later discovered the reason why I found so many Bavarian plates and dishes on display in Sheffield homes.

Dad was even not averse to setting alight the straw with his discarded matches thus accidently setting either the yard or the stall alight. This he turned to his advantage my announcing a 'fire sale.' Mother sold most of the items for sixpence.

In later life many people showed me 'antique' Bavarian pottery they considered prize possessions. I didn't have the heart to explain what they really were.

Once Gibby brought a large quantity of trees, which dad had bought as rose trees. However, they were unlabelled and mother found them difficult to sell because her customers thought it strange for a junk shop to be selling trees. So mother planted the majority in the garden of the bungalow and we ended up with a beautiful rose garden and rose pergola.

Another reason to remember Gibby was the sweets he gave us - twisted barley sugar sticks. How, or where, he got them during the war is still a mystery to me and my brothers. Nevertheless, and possibly because of the sweets, we were always there to help him unload his three-wheeler.

Dad also bought splash tins or enamelware 'seconds,' having chips on them. The salesman, Charlie Everson, was also the boss of the manufacturers. Dad had an outhouse connected to the shop but you had to gain access from the yard. This was where he stored the splash tins, so we naturally referred to it as the 'splash tin house.'

He paid Charlie by cheque but he would always round down the figure. For example if the bill came to £18.7s.6d, he would give him a cheque for £18. One day Charlie presented him with an invoice for £25. Dad asked what it was for and Charlie said it was what he owed him. 'I don't owe you a penny – I pay every time you give me a bill,' said dad.

'Aaron,' replied Charlie, 'That is for all the bits you have knocked off over the years.'

'I don't care,' he declared, 'I don't owe your firm anything.'

Charlie replied, 'I told them what you would say, so I paid it myself. It will stop the accounts department from carrying it forward.'

Above the splash tin house was the place dad kept the pictures or mirrors with gilt frames. He would take out the mirror or watercolour and save the frame. The paintings, mostly Victorian, were burnt, but I would like to have them today. The mirrors were sold to Newman's. When the room was full of gilt frames they were taken to the Sheffield Smelting Company. A vanload was worth £25.

Also during the thirties dad acquired quite a lot of chairs from a village hall and church at Ladybower which was due to be flooded and become Ladybower Dam. Mother had the job of selling a large quantity of the chairs. She explained to every customer how useful an extra chair could be and also that they came from Ladybower, meaning the village. Suddenly she had a queue, all wanting Ladybower's chairs. No one seemed to realise that the chairs came from a village hall and the church, and not the home of a titled lady, Lady Bower!

Chairs, frames, ceramics, even bottles of furniture stain! Dad spotted a stranger at the market selling tiny pots of stain – light and dark, oak, walnut and mahogany. It turned out the man had gone bust when his only customer, a large store, cancelled their contract. This store had ordered so much the man had stopped supplying anyone else. But each time they ordered a new amount they demanded a lower price until he was forced out of business. The man had managed to hang on to one last vanload which he was trying to knock out at the market. In the end dad bought the lot.

Up until that point all dad's re-polishing work was done by a Scotsman called Mr. Packstone who had a workshop in the yard that housed the spiritualist rooms in Sheffield. Like dad, he smoked a pipe and the combination of French polish and Twist tobacco produced a vile smell. After he bought the stain, anything that remotely needed polishing received dad's personal attention – and he always put plenty on the article. Toilets were one of his specialities. Often we would get stuck on the seat because it hadn't dried. Even at a shilling a bottle the stain didn't sell. We had it for years.

6

The War Years: 'We three sons were cheap labour'

The Sheffield blitz in 1941 was frightening for everyone. Several memories stick out. The first was dad doing his Air Raid Warden rounds, making sure every house was blacked out. When the sirens sounded he came back to make sure we were all right. One day he was standing in the entrance to our shelter as a bomb dropped across the road. The force of the blast blew him into the shelter.

On another occasion he took Philip and I to the Gaumont Cinema while mother and Aunt Leah went with Irvine to a different cinema, the Hippodrome. In the middle of the film the manager appeared, the film was turned off and an announcement made that the city was being bombed.

Dad took us straight out to make our way back to the shop. We caught a tram and the driver halted after a couple of stops at the bottom of Angel Street to take shelter. After 15 minutes dad persuaded the driver to continue. We arrived at the shop to find mother, Aunt Leah and Irvine already in our shelter. The next day we heard that the place the tram driver stopped to take shelter had received a direct hit. Yes, we were lucky. In the same raid one of our neighbours, who lived next door to the bungalow, was killed in Marples public house in Fitzalan Square.

I also remember being in the bungalow when the area was attacked by the dreaded 'doodlebug' flying bombs. We had a table shelter at the bungalow. Irvine was left in charge as mother and dad carried out their wardens' duties. After a while, hearing a funny sound, Irvine went outside to see what was happening. It was of course these V-1 Bombers going over. Being dutiful brothers we soon followed Irvine to watch the spectacle. It was quite safe until the engine stopped, and then there was trouble for someone. However, as we were in the middle of a five-acre field it was unlikely that we were the target.

By this time dad had become President of the Sheffield Branch of the Market

Traders Association representing the interests of all the independent traders in the city. He thought it unfair that traders called up to serve king and country should lose their right to their market stall and successfully persuaded the local authority to change the rules. This proved particularly invaluable to a friend called Nat Elston whose parents had a stall in the market. His parents had died just before the war and Nat had only occupied the stall for a few weeks before being called up to join the Air Force. Sure enough, after the war he was able to resume trading on his old pitch.

Nat became almost one of the family. His brother lived a few houses from our bungalow on Gleadless Road but Nat didn't get on with his sister-in-law. When he came home on leave he spent most of the time with us. Mother made him welcome, saying, 'I've got three boys already, so one more won't make any difference.'

When grandfather Patnick died, dad sent a telegram to Nat saying, 'Dad died come home at once.' Nat was surprised to say the least because his father had been dead for two years. Even so, he was given compassionate leave to attend the funeral.

Dad had bought a car just before the war, a Ford Pilot V8, with the registration number DWA 554, which he kept in a garage at the bungalow during the hostilities. Grandma Patnick died in 1946. By this time Nat was demobbed so he drove to the funeral in the car. With him were his girlfriend Biddy, my cousin Enid, and her boyfriend Carl.

To impress the girls, Nat put his foot down and overtook the family and the hearse. Dad couldn't believe it. It was something Nat will have remembered for the rest of his life because of the rollicking he received from him.

As I have said before, dad was obsessed with books. He often visited a shop on West Street – Cadman's second-hand bookshop, to either sell or just have a chat with Mr. Cadman. Dad really envied Mr. Cadman; his shop was very close to Sheffield University and was frequented by students.

Dad heard of Mr. Cadman's death and was considering if he should buy the business. It would have fulfilled an ambition for him, but he was beaten to the punch by Mr. Duffield, who as a young man had been afflicted by polio. He was more or less confined to a wheelchair and believed this gave him the right to be rude or vulgar; at least that was the impression he left with me. Duffield had sent for dad to buy the books he didn't want. Dad never really forgave him for being so quick off the mark.

In 1946 dad was asked by an auctioneer to look at a house in Paradise Square in the heart of Sheffield following the death of the owner. It turned out it belonged to Wards, who had a bookshop in Sheffield Norfolk Market Hall. Dad, who loved all books, couldn't wait. And what he found was amazing.

The whole four storeys were crammed with books – every room, the hall, the stairs, even the kitchen table which just about had enough space for one plate. The stairs and passageway allowed just one person to pass at a time and the rooms were full from floor to ceiling.

We, the three boys, were commandeered to assist in moving them either to the shop or the dump. We were at the 'bookhouse' every day, even Sundays. I remember throwing sacks of waste paper through the attic window onto the van. That was our job after Hebrew classes, so dad could take them to the waste paper place on Monday. It is hard to imagine, but he took 40 tons of waste paper out of this one house. Dad handled every book personally. Only he could decide which to sell, which was for waste paper and which to hold on to.

The furniture that was uncovered after moving all the books was unbelievable. There were beautiful antiques, some of which dad bought, including a black bedroom suite with a matching bed and a lovely black court cupboard, which graced brother Irvine's hall for his whole life. But that wasn't the only gold in that house.

Twenty years later dad was particularly worried about a mortgage I'd taken on. It was for £4,000 – a great deal of money in those days. He said he couldn't sleep worrying about how I would ever pay it off. I rather flippantly thought, 'Good. That means I can sleep. There's no point in both of us staying awake.' However, I bit my lip. Dad then said, 'Take these books and get them auctioned at Sotheby's. It will help pay off your mortgage.' Sure enough, the proceeds did indeed pay off my mortgage.

Mother decided she was going to America to see her sister Esther. She had been before, in 1939, travelling on the Queen Mary, but while she was away and with war imminent dad insisted she return on a neutral ship. Mother had no intention of missing out this time and booked her ticket on the Queen Elizabeth.

US Regulations stipulated she had to have a letter confirming that her sister would support her while she was on holiday and that her sister's husband Norton would pick her up in New York from the ship. They lived in Chicago, quite a drive!

Dad took her to Southampton. She spent the first day exploring the ship and couldn't believe the wonderful facilities. But with only £25 from the Government Holiday Allowance this wouldn't be easy and she raided her Midland account that had a branch on board.

The next day mother had her money and enjoyed every minute of the crossing, from hairdressers to massages. The only other thing I remember about the trip was she bought me a ventriloquist's dummy of Babe Ruth, the famous baseball player. I have no idea what happened to it. I can only assume that like most things she sold it!

My parents were quite a sociable couple. On Thursdays they loved going to the Empire Theatre in Sheffield city centre, and enjoyed live variety and plays at the Lyceum. Whenever theatres needed props they always came to the Patnicks to see what they could find. Dad never charged them but usually got free tickets or a mention in the programme.

I inherited this commitment, being told, 'Your father always provided us with props.' So I carried on the tradition, though I do remember wanting to see a show or play at The Crucible and being told they had no tickets left. I was furious because the week before I had provided a large carpet and we had to deliver it too, at our expense. So I said, 'You haven't got a ticket for next week, but you know where to come when you want to borrow furniture and props don't you?' I received a blank stare and left without a ticket.

Mother and dad never went out on a Friday night. Maybe it was their Jewish upbringing. It was the start of the Sabbath and they stayed in to welcome it. People soon realised that Aaron and Bessie were always at the shop on a Friday night and along came non-Jewish friends for a chat, all putting the world to rights.

These visitors were experts in their fields. Mr. Collins taught father about coins and jewellery. He used to say if you were flushed you should buy a gold coin or jewellery for your wife. Mr. Howson was an expert on books. He also advised dad on his will, pointing out that everyone should make a will. Even so, Mr. Howson died intestate. Cyril Plant, an expert in silver and old Sheffield Plate, also had an interest in greyhound racing. He owned several greyhounds and would tell dad when his dog was likely to win. But he had no interest in gambling. He always said he gambled too much in his business and always knew that if he made a mistake and paid too much for goods he would always get some of his money back, which wouldn't happen if the dog lost.

There was also a man called Harry Hunt but I never found out what his role was. Their discussions would go on late into the night with mother providing tea.

7

Coming of age

In 1947 when I was 11-years-old, I was taken ill. Wednesday afternoon was football at school, which meant a trip to Myers Grove playing fields and back to school. Then I had to take the bus to Psalter Lane for Hebrew classes and after that two buses back to Gleadless.

I didn't realise I had a sore heel, probably from my shoes or football boots being too tight. After receiving a kick or two at football, the journey home was far from easy, Philip kept telling me to hurry up and I was walking slowly and with difficulty.

On arriving home I was quite ill. Mother sent for the doctor and I finished up in the Royal Infirmary. The specialist Mr. Holdsworth certainly had no bedside manner, but I owe my life to him. I was in a ward of about 21 men for three months being pumped with penicillin every three hours and with a heavy weight attached to my leg to keep it straight.

I learnt later I had suspected osteomyelitis, an infection of my hipbone. I refused to eat the non-kosher hospital food and after two days the ward sister asked to see mother. She said I was dying from malnutrition. Mother explained I was always a funny eater. Every day after that she appeared just before noon with chicken soup (Jewish penicillin) and chicken pieces saying this was all I would eat. The sister's only comment on seeing my food was, 'No wonder he won't eat our food.'

Three months was a long time but, after those first two days, mother never missed her daily food delivery. My bed was at the bottom of the ward facing the door. She just waved from the entrance and handed over my lunch and dinner for the day.

No one seemed to realise that I was in bed all the time, never being allowed out or given any exercises to do. I was injected every three hours day and night, although a few days before I was discharged I complained the needles were hurting and they were stopped.

When I was at last allowed to go home I was unable to walk and had to be taught over again. I also discovered I had flat feet. Mother made sure I went to Edgar Allen's clinic where they gave me exercises and also inner-soles for my shoes.

Soon after, Irvine went into the Forces for his National Service and my first trip out was to Catterick Camp to see his passing-out parade. It was quite an effort for me but everyone was very helpful, the officers saying how pleased they were to meet mother and dad and what a wonderful soldier Irvine was.

He'd always liked playing soldiers and was a member of the Hillsborough Cadet Force and the Jewish Lads Brigade. He was assigned to the Artillery and posted to Tripoli. Everyone believed he would be commissioned but the Israel War of Independence put paid to that.

He was told, unofficially, that since he was Jewish they wouldn't be training him. The logic was that after completing National Service he might be persuaded to go to Palestine and train the Jews there to fight against the British Forces who were trying to keep the peace between the Jews and the Arabs. They were having problems with terrorist attacks from the Jewish inhabitants.

The next significant episode in my life was my Bar Mitzvah a year later. Dad was now a vegetarian after giving over his rations of meat to his sons during the war. The only place he would eat out was in the Sunshine Café, in Orchard Street, Sheffield. This was booked for the Thursday after my Bar Mitzvah ceremony held in the small Brunswick Street synagogue.

Mother decided to make the best of the occasion and sent liner tickets to her sister, Esther, in America for her and her two children Steve and Judy to attend. Plus she wrote to Irvine's commanding officer. She explained that it was my Bar Mitzvah and her sister would be coming from America to attend and how important it would be for her eldest son to be present. She also stressed that her husband would pay his airfare from Tripoli. Gunner Patnick was given leave, the only stipulation being he had to travel in civilian clothes. Irvine was pleased because everyone else on the plane was an officer.

My memory of the event is vague but I do remember mother's cousin's son entertaining guests with an impromptu opera aria unaccompanied, which certainly wasn't to my liking, and the singer's father telling everyone to 'stand back as far as you can.' I never knew singers needed room to perform, but perhaps he told us to stand back so that we wouldn't be able to hear his son's terrible singing!

Irvine returned to his unit after his two weeks sojourn at home. I accompanied my Aunt Esther, Aunt Leah, together with my two American cousins, to Dublin. The crossing was awful as I was seasick all the way, while the cousins, Steve and Judy, ran round the ferry getting into all sorts of mischief.

The rest of the time was spent going from shop to shop helping Aunt Esther to find cheap goods to take back to the States. Yes, she could certainly shop! In fact most of her time in England was seeing what she could acquire. Mostly she managed, by devious means, to get relatives to give her stuff.

My cousin Steve was a nightmare. Grandfather Levine was by then living in Barrie Crescent, in Parsons Cross, after being re-housed from Albert Terrace Road in a compulsory purchase order issued to make way for Banners Store. He had a light-coloured bulldog which Steve painted black. Believe me, everyone was relieved when Steve went back home.

For my Bar Mitzvah, dad decided that, along with himself, mother and brother Philip, I should go on a sightseeing tour of Italy. He booked a coach holiday for the four of us, which included a two-day stay in Lugano, Switzerland, both going and coming back.

The sightseeing included Milan, and I distinctly remember being shown where Mussolini was hanged after his execution by the Italians. We also went to Florence and walked around every church and museum of interest. Dad would have been about 59 at the time. Being on an escorted tour we had guides everywhere we went, he always seemed to be in front going into the next room before anyone else. Mind you, at that time in his life he seemed to run everywhere.

On one occasion he came out of the next room before the guide had explained what was in there and told the three of us, 'don't bother with this room, there isn't a decent painting in it.' To which mother said, 'Aaron, let's listen to the guide, he's paid to know about the paintings and will know more than you about them, thank you.'

The guide than gathered everyone around and said, 'This room contains all the not-very-good forgeries.' Dad smiled without saying a word.

Michelangelo's David will stay in my memory for ever. We were also treated by seeing the leaning Tower of Pisa and the town of Die. Before that I had often wondered why people say, 'See Florence and Die.'

Moving on to Rome, I can remember the opulence of the Vatican, and the poor people lighting candles, offering up what seemed to be the only lira they had to do so. I must admit the outstanding moment was the Sistine Chapel. Mother didn't care for the catacombs. As she held on to dad's arm she was constantly complaining about the narrow paths and it being so dark. We also took in an opera, 'Madame Butterfly,' performed in the open in the Colosseum. I slept through nearly all of it.

We certainly needed the two days stay in Lugano to recuperate, relaxing and taking in the scenery, which was outstanding. I never understood how we could afford the money we spent on the holiday as the holiday allowance wasn't great. Philip told me that mother had every letter Irvine sent from Tripoli with her and she had placed £2 in every one to supplement our allowance.

Because it had made such an impression on me over 60 years before, after my retirement, my one ambition was to take my wife Anne to Florence and Rome, since she had never been. We went on a cruise that took in both cities not realising the ship's call at Florence was a Monday when the art galleries were closed so we never saw Michelangelo's David and our tour of Rome didn't include the Sistine Chapel!

8

Wadsley Grove

We all went to Walkley County School at the northern end of the city. This was fine when we stayed at the shop on Langsett Road but if we were in residence at Gleadless it meant an early start and two buses to get there. This wasn't too bad in summer, but in winter the journey was dreadful.

The winter of 1947 will stay in my memory. As we walked to the bus along Gleadless Road the snow seemed higher than my head. People had made a path through the snow so it must have been piled high on each side giving the impression of a tunnel. Somehow we managed to get to school.

During my last year at Walkley my bus skidded on ice and smashed into a shop, narrowly missing pedestrians. Along with the other rather shocked passengers I scrambled out of the wreckage and had to walk into town to catch the second bus, arriving at school after 11am. The teachers were very sympathetic.

My schooldays were not outstanding, much to mother's chagrin. She had our career paths all mapped out. Irvine was to be a builder; Philip an estate agent, and I would be a lawyer. She even made sure we all had two first names so we would be able, if needs be, not use our surname.

None of us passed our 11 plus, although Irvine did pass an exam at 13, which enabled him to go to the Sheffield Technical School and then transfer to the building section. He then went on to college and after completing his National Service gained a Higher National Diploma in building.

Philip and I stayed at Walkley until we were 15. He did start working for an estate agent but it was impossible for me to go into law because I didn't pass any exams. However, my maths was very good and it was suggested accountancy would be more appropriate. Mother of course wasn't going to be beaten easily. She found a school to help to get me get into university: Claremont Edge Tutorial School, run by a Doctor

Rushton. Trying to be funny, I called it Doctor Rushton's School for backward children, never realising people would take me seriously. Even my wife Anne told one of her family how well I'd done considering I'd attended a school for backward children. I left with five O levels, but never mastered Latin or A levels, so university wasn't an option. I did start to work for an accountant but never enjoyed it.

Mother and dad took a liking to a house on Worrall Road near Hillsborough golf course owned by Longdens, the building firm. Wadsley Grove, as it was called, had three reception rooms, a kitchen, and a large breakfast room with a servants' bathroom off; there was also a garden hall as big if not bigger than most lounges, a hallway as big as most houses and a downstairs toilet.

Upstairs was a lounge with its own entrance from outside, plus four bedrooms, the master bedroom having a dressing room off. The house was in acres of grounds with a separate ballroom and a large detached garage with its own drive off the main driveway.

It wasn't ten minutes from the shop and they heard it was coming up for auction with J. J. Greaves. Before the sale dad went to see Alec Greaves to get some idea of how much it was likely to fetch. He was surprised at the price, but was still keen. The day of the sale Alec told dad that he was out of the running because a man had already indicated he was willing to pay far more than his best offer. He pointed to the man who was waiting for the auction to begin.

Mother had already taken her place on the front row keeping a place for dad. I must admit I can never remember him sitting on the front row of any auction, though at furniture sales he would walk round with the foreman who was showing the lots being sold and often got in his way. When the sale got under way, dad sat silent, only joining the bidding late on. It seemed an eternity before Alec Greaves finally brought down his gavel in favour of dad.

They were thrilled. Dad went with mother to Alec's office to sign the contract. Alec said, 'Aaron, I can't believe you actually got the house. The man I mentioned to you, who offered far more than you actually bought it for, didn't bid at all.'

That wasn't the end of the story. Later that day a stranger called at our home wanting to speak to dad. I explained that he wasn't in but was expecting him home at any time if he cared to wait. It transpired that this was the same man who had expressed an interest in buying the house.

He explained that he'd wanted to buy it all along, but hadn't realised dad was actually bidding. This is odd because several times during the auction Alec had said openly that the bid was with dad on the front row. He offered there and then to buy the house handing him a handsome profit. But dad refused.

So began dad's obsession with Wadsley Grove. The Morning Telegraph was scrutinised for auction sales, especially house sales in the country. He visited every one looking for antiques to grace his new home.

With dad hunting for furniture, mother had the task of carpeting and curtaining the home. Nearly every evening Edna Wilde would be at Wadsley Grove sewing curtains while the gentleman with her fixed curtain rails. Why she needed to sew the curtains actually at the house I have no idea, unless they were unfinished and she had to make sure they fitted.

Mother referred to the fitter as "Him Who Walked Back". I later discovered he had been a prisoner of war and had escaped and managed to walk back to the Allies. He had, mother informed us, 'Walked the soles off his feet.' Whether he was Edna's husband or boyfriend or just a worker we never knew.

Dad bought a large breakfront mahogany bookcase for the reception room, or 'the Blue Room,' as it was known, along with a large chandelier acquired from Welbeck Abbey. It was so big it filled the 7.5 ton removal van and had to be suspended on ropes from the sides.

In the bookcase he kept an unusual glass paperweight, with a dump bottom and a drinking glass top. Dad delighted showing people around his house, pointing out his various acquisitions. After showing one customer round, he discovered the paperweight had disappeared. He didn't speak to this customer again.

Another of dad's purchases was a Georgian breakfast table and eight chairs. Mother acquired a bulldog which slept in the breakfast room. Unfortunately it took a liking to the legs of the table and chairs taking great chunks out of them. Needless to say the dog didn't last long, nor did the table and chairs. Mother sold them and found a new home for the dog.

Dad attended a sale at a gentlemen's club in St. James Street and bought the contents of the cellar. This was something he did quite often, though I wondered if he actually viewed the contents beforehand.

The cellar was full of wine, dad paying about £40 for the lot. Everyone was surprised at the contents and the number of bottles, including a large quantity of 1906 pink champagne. Us boys carried three van loads from the cellar in St. James Street and then down into the cellar at Wadsley Grove.

Without a licence, dad was of course unable to sell the booze at the shop. Mother decided to have a house-warming party. After making a list it was decided they would need two parties, even taking into account the large ballroom. One was organised for a Sunday, the other for the following Thursday.

They were quite a success, I suppose, mainly due to dad's wine cellar. Everyone particularly enjoying the pink champagne. Mr. Lee, one of his stall workers, came dressed a bit like a butler and was stationed at the front door greeting and directing people around the side of the house to the ballroom.

The front door had the largest key I have ever seen, dad always insisting to enter his own house through the front door, reasoning, 'I always have to go to back doors when I am out buying or working.'

One room he never opened was what I presumed had been a cloakroom, but became where dad kept his safe and gold coin collection. These were only shown to special people whom he trusted. The safe was four foot six inches high on a plinth. The coins were kept in cases with trays that pulled out. Dad just enjoyed owning them, but again remembered when and why he bought each coin.

Unfortunately for him, the Labour Government introduced a law that no one could own more than one of each specific coin which meant he had to sell quite a number of his collection.

I later had the job of taking the coins to Henry Spencer's saleroom at Retford. On my second visit I was told Rupert Spencer wished to see me. He greeted me like a long-lost brother, saying, 'The last sale we had with the coins you brought was the best we ever had.'

Mistakes do happen. Dad always took full responsibility on any deal. He took the view that if things went pear-shaped it was his own fault for not doing his homework properly. He bought some framed gold coins from Eadon Lockwood and Riddle. They were hanging on the wall, and since they were behind glass, very difficult to inspect. They certainly weren't cheap. On arriving back at the shop he received a visit from Billy Hill, a jeweller who doubted they were gold.

Dad said, 'They must be, Billy. That's how they were described at the auction.'

But further examination convinced them both that in fact they were not as they seemed.

'You should return them, Aaron and get your money back,' Billy suggested.

But dad told Billy it was his own fault as he hadn't inspected them properly. Later that day the auctioneer arrived at the shop to say they had doubts about the coins and would like to look at them. Dad received his money back but he had never gone back on a deal or complained about a purchase before or after.

Wadsley Grove was next to the golf club, in fact it had a gate that led to it. Mother informed us boys that we could never join because they didn't accept Jewish members, though I did find out later they did have two members who were Jewish.

Ironically, every Christmas the club would ask if they could borrow our trestle tables and tablecloth for their annual parties. Mother always said, 'Yes, no problem, just pop down and pick them up.' I must admit that I couldn't understand mother loaning her tables and cloths to them when they would not allow us to join the club because of our religion. Years later, in the eighties, I was introduced by my friend Harold Needham to the then chairman or Captain of the club, a Mr. Hornebuckle. The first thing I said was, 'I understand you'll not have me as a member.'

'That's right,' he replied, at which I responded, 'Yet you don't object to borrowing my mother's trestle tables and table cloths.'

Harold was very embarrassed: he hadn't a prejudiced bone in his body and couldn't understand anyone who had. The club continued to borrow our tables for years. In fact, any organisation was allowed to hire our ballroom for free no matter what the religion of its members, provided the function they were holding was for charity.

Mother was also asked to crown the May Queens at churches throughout Hillsborough and always presented the lucky young lady with a new bible. She delighted in referring to the 'Ladies of Ecclesall and the women of Hillsborough.'

9

Sheffield Markets

I was part of the Sheffield market scene before I could even walk or talk. Mother told a story of a lady asking how much a baby's bonnet was. The reply came back, 'You can't have that, it's my baby!' I believe this was a story about grandma Patnick, but it could have applied to me or to either of my brothers, since we were all put on the stall whilst mother served.

Before the war mother employed nannies or local girls to help in our upbringing. But there were always customers willing to change or nurse us. When he stood for the local council elections many years later, my brother Irvine swore blind he must have been the dirtiest child ever judging by the number of ladies who asked, 'Who do you think you are, I remember changing your nappy.'

Stories abound about the characters that traded. One man sold miniature candlesticks made from gold, reportedly given to him by an Afghan chief whose life he had saved in the Khyber Pass area. Well, if you believe that… I grew up watching the wonderful pitchers and demonstrators, the medicine men, or 'crocus' workers, selling their fake potions and cures to the gullible public.

These were all wonderful characters and I just loved listening to their patter. There was Rex Amond, who sold patented medicine that he claimed would cure any ailment. Leo Marlow Huntridge was another. He attracted a crowd by sprinkling a powder which would burst into flames. He also dropped a piece of meat into a glass of milk at which the milk instantly turned sour. People naively bought his potions believing they would actually cure their ailments.

There were others of the same ilk, men such as Monty Green who was so smartly dressed, people stopped just to admire his immaculate suits, thus attracting a crowd he could work to and so sell his curtaining; Dot Woskow and her brother Harry Livingstone both sold bedding in different parts of the market; people weighed

This photograph shows the then Lord Mayor of Sheffield Ald. Grace Tebbutt weighing the Lady Mayoress with my mother standing next to the seat and the lady that owned and ran the weight scale, Mrs. Nutt, between the Lord Mayor and her Consort. Circa 1949

themselves with Mrs. Nutt's special seat. You sat on one side and weights were loaded onto the other. It was all made out of brass except for the seat which was upholstered in velvet and was always immaculate.

Then there was the Edwards family, who sold pots. Boy, could they gather a crowd. The father, Arthur and his sons Joe, Arthur, Bill and Michael, who was my age, all demonstrated pottery. There was also Elizabeth, the boys' aunt, who used to gather a crowd by knocking a six-inch nail into a piece of wood with the edge of a dinner plate. I spent hours listening to their patter.

Dad had an old man, Mr. Lee, to help him. He would arrive about 2pm and hang his bag made out of upholstery material on one of the roof supports ready for work. Dad just had books on his quarter, with mother looking after the other three stalls.

We shouted to let the customers know what we had for sale, which of course depended on what dad had bought in any particular week, but it invariably included 'Please keep the books straight,' and 'Come on you book worms.'

To Mr. and Mrs. A. Patrick From Mr. T. Lee.

Wishing You Both, a Prosperous and Healthy Long Life. In gratitude, as recompense for your good, and most kind Charitable Friendship to me; Now – and for many Years Past. Dec. 22, 1951.

J. Lee

This Greeting Card is Original Produced for the first time.

Here is one of Mr. Lee's illuminated greetings cards, produced especially for Aaron and Bessie

We always had to remind the ladies to be wary of pickpockets, so we would often add, 'Ladies, mind your purses.' Years later when I took over the business, I had a habit of keeping the bank notes in my trouser pockets. Mother, Anne, Beryl and Dot, the two girls who worked for me, always used a 'market pocket.' Mother's was a large leather one, specially made with three zipped pockets. Two were for notes and change, the third was her 'weeding pocket,' money kept for herself and never declared in the day's takings, though dad knew all about it.

I insisted my notes were all the same way round and straight with the Queen's head always the same way, £20 notes first, then tens, finally fivers on top. I constantly took them out of my pocket and put them back to give change or just putting the notes away.

Once I felt someone behind me with their hand in my pocket. I swung around, grabbing the person's hand and hitting them, not realising it was an old woman. The crowd went mad, shouting, 'Leave the old woman alone. You should be ashamed of yourself.'

I replied, 'She had her hand in my pocket, what am I supposed to do?'

I might as well have been speaking to myself. After this episode I always gave the money to one of the girls with a market pocket.

A regular visit for dad was the transport lost property sale, a rich source of things like umbrellas, gloves, even false teeth and lost false limbs! How anyone came to lose their dentures on a tram or a bus defeated me. Dad bought them for the gold wire or palates. He could turn a profit on anything.

The brollies came in bundles of 12; the gloves were sold in sacks, including odd gloves. No one ever bothered to inspect them beforehand; they were taken back to the shop to be sorted. Dad repaired some of the broken brollies but many had to be binned. They say that opening umbrellas indoors brings bad luck. If that's the case we were doomed!

It was our job to sort the gloves. The odd ones were separated into left and right, then into colours and patterns and so on. Mother sorted the pairs, which she put into boxes marked winter, summer, leather, wool, fabric, or too good to sell. These were given to the family or our best customers. The stocks of odd gloves were poured out onto one of the four stalls. We sold the odd ones and mother the pairs. I used to shout, 'odd gloves, sixpence each. There are no pairs.' I lost count of the number of people who asked if I had the matching glove!

Spectacles were another of dad's unusual punts. These sold well, both in the market and the shop. Mother would leave a newspaper and a book next to the box so that customers could try them out to suit their sight. Dad's own eyesight wasn't very good. In fact his left eye was very bad indeed, so he had a thick lens. He had two pairs in case one got lost or broken. One day he couldn't find his spares.

He said he'd spent ages looking for them, which actually meant mother searching everywhere whilst he sat in his Captain's chair, smoking his pipe, with his feet on the fireguard, watching her look in every nook and cranny.

'Aaron, I don't know what you've done with them. When did you have them last?'

Dad replied, 'Knowing you, you'll have sold them.' This was unlikely in that no one could have used those glasses but him. In desperation mother brought the box of specs out of the shop and examined every pair but with no luck. Argument continued into the evening with dad convinced she'd sold his specs. The next day he went out to the van and there they were, on the front seat.

He was really miffed when later the Government brought in a law that second-hand spectacles could no longer be sold and that only an optician could sell glasses. After this the auctioneers would sell frames and cases only.

At one sale dad bought thousands of mixed buttons. There were all kinds, including many pearl ones. We sold them at sixpence a handful. The factory they came from must have closed. It depended on who served you how many buttons you got. The weights and measures people would have had field day if they had been around then.

We certainly had variety. No one knew what we would be selling from one week to the next.

Dad had a business acquaintance, Frank Greenall, who had a stall in the market. He sold mostly second-hand electrical wire, fuses and motors, plus all sorts of parts. He was addicted to snuff, always sniffing it and dropping some down his clothes which were always stained. On bringing out the snuff he would enquire, 'Do you want a little bit up?'

His stall was down an alley past the pet market. He had a green wooden lock-up building. His main business was buying scrap electrical goods which he took to pieces, carefully separating the brass, copper etc. It was Frank who introduced me to Sheffield Wednesday, lifting me over the turnstile at an early age.

Just about the time dad bought Wadsley Grove, Frank acquired 12 Hepplewhite chairs which he took in place of a £60 debt. He mentioned them to dad who said he would be interested and would pop and see them.

Before he got there an antique dealer saw the chairs and asked how much they were. Frank said he was waiting for Patnick who wanted them for his home, but the dealer could have ten for £100, keeping two for Patnick. After a bit of haggling, they eventually agreed £60.

Dad was furious that Frank hadn't waited for him to view the chairs but accepted the two. The next day, he saw to his amazement the ten chairs on sale in Derbyshire for £1,000. Dad never begrudged anyone a profit, but tenfold was a bit steep and thought Frank had been turned over. He remained a friend but dad was always wary of the antique dealer.

As well as working in the market we were often commandeered to help move furniture from houses dad had bought, usually the estates of the deceased. We would be employed after school or at weekends and during school holidays.

On one occasion we were moving furniture from over a shop. It was obvious the wardrobe wasn't going to come down the staircase, so Irvine proceeded to take out the sash window and lower the wardrobe by ropes to the ground. Usually a ladder was needed to help to lean the robe on, but since we didn't have one, a rope was tied around the robe and Irvine and myself were to lower it to Philip on the pavement.

Unfortunately the rope broke and the robe dropped to the ground. If it had fallen forward it would have severely injured Philip. Since it fell backwards it smashed the shop window. Dad came running out of the building where he had been chatting to the people who were selling the furniture. 'You haven't damaged the wardrobe have you?'

Yes, that was dad, not 'Are you all right.' No one was blamed, but he had a new window fitted straight away. He believed you learned from your mistakes and I certainly did that day.

Our rewards came in unexpected circumstances. Dad took us to an auction in a large house. He said it was a treat. He wouldn't have dreamed to take us to a park. We walked round with him as he inspected the lots. In one room there was a matchbox on the floor. I kicked it to Philip but instead of kicking it back, he picked it up. To our surprise it was full of money. Philip took it to dad who was chatting with the foreman. The man said, 'I don't believe it. I've kicked that box more than once since our arrival and so has everyone else. You keep it son, you found it.' Philip was delighted to have extra pocket money that week.

Dad's habit of not inspecting the goods beforehand backfired spectacularly at an army surplus auction at Runnington near Nottingham. Most bidders got there early to view the lots, but not my old man. Armed with the catalogue, an apple or banana and a bar of Cadbury's Dairy Milk, he would leave Sheffield at 8am, arriving at 10am, leaving just an hour or so to look around. Mostly he would bid on instinct, relying on the catalogue and the auctioneer's description. This of course left a lot to chance.

On his return we would all wonder what would be in the back of the van. One time there were sacks of army boots. We emptied them onto the kitchen floor to discover they were all brand new. However, every left boot had been cut from the top to the sole, making every pair unsaleable. Dad was furious, but he had no comeback. He should have viewed them beforehand. It wasn't up to the auctioneer to point out the defect.

My parents complained to the local Conservative MP for Sheffield Heeley, Sir Peter Roberts who came to Langsett Road to inspect them. Dad explained that he accepted his responsibility for not viewing the goods before the sale but questioned the Army's policy of cutting brand new boots so no one else could benefit. Sir Peter said he would ask questions in the Commons but we never heard another thing. The boots ended up in the destructor. Not one of dad's better buys.

He then bought 12,000 entrenching tools, though I never knew them as that. To me they were 'fourpenny shovels.' They were not fast sellers until one day a man enquired how much the shovels were. Mother started telling the gentleman how useful they were. 'You can chop wood with them, do gardening, stoke the fire; they are probably the best tool you'll have in the house.'

The gentleman again enquired about the price. Mother finally said fourpence. He then asked how many did she have?

'About 10,000.'

Mother was then asked, 'If I bought the lot, would you deliver them?'

She replied, 'Of course, no problem and there will be no charge sir.'

Having got the man's address – 'North Shore, Blackpool' – The deal was done. Next she had to break the news to dad, who said, 'Good, but I'm not delivering them. That's not my job, I just buy and bring things to the shop.' And then he went to bed. Mother arranged for Reg Linley to take the shovels to Blackpool and mother turned it into a day trip for all of us.

On another occasion dad was at Runnington as usual looking for that one bargain which everyone else had missed. There were always the big buyers present, including from Sheffield, Jack Mortimer, who specialised in army surplus both in the market and in his shop in The Wicker.

Dad had a lean morning and bought nothing. The first lot of the afternoon was hundreds of flying jackets, in fact a complete roomful. Not many people seemed interested. The large buyers were all talking at the back of the hall telling each other jokes. The auctioneer again asked if anyone was interested.

'A very large quantity of flying jackets, who will give me £100 to start? What about 50? Right then, 20. Come on gentlemen, there must be some interest, what about £10?'

Dad thought he'd stolen a march on his rivals and couldn't resist.

'Ten pounds I have a bid, any advance on ten pounds? Fifteen pounds I have bid.' This was probably the auctioneer trying to get other people interested and is known in the trade as 'trotting,' an illegal practice, but one often used by auctioneers to enhance the price. Dad then bid £20, thinking the jackets must be worth a lot more. He was certain the large buyers would soon wake up.

Finally the gavel came down and dad had bought the jackets. The army surplus sales had the same rules as any auction. On the fall of the gavel that was a contract. You were obliged to pay ten per cent on the spot and the rest before collection. He paid in full and made his way to the hangar.

Now, everyone knows what a flying jacket looks like – leather outer with a sheepskin lining. That was dad's vision too. What he was greeted with was what I knew as a 'Mae West,' or to give them their proper title, life jackets. Dad knew why no one else had bid but was reassured with the knowledge that Bessie could sell anything. He put some in the van and drove back to Sheffield. He arrived back at Langsett Road, and demanded his usual cuppa with two sugars.

My grandson
Rafael with a
model airman
showing a
'Mae West'

'You buy anything, love?'

'Yes, a large quantity of flying jackets.' She rushed outside but couldn't believe her eyes. 'These aren't flying jackets. They're Mae Wests.'

'Don't worry Bessie, you'll sell them at half a crown each.'

'Don't you realise, Aaron, No one needs a life jacket around here. We are 90 miles from the sea either way. The only time anyone goes to the seaside is with the church on a day trip.'

'They only cost £20. I'm sure they'll sell. There are loads more and you'll need to make room.' We had a large garage at Langsett Road, big enough to accommodate ten or more cars. Mother of course had to organise transport to bring the jackets back to Sheffield as well as clearing out the garage to receive them.

The large 7.5 ton vans were sent and the garage was filled with the Mae Wests. No matter how hard mother tried she couldn't sell them. They stayed in the garage for years. One day dad arrived home and noticed I was reading The Eagle comic. 'That man's wearing one of our flying jackets,' he said.

'Dad, it's Dan Dare and he's in a space jacket.'

Dad left the room and came back with 12 Mae Wests. 'Here they are, six for you and the same for Philip. Give them to your friends and tell them they are Dan Dare space jackets and are on sale at Patnick's for a shilling each.' We sold out within a month but I never knew if we made a profit.

Dad did buy other items at the army surplus sales but never made a fortune out of them if indeed anything. I remember some RAF small carriers for ammunition, which fitted on to a belt that was not included. Needless to say they were not good sellers either. Dad finally realised that the army surplus sales were not for him.

On one occasion I attended, with dad, a J. J. Greave's sale which was probably a bankrupt stock of a quantity of suit lengths. We arrived an hour before the sale commenced. The auctioneer began promptly at 2pm and dad was straight in at 10 shillings a length, which proved to be the only bid, so he bought the first lot and was offered the first 15 lots at this price which he took. Then dealers began arriving. He bought the next 15 lots at three pounds a length. More dealers arrived and dad didn't buy another lot. They were now fetching over £6 a length. He just wished the other dealers had spent a little longer in the local pub.

10

National Service

It was 1955 and like thousands of young men up and down the country, I was required to do my National Service. My brothers had already served before me, Irvine in Tripoli, and Philip in Fassberg, Germany. Sadly, I spent my entire time in England – two years of my life which were a complete waste of time.

I was billeted at Bletchley in Buckinghamshire but spent most of my days at RAF Stanbridge near Leighton Buzzard. My Air Force career began at Cardington where I was kitted out, then on to Hednesford for the dreaded square bashing.

It didn't get off to the greatest of starts. My service began during September which straightaway clashed with the Jewish New Year and the Day of Atonement. I applied for leave, but had to convince an interrogation officer that I was genuine. He was certain that a number of East Enders from London were pretending to be Jewish to get time off.

The first thing of note was being asked to take part in an inter-squadron boxing competition. I had previously attended Hillsborough Boys Club which was renowned for its boxers, but although I'd trained, I'd never actually boxed in my life. Nevertheless, I was drafted into the squadron team. The good thing was that everyone in the team missed two weeks of square bashing.

I weighed in at 12-and-a-half stone and was delighted to hear that the team we were fighting against had no one of that weight. All I had to do was step in the ring, take a bow, and leave. Marvellous!

Unfortunately on the day of the fight the opposition turned up with an English Boys Champion who was stepping up a weight just to fight me! I couldn't drop out and was told to do my best.

Early in the first round I managed to land a right-hander which hurt him but hurt me much more. I discovered later I'd broken my knuckle. I did finish the fight, but he deservedly won on points. I was taken to hospital and my third and fourth fingers were bandaged and were to remain bent back for a month.

Our Squadron Leader said how much he'd enjoyed the fight. I was pleased he did because I certainly didn't. However, I was excused the training and passed out with the rest. That suited me fine but my hand was certainly painful. After returning from hospital I went straight to bed, but didn't sleep. I was surprised to hear someone shout, 'NCO present, attenshun!' Another voice said, 'At ease,' and then I was staggered to find a sergeant sat on my bed. He asked if my name was Patnick and did I have a brother Philip?

'Philip was the best friend I had in the Air Force, but the worst airman you could ever wish to meet. He told me you would be arriving shortly.'

That was more or less the end of our conversation and I never saw him again.

The next four weeks were difficult to say the least. I couldn't salute because of my bandaged hand, and if you didn't salute and give your number you didn't get paid. So every time I was supposed to salute I had to explain why I couldn't salute.

I was given little jobs, like painting bricks white, but I still passed through my six weeks without doing any actual training. I was than posted to Stanbridge to complete my National Service. I was trained to be a teleprinter operator. Believe me you didn't have to be very bright to do this job. We worked shifts; mornings, afternoons, evenings and nights. After a night shift you were off until the evening two days later, which usually meant I could get home.

I could never understand why the cookhouse was closed at night, which meant we only had cold sandwiches and even these were left over from day before. One day there was a commanding officer inspection which meant a parade with rifles. I had to explain I'd never handled a rifle, never mind marching. Luckily it must have been on my records so I was excused. I soon realised how stupid the officer and flight sergeants in charge of our shift were. All one had to do was walk around with a tape round your neck and no one came near you.

Stanbridge was the central signal section for the RAF but the people who ran it hadn't a clue. The Suez crisis happened while I was there. I was working in the office dealing with queries when one of the flight sergeants suddenly said, 'We don't know what to do about you Patnick. Just carry on working until I to find out what to do with you.' This was because I was Jewish. I'm still waiting to know, though the priority messages were all handled by me on our shift.

After completing my time I was interviewed by our squadron leader, the only time I ever met him. I told him exactly what I thought of the RAF, once again complaining about the cookhouse being closed at night. All he could say was he'd never had anyone complain or criticise before but he would take on board what I'd said. I never knew if the signal section at Stanbridge benefited from my complaints but I hoped future recruits and regular airmen did.

While I was in the forces Philip celebrated his 21st birthday with a party in the ballroom at Wadsley Grove enjoying of course some of the contents of the wine cellar including the pink champagne. I celebrated my coming of age in the Air Force. I had to wait until my 38th birthday before having a party. I was born six months before my cousin Doreen and since she lived at the bottom of the five-acre field, I always shared my party with her. My mother was always too busy to bother with parties.

11

Following in dad's footsteps

I had decided before leaving the Forces that I would like to work with dad as a junk dealer. Convincing him proved harder than expected but I somehow managed it. I had no qualifications for any job and I certainly didn't fancy being an accountant. Sitting adding up rows of figures didn't appeal.

My first task was to learn to drive. I passed first time and bought a Standard Eight. It didn't need a key for the ignition, just one for the driver's door. By this time I had become friendly with the assistant manager of the Odeon Cinema and would get invited to previews. These took place around 11pm.

One evening coming out of the cinema I saw my car being driven along the road and ran after it. I caught up with it in the traffic and tried to get into the passenger door. I'm sure the driver leaned across and instead of locking the door opened it. I grabbed him and asked what was he doing with my car. He said he was borrowing it to go to Blackpool to see his girlfriend. In those days there was a police box in Fitzalan Square which was nearly always manned and the lad was arrested.

Shortly after I started working for dad, the Government decided that anyone whose child was employed as an articled pupil would receive tax relief. He read this in the paper and set up a meeting with his lawyer.

I was taken to Waite and Co and became articled. I suppose I'm probably the only person who's ever been articled to a junk dealer for five years. Yes, that was me, five years at five shillings a week.

They were interesting times accompanying my father on his travels to auction rooms and deceased estates as well as sitting in the van for long periods while he chatted. Dad attended every auction he could and also bought privately, often taking his buys straight into an auction room to be sold. This saved him having to unload the van at the shop or deliver the goods after they had been sold.

He tried to be honest in his dealings and expected others to be the same. One small clearance will remain in my memory. He bought the contents of a bungalow. I, along with dad and our other helper George, a Korean War veteran, had almost completed the clearance and he checked we hadn't missed anything. He looked in a broom cupboard and brought out a stepladder. The lady who had sold the goods said she'd decided to keep them. Dad replied, 'That's fine dear, keep the lot. Edward, unload the van.'

The lady said, 'They're only steps,' to which dad replied, 'Yes they are, but I've bought them and paid for them and what you are doing is stealing.'

George and I were not too pleased, but sure enough we left with an empty van.

Dad was, as I have said before, a very generous person especially to our wives, but also to me. I needed an operation and after this had been confirmed he insisted I have it done privately in Claremont Nursing Home. I used to say, jokingly, this was because father needed me back quickly as I was cheap labour. Dad didn't even believe in medical insurance so had to pay for the treatment and the nursing home.

Irvine had a cartilage operation and dad arranged for him to be treated privately in the Sheffield Royal Hospital. On entering his private room the bed was surrounded with some 20 people all drinking tea. A nurse entered and enquired if we required tea. Dad looked round and said, 'I don't think I can afford one, looking at how many I'm paying for already.'

It wasn't long before I began to go out buying on my own, never to auction sales, just private homes for which mother had made appointments. Dad taught me to assess and how much to pay. Part of my education was to learn from my mistakes and I certainly made many.

He'd told me when assessing a house or stock to count the number of articles worth £5 or more and that should be the amount you pay. Sometimes I would count one article as two or more, or even count each article as £10. It certainly helped me over my 50 years in the business.

Dad also said that if a single item was cheap it followed that the rest of the same stock was cheap too and to always buy the whole lot to prevent being undercut. Dad always advised me to look, feel and touch, and not let other people see what I was doing. 'If you feel a chain that is yellow coloured and it's cold, it's brass. If it's warm, it's gold.'

I once viewed furniture with a bank manager. Pulling a gold-coloured chain from a drawer I saw he was watching me so I enquired if the family would like the chain. He said no, they didn't want brass. He was a bank manager, I was a trainee junk dealer, so he must be right. I still have that chain, and as my mother said, 'It hasn't gone green Edward, and I'm sure every link is stamped 9 ct. gold.'

Dad also taught me to recognise sterling silver by the colour, especially when it hadn't been cleaned. Sterling silver is black, whilst plated ware has a brown tinge coming through. Not just the appearance, you can tell by sound too. Sterling has a nice clear ring to it whereas nickel makes a more deadened noise. Old Sheffield plate has copper showing through, electro plate on Britannia metal has a tiny sound and the teapots didn't hold very hot water and usually develop a hole in the bottom.

I remember finding an old Sheffield plate candle snuffer and tray in one house which I thought I would keep. We were having a party and Anne decided to have the snuffer done up as the copper was showing through. This happens with age and is called "bleeding". Anne decided, without consulting me, to have the snuffer and tray re-plated which was duly done. Though we still have the snuffer it is now no longer Old Sheffield Plate, but an electro plated item on copper. "A little knowledge can be dangerous". Anne of course was an exceptional hairdresser but hadn't had my training as a junk dealer!

Although I took his lessons on board I still made mistakes, even long after dad died. I once saw a silver-coloured tea service in a glass cupboard in a house in Dronfield thinking it had to be sterling without opening the glass doors for a closer look. It wasn't even a plated item but pot, Lusterware. The metallic glaze had fooled me.

My first stock purchase was from a grocery shop. We were called in by the bailiff, Clifford Spencer, of Cooper Sons and Spencer Auctioneers, to tender for the entire stock. I was sent to view it because dad had another sale to attend and mother was busy in the shop. The shop was on St Michael's Avenue, Ecclesfield. I had never done any grocery shopping in my life, so hadn't a clue how much anything cost. I dutifully counted shelves that were worth £5 or more and made my offer, first checking with dad if he would like to take a look.

Dad was adamant it didn't need two of us. A week later mother received a phone call to say my tender had been accepted. I collected the keys then collected dad and George and proceeded to the shop to collect the stock. On opening the door, the stench was awful. I was physically sick in the road. He came out after a few minutes and said, 'That's fine, take me back to the shop.'

I got back in the van, pausing to ask what the stench was.

'It's the freezers. They've been off for a week, no electricity. I've told George to empty them into the bins. It won't be too bad by the time you get back.'

I didn't make that mistake again. If the bailiffs are involved this means there is no money to pay bills so the electric and gas are immediately turned off.

Dad bought the contents of many private houses from professional people –

lawyers, estate agents, bank managers and the Social Services – but few from private individuals.

One house that sticks in my mind was in Whitley Woods Road. George and I filled our Luton van first with chairs, then with the large furniture, filling the wardrobes with smaller items after they were on the van. Dad either chatted to the people who had sold him the contents or packed small items in boxes, occasionally bringing out one small item to the van. Usually something so small it would only need one hand.

George was a character. He'd been wounded in Korea and had a plate inserted in his head. He detested carrying the books. Dad of course spent hours sorting them. They were never boxed but put in piles earmarked for different destinations – the market, shop, speciality buyers or the big house, as dad called the salerooms. We therefore had to re-stack them to carry them to the van making sure we kept the categories distinct. The way I was taught by dad was to put a large book on the bottom and stack two columns on top, finishing with a large book across the top, fitting just under your chin. It was useful to have a table about waist high to stack the books on, if not we used our knees.

George was in the attic gathering the books while I was packing small items in the wardrobe on the van. George then summoned me to the attic to give him a hand with a wardrobe. I was the one who always walked backwards, George never did. This wardrobe seemed very heavy but it had to come down, I knew that. We negotiated the first flight safely. I had the difficult part of stopping the robe falling down the stairs with my shoulder as well as lifting it above each stair.

George really hadn't a grip and I had all the weight. I just couldn't hold it and it shot down the stairs smashing against the wall, with books flying everywhere. No wonder it was heavy. George had filled it with books. Dad came to the foot of the stairs and said, 'That robe needed smashing up,' and went back into the living room, never enquiring if I was all right.

Yes, I was always the one to walk backwards with George. This made deliveries awkward for me because I was the one who had to balance the article, usually on my knee while trying to knock on the door. Not easy. On one such occasion we were delivering a sideboard to a house on Burngreave Road that had almost a flight of stairs before reaching the front door. After entering the house I asked where it needed to be put. The reply I wasn't expecting was, 'upstairs'. George just dropped his end saying, 'wardrobes upstairs, sideboards downstairs', and walked out of the house back to the van. I quickly followed.

Dad bought a house contents telling us there were only three items to be kept, the rest could be smashed up. We duly carried out his orders but when the seller appeared he couldn't believe what we were doing. He informed dad that he had no intention of giving him his money back since the furniture was in good condition when he sold it to him. Dad gave us a right rollicking for smashing all this wonderful furniture and said we were new to the job.

Another early purchase of mine was a bedstead, dressing table and a wardrobe. They went straight into the shop but a few days later we received a visit from a private detective who'd been hired by a large furniture store to recover goods that hadn't been paid for. He was very offensive and demanded we return what he described as a 'bedroom suite.' Dad looked at me and said, 'Did you buy a bedroom suite from Bamford Street last week?' I just replied 'No.'

The gentleman said our van had been identified as the one moving goods from the house. Dad asked the man to wait until he had phoned his lawyer. Dad returned and told the private detective to go with me into the shop and point out the bedroom suite he wished to repossess. The detective said it was 'the one your son bought from Bamford Street'.

Dad said, 'That's fine, just go into the shop and point out which bedroom suite it is and you can take it away.' Of course the man couldn't identify it as he had never seen it and I hadn't bought a bedroom suite, just a bed, dressing table and wardrobe which didn't constitute a suite. Dad then told the detective to leave. I had learned another lesson – check if the goods you are offered are paid for and belong to the person selling them.

Like any apprentice, I needed reassurance. After buying a shop full of toys for £500 I took the load to dad, who, as usual was at an auction sale, hoping for some sort of 'Well done.' All he said was, 'Just in time. Put this stuff I bought on the van.'

'But dad. I've bought a stock for £500, it's on the van'.

'Is it all right?' he asked.

'Yes,' I replied.

'That's fine. Put this on the van, it cost a tenner.'

He never even glanced at my purchases. But I had done my job well and the toys sold quickly and at a good profit.

Mr. Spencer asked dad if he could borrow George and I to do an eviction. He readily agreed and having nothing better to do, came with us. I parked the van close by and Mr. Spencer duly arrived with two policemen. I enquired, 'Why the policemen?'

'In case there's trouble,' he replied.

Mr. Spencer gained entry, with me, dad and the police a discreet distance away.

George and I were eventually called in and finding no one around proceeded to empty the premises one room at a time.

In one of the upstairs bedrooms, George let out a scream and bolted down the stairs with me following. A man was in bed asleep, though he soon woke up amid the commotion.

We both made it to the police officers and were informed the man had a violent history and this was the reason for their presence.

Mr. Spencer said we had done a good job and not to bother about the last room. I'm not sure the pound we received for our work was recompense for our endeavours but it certainly enhanced my five shillings salary.

It takes all sorts to make the world go round. In one house George discovered a hole bored in the ceiling of an attic so that the occupant could look down on next door's bedroom.

Around this time I became friendly with Michael Edwards who was later to have his wedding reception at my house. Michael's family were established market traders. He was the youngest of four brothers who'd all inherited their sales patter and selling skills from their father. I can see them now, banging a dinner plate on the stall to get attention and then fanning the plates out in sixes, starting high and gradually lowering the price during the patter.

'A lady over there, another over there, and that gentleman there,' all subterfuge to create the illusion of heavy demand. They would add quietly, 'nish parcels,' — Yiddish for no sale. In the meantime they would throw the plates across the stall to an assistant who would catch them, still in the fan, gather them together and place them in a bag ready for their first genuine customer. The plates flew quick and fast which was all part of the act. Some pitchers actually employed people to put their hand up to buy the first lots, to encourage real customers to buy.

Michael's eldest brother Joe was the most flamboyant in both dress and patter. Occasionally he would drop by to have word and even help if they weren't doing well. One day Joe turned up at the stall in Sheffield in his hunting clothes, red jacket, breeches, the lot. This certainly attracted a crowd. One man who helped the boys said, 'Where's thou parked the horse Joe?'

One Thursday Michael asked if I would like to go to a fair where Joe was working in the Midlands. Little did I realise what this meant. When we arrived Joe was complaining it had been hard. 'Right, now you're here, let's get going,' he said. He started with the plates, banging the edge of one on the wooden stall, then fanning the rest out in sixes, shouting his usual patter and throwing them through the air to me. All very well, except that I wasn't expecting them. I just managed to catch them but only because they were expertly thrown, straight into my arms.

'A lady over there, a gentleman at the back and a lady over there,' then of course the words, 'nish parcel.' It's amazing how fast they come across to you and how quick you have to be to get them bagged. I must admit I was pleased when we were on our way home.

My early market experiences weren't all bad. One day I had been with mother and we bought a parcel of babygros from a children's clothes shop in City Road. We decided to go out with them at seven shillings and sixpence. To say we were knocked over is an understatement, selling out at lunchtime for a healthy profit.

Sheffield Market had a rule that you couldn't pack up before 5pm enforced by two peaked-capped 'Tobymen', in black uniforms called Mr. Lawrence and Mr. Butler. After paying our rent we started to pack up. But they insisted we had to wait until five. 'But we've sold out,' I argued. But they were adamant. I picked up mother's bag that contained our flasks and what remained of our sandwiches and we walked out of the market to the van, saying goodbye to the Tobymen as we left.

The late fifties saw two significant events for the Patnick family – Irvine's engagement and subsequent marriage to Lynda, and the start of his political career. The pink champagne took another hammering at the engagement party at our house – one of our friends, sitting on the settee, saying it was like drinking lemonade. He spent the night on that same sofa!

The wedding at Wilson Road synagogue, followed by a tea dance at the City Hall, was a problem for mother because dad had always refused to attend that synagogue and we all wondered what he would do. First, however, there was a family dinner at Lynda's parents. Dad had a habit of inspecting cutlery to make sure it was made in Sheffield. Lynda's mother saw him examining a spoon. 'Thank goodness I gave you the silver one,' she said.

Dad was as good as gold, attending the synagogue on the Saturday before the wedding and the ceremony without any problems. And for the first time he stood for the Israeli national anthem. He believed this shouldn't be sung while we lived in England, it should just be God Save The Queen. He liked to stick to his beliefs.

Some time after the wedding Lynda took a liking to a spinning wheel that stood on the top of a cupboard in our hall. Dad was generous with all our wives but didn't like parting with anything he had bought for his home.

One day I drove him some distance to an auction in Derbyshire so he could buy a similar wheel for his daughter-in-law. But when we got there the item had been withdrawn. Dad demanded his travelling expenses from the auctioneer complaining he had wasted his time. The man said there was no guarantee that dad would have been successful. Make no mistake. He would have paid any price to give Lynda that gift.

By now Irvine, who'd qualified with a Higher National Diploma in building, had started his own building firm and the couple renovated a cottage. He'd been a member of the Young Conservatives for many years and a long and successful political career was around the corner.

It began in a peculiar way. A Conservative agent, Gerry Goodwin, visited the shop to see if either mother or dad would consider standing as a candidate in the local election. Both declined, but mother put forward her eldest son who was duly adopted as candidate for the Central ward, a Labour stronghold. We all went out canvassing but soon realised that the only votes were likely to come from the local pubs. This meant a drink in every one we visited, proved rather expensive, and left us all feeling the worse for wear. The count proved equally disappointing. In fact, Irvine received so few votes that Philip, seeing a cross for his brother shouted, 'Bingo.'

However his fortunes were to change. This was the era when the Tory Prime Minister Harold Macmillan told the public, 'You've never had it so good,' and Irvine was adopted as the party candidate for the more winnable seat of Owlerton. Philip ran the campaign and it was nip and tuck. We knew during the count it was going to be close. In the end Irvine lost by just 50 votes. We left the building dejected, our mood worsened by the party agent who told us we should have demanded a recount. Our lack of experience showed, because we hadn't a clue that we could. All it needed was for a small bundle of votes to have mistakenly put in the wrong pile for Irvine to have won.

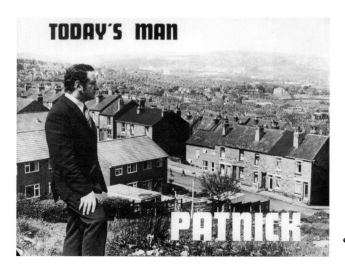

Brother Irvine on the campaign trail, circa 1969

12

A friend in need

There's a cliché in selling that the customer always comes first. Dad certainly thought so. One day a man came in asking if we had a large family-type bible for sale. He told him he didn't have one but the next time he saw one he would put it aside. Sure enough, months later the man returned. Dad went out to the back and produced the Good Book he'd saved for the man. 'Is this what you want?'

'Perfect,' came the reply, 'How much do I owe you?'

'Five pounds,' said dad. 'I've kept it a few months. I'd a feeling you would be in again.'

Years later, dad's youngest brother, Bernard, who had a small upholstery business in Bond Street, called 'Bond Upholstery,' saw advertised larger premises in Spital Hill. The name of the firm was dad's idea, 'My Word Is My Bond.'

Dad spoke with the principal dealing with the Spital Hill property and made an offer on his brother's behalf. Then he got a call saying that the owner wished to meet before agreeing any contract. At the meeting the owner looked at dad and said he could indeed rent the property. He explained he didn't want it himself, he was merely acting for his brother. The man was adamant that it was dad who could rent the property not Bernard. He couldn't understand, neither could the agent, but the owner said, 'I remember buying a large bible from you on Langsett Road. Anyone who keeps his word like you do can rent one of my properties.' Dad agreed to act as guarantor and the lease was signed.

Police sales were another source of profit. I became puzzled by some of the high prices being paid for lost or reclaimed property, particularly scrap. I soon discovered why. It was handy for dealers to have a receipt from the police in case they got a pull over some dodgy goods. I was even told that old safes with no backs were useful for safe blowers to practise on.

Dad was always ready to take a gamble or act on instinct. One day we went to the West Yorkshire Police sale in Wakefield. This particular day, he bought a roomful of goods but it was only later back in Sheffield that I learned what it consisted of.

That evening he asked if I wanted a new watch. He handed over an Omega from the police sale. I wore that watch for almost 40 years until one morning walking the dog I slipped on black ice and didn't realise the strap must have broken. I went back to the spot but the watch was nowhere to be seen, a huge sentimental loss.

That day's parcel also included 30 bags of sergeant stripes. I've no idea why they were surplus. Perhaps there was a shortage of sergeants that year, or they changed the design. Anyhow, we had them for weeks. What would anyone want with bags of sergeant stripes?

Around this time I was active in Sheffield Maccabi, a Jewish Youth Club, playing both football and cricket for them. I also served on the National Maccabi Committee, which meant frequent visits to London. National Maccabi also organised the Great Britain team to take part in the Maccabiah, the Jewish Olympics, in Israel. I had no chance in going as an athlete but they were running a supporters tour at the same time. This appealed to me as I had never visited Israel before and it also included a sightseeing tour.

The cost was £150. This was the difficult part. I had two years to save the money but on five shillings a week it was rather unlikely. I did drop a lot of hints, but to no avail. A year before the trip dad said, 'If you want to go to Israel, take those sacks of chevrons to the Sheffield Smelting Company and you can have what you receive for them. They should pay for your trip.'

I loaded the sacks onto the van and drove to the smelting yard. The foreman recognised me, asking if I'd brought another load of gilt frames.

'No, some of these,' I replied, showing him one of the sergeant stripes.

'Not here. Try West Bar police station down the road.'

I left the office annoyed that my father had sent me on a wild goose chase. As I was making my way to the van I bumped into a man who said, 'Aren't you Aaron Patnick's son?'

He too thought I'd brought some frames but I showed him the stripes. 'Come back in the office,' he said.

Inside, the foreman looked up and said, 'I've already told him to take them to West Bar.' To which the man, who I assumed was the guvnor, replied, 'You test them. If Patnick has sent them there's a reason.'

It transpired the stripes were sterling silver wire and worth good money as scrap. Dad's gamble had paid off again. And I was heading to Israel!

Israel was a wonderful experience. We toured everywhere except the part of Jerusalem then occupied by Jordan. I was fortunate to go the Maccabiah three more times. I became a member of the organising committee as the Northern Liaison Officer at the 1965 Games, and was given the job of managing the wrestling team. I had no knowledge of the sport whatsoever. Luckily it only entailed organising training, attending meetings and making sure the wrestlers turned up at the venue on time.

Compared to the rest, the British wrestlers were not very good despite my support from the sidelines. I was then drafted to the cycling team to encourage them, though they had a manager who understood the sport.

In 1969 I was manager of the football team, much more to my liking. We lost to the hosts in the first game 1-0 to a dubious penalty awarded by the Israeli official. We also visited the Western Wall, not possible on previous trips, and the entire team prayed there. Then in 1973 I was made manager of the football team, plus vice captain of the whole British team.

I was now earning £15 per week and was more or less doing most of the buying. If I had nothing better to do I would take dad and stay at the back watching the antics of the dealers who were all characters: Billy Hill always had a pocket full of diamonds, Freddy Robinson gold sovereigns, antique dealers reading newspapers, occasionally looking up when the auctioneer announced something they might be interested in.

One in particular, when an oil painting was put up for sale, glanced up and shouted, 'Another bloody ship,' then continued reading. I only wish I'd bought all those 'bloody ships,' I could have made a fortune in the 1980s.

Dad once bought the largest watercolour I'd ever seen to hang in the hall of Wadsley Grove and later at their home in Psalter Lane. It must have been five feet wide and three-an- a-half feet deep. It was a drawing room scene for which he paid £500.

I was travelling to London quite a lot to Maccabi meetings. Dad didn't miss a trick, handing me goods to take to London international salerooms. It was quite a feat to get past the secretaries at the front counter. My art was wrapped up securely with instructions from dad to insist that I would only unwrap the parcel in the presence of the appropriate expert.

On one occasion all four paintings were accepted, two of them to the Old Masters' Department. Dad eventually received a letter saying that these had been lost with an insurance cheque for £50.

Another time he sent a painting to London convinced it was a Gainsborough and was signed as such, but he couldn't provide the provenance for it, so it was sold as an oil painting. Someone got a bargain. When all was said and done, dad was only a junk dealer and they were world-renowned auctioneers.

Many years later that London experience proved useful. I was playing cards at a friend's house and the host pointed to a portrait he'd bought. I can't say I'd noticed it. He asked me if I liked it, but I was non-committal.

'Edward, you don't like it, do you?' John asked.

'It doesn't matter what I think. It's more a question if you like it,' I said diplomatically.

Refusing to drop the subject he enquired, 'How much do you think it's worth?'

'I've no idea. It is not something I'm qualified in. To be honest, I'm just here to play cards,' I replied.

He continued to pursue the topic all night. Finally he confessed he thought it was worth more than £1,000. I was amazed. He must have seen the surprise on my face. 'Okay, you give me your valuation,' he said.

Frustrated more than anything, I offered to get someone to value it. If it was worth £1,000 I said I would pay for the valuation out of my own pocket. He agreed and I contacted an auctioneer Michael Haigh who said he would be pleased to help even though he was not an art specialist.

Michael arrived with an assistant and I politely stayed outside the room while they inspected the painting with my friend. Eventually Michael emerged. 'Why have you brought me here?' he said, adding that I could easily have valued it myself and the work was worth £50 tops.

'Michael, you have to tell him that. But I'm staying here,' I said. He duly broke the news to my friend and refused to take any money for the valuation.

John was still sceptical and so I offered to go with him to Sotheby's in London to get a more professional opinion. I was so confident that I agreed to pay for the day out, including the valuation, if it was valued at a grand.

We went down on the train with the painting neatly wrapped. Following dad's advice, I refused to open it unless it was in the presence of an expert. I asked to see an American oil painting specialist. After questions and my refusal to show it to a receptionist, an expert appeared. John unwrapped the painting. The lady said, 'I'm afraid it's not the sort of painting we would sell, I suggest you try Bonhams.'

Off we went there, using the same procedure. A gentleman appeared, looked at the painting and after a while said, 'Yes, we could offer it for sale. It may fetch £50 and I would recommend a reserve of £25.'

John's face dropped. We rewrapped the painting and left. We had a very expensive lunch and headed for the train home. I learned he'd bought the painting as a gift for his wife from a relative in America who happened to be an art dealer. It was priced at £850 but she accepted £650 and suggested he insure it for £1,000.

I told John it didn't really matter. If they liked it, and wanted to keep it, its value was irrelevant. John was adamant he wasn't going to keep the picture and gave me the job of sending it back to America. It cost £45 to send back which was about the price the picture was worth.

Art is such a personal thing. I am reminded of once visiting a friend's house and being asked what I thought of certain things. One was a sketch of a naked pregnant lady by Epstein. I thought it was hideous but it was signed. Since it was rolled up, I asked where it was kept and I was informed under the stairs in a cupboard. All I could say was, 'that's the best place for it.'

How wrong you can be. Years later it was framed and sold by auction for a very handsome price.

Another friend received an oil painting as a gift from a local artist whom we both knew. I said, 'What's it supposed to be?'

She replied, 'It's a castle. I was told by the artist that every lady should have a castle in Spain and this is mine.'

I thought it repugnant but said she couldn't sell it in case he ever visited. 'Where do you have it displayed at present?'

'Oh, it's under the stairs. I wouldn't put it on display,' she said.

13

Dad develops 'hacksawitis'

Just as I was getting the hang of things dad was taken ill with a rash from head to toe. Our doctor was baffled and a specialist later admitted him to Claremont Nursing Home. We visited every day and he always enquired about business. His condition was being treated with a white lotion applied virtually to the whole of his body. But it didn't seem to help and he was confined to the hospital. Except I then got a phone call from an auction room requesting that I pick dad up from the saleroom with the van.

'I think you're mistaken. He's in Claremont,' I assured him.

I was then informed he'd been at the sale all afternoon and had bought a quantity of lots. I still doubted the auctioneer's word but proceeded to town to see for myself. Sure enough dad was there with his purchases – a quantity of pipe tobacco. He'd absconded from the nursing home to attend the sale of tobacco. I delivered him back to the nursing home and he kept a couple of tins for his pipe.

Just before dad's illness, I was called to Slack Sellers, where I was shown a quantity of hacksaws made for export but the order had been cancelled. I looked at one and decided they were very saleable. I was informed there were 20,000 which put me back a bit, but remembered the old man's maxim that if one was cheap, they were all cheap. I offered rather cheekily £500. To my surprise it was accepted.

I drove the van to the shop to show dad my purchase. He looked at one but made no comment, just writing a cheque for £500 which I delivered. The hacksaws didn't fly out either in the shop or in the market at one shilling and sixpence each. In fact we didn't sell many at all.

With dad out of hospital but not cured I bought furniture from a house in Nether Edge. It was a Jewish family whom I knew but was not particularly friendly with. I didn't mix in their circles. The eldest son said they wanted £3,000 for the entire contents.

Dad at the auction sale

I replied that the bricks and mortar were worth more than that!

He laughed and said he would accept less because the house needed to be cleared.

I took the entire estate into a saleroom which I attended with dad. He was now being treated at home, but still didn't know what had caused the rash or why it was so persistent. He sat in the middle of the room, unusually, while I stood at the back. I suppose the illness was making him tired and he needed to sit down.

One of my lots was a framed newspaper cutting showing where movie stars lived in Hollywood. It was virtually worthless. The bidding started at £5 and inexplicably reached more than a hundred. I couldn't understand it and looked around the room to see who on earth was driving the price so high. To my horror I saw one of the bidders was dad. I rushed to him and said, 'It's mine from the house in Nether Edge. It's useless, just a newspaper print.'

Fortunately, he got out just in time and the print was sold for £125. He said afterwards that his eyes were bad from the rash and he thought it was a genuine map of Hollywood. I still didn't understand. There had to be two bidders, so someone else must have been fooled too, and had indeed bought it. 'Yes,' said dad, 'That's Wilf. He watches me when I bid for art. He doesn't understand paintings so competes with anything I bid for. I am pleased to say he definitely got his leg in this time.'

The story doesn't end there. I was in trouble with the family from whom I bought the contents. The sister saw how much the Hollywood print fetched and thought I'd fleeced her. It was hard to explain that it only reached that amount because dad was bidding.

We soon found a way to beat the people preying on dad's superior judgement. He sat at the front whilst I stood at the side. He told me to bid for articles only when he had his pipe in his mouth and to stop bidding when he took it out. There was nothing illegal about this, of course. It was just a form of communication between us. He didn't believe in doing anything shady.

One illegal practice that is still quite common is 'knocking,' where dealers agree collectively not to bid against each other. One buys the item cheaply and then later the dealers have their own private sale. It is difficult for auctioneers to prove and vendors suffer through not getting a fair price for their goods.

Dad still had his rash. And we still had the bloomin' hacksaws. One of Irvine's friends Brian Viner even joked that dad was suffering from 'hacksawitis.' I was getting worried because even mother couldn't sell them. I found out why almost by accident. I was doing some repair work at home with one of the saws and broke the blade. Now to replace it I could have gone to our shop and got one of the thousands of blades that were slowing turning to rust but for some reason I took the broken blade to my local ironmongers, Lingard's.

An early photograph of Lingard's shop opposite ours on Langsett Road

'Sorry, we don't stock that size blade. It's a five-inch hacksaw and as far as I know no one else does. The smallest is a six-inch,' said the ironmonger. It dawned on me why they weren't selling and why I'd got them so cheap. As usual, dad had the answer. 'Come on; let's go to Slack Sellers'.

We saw the director who normally dealt with us and dad bought 40,000 five-inch blades cheaply. Back at the shop he simply said, 'From now on you sell hacksaws with two extra blades for two shillings and sixpence.' Believe me they then started to sell.

I learned another lesson – an article can be too cheap, either buying or selling. Stop and ask yourself why. Yes, the hacksaws were cheap, but they were also a cancelled export order. Why was the order cancelled? Dad never criticised me for making an error and always waited for me to admit the mistake before advising or correcting it.

Another boob of mine involved buying furniture from an upstairs flat. There was a beautiful grand piano but I hadn't considered how, or the cost, of getting it down the stairs. I called dad to the scene to pick his brains.

'No chance. The stairs have been altered since the piano was put there,' he said shaking his head.

I had to employ a specialist removal firm and stand and watch as they took the legs off, removed the sash window and lowered the instrument to ground.

Another costly mistake was not checking furniture for woodworm or rot. I'd bought the contents of the flat of the Cantor of the synagogue who was retiring. As we lowered the furniture out the window the wardrobe broke into pieces. It was only then I noticed the woodworm. 'What is woodworm?' the Rev Khan asked.

Minutes later, Ralph, my help for the day, found a bottle of woodworm treatment in a bedside cupboard. He held it up and laughed, 'What's woodworm!' When we finished clearing the effects the Reverend did give me a pair of beautiful Russian candlesticks as a wedding present if I ever got married.

My father still managed to attend nearly all the auction sales in the area. One such auction in the Dewsbury area was a sale dad started attending that sold bankrupt stock. Dad bought calico there very cheaply and mother sold it by the yard in the shop and market. A yard, according to mother, was from the tip of her nose to the end of her fingers, not very precise but the customers never complained.

I attended a sale with dad, which had a large amount of calico. Soon he was bidding for the calico, this sale had quite number of lots and the auctioneer usually gave the buyer of the first lot the option of taking as many lots as he wanted.

The auctioneer started the first lot of calico very cheaply. Dad bid and there didn't seem to be another bidder. I thought he had really pulled of a wonderful deal since he could take the next 15 lots when the hammer came down. The auctioneer suddenly said, 'I am withdrawing all this estate, we will now move on to lot 25'.

We bought some very small lots of cloth, which dad paid for and I loaded them on the van.

He was waiting to speak with the auctioneer.

I waited with him and he asked what he had done wrong. The auctioneer assured him he had done nothing wrong whatsoever but the goods had been accepted without reserve and the owner was trying to bid for his own goods, which wasn't allowed, so I withdrew the lot. Dad was very disappointed but realised that the auctioneer was right.

I decided to take a break from life at the auctions and to enjoy some foreign sun. My parents had always looked after us regarding pocket money and along with brother Philip and a friend called Brian we booked to go on a cruise to Europe, sharing a four-berth cabin with a stranger on the SS Batory.

Any hopes of lying in the sun were soon dispelled. I developed a prickly heat rash. The ship's doctor gave me some cream but suggested I stay out the sun for the rest of the trip.

In Tangiers we all went to a nightclub, including our cabin companion. The drinks were outrageously expensive and we refused to pay. The manager said if we did not pay the full amount he would call the police. A short time passed and a man in civilian clothes arrived saying he was a policeman. I asked to see his credentials and he produced a revolver which he pointed at my head. I said, 'That's good enough for me.' We promptly paid the bill and left.

At Cadiz we went on a trip to a sherry-producing vineyard and were brought glasses to try. Philip was always and still is very generous. He gave the waiter some money and more sherry arrived. Each time Philip tipped the waiter we were given more sherry. Then we were asked which one we liked, each of us picked a different one. This time the waiter bought a bottle of each. Four bottles were devoured, plus the samples. By the time we left we were all well and truly drunk.

At last I completed my articles and dad presented me with my reward - a Ford Escort shooting brake. It had to be a shooting brake because there was no purchase tax. Dad knew every trick, but at least it was my first new vehicle and he paid the running costs out of the business. So, I was all set with a career and a car.

Little did I know what was around the next corner!

14

Engagement, marriage, honeymoon

I'd been to Israel for nearly three weeks and was keen to show off my tan. I met two of my friends, Michael and Melvyn, in the Grand Hotel cocktail bar in Sheffield. Michael mentioned there was a Junior Israeli fundraising event on nearby.

I'd seen this lovely girl called Anne Green at previous Maccabi football and cricket events in Leicester. She was engaged and not surprisingly her fiancé guarded her from all other beaus. Anne was my mother's cousin's daughter's best friend and on this occasion the fiancé wasn't to be seen. It was easy for me to get an introduction through my cousin who also informed me that her engagement was over. I spent most of the night dancing and talking with Anne and her friend Stephanie.

I told Anne I had a meeting in London the following Thursday and would call in and see her on the way because I had bought her a present in Israel. It so happened I had brought an extra present back with me, a leather cigarette case.

Philip, Irvine and myself looking at plans for the new sports field on Wadsley Common

**Anne at her first
Maccabi Gala
Night in 1965**

Our courtship wasn't all a bed of roses. On the occasions I went to Leicester, I always stayed at the Grand Hotel. One Saturday evening I was invited to a party and booked in there. Anne just about ignored me all night. I assumed that all wasn't well with our relationship and her ex-fiancé was on the scene again. I returned to the hotel wondering what to do.

The next morning at breakfast I was continually being paged to take a phone call but I ignored them. The young lady on reception said I'd had a number of phone calls from a lady who wanted me to ring her which I did an hour later. Anne apologised for more or less ignoring me the night before and invited me for Sunday lunch at her mother's. This I accepted and everything worked out fine.

When Anne first came to Sheffield, she stayed overnight at the Hallam Towers Hotel. A Maccabi Gala Night had been arranged there and since I didn't know what time I would get away it was easier for her to be able to change and sleep there. Ted Ray was the cabaret. This event was to raise money for a new sports field for Sheffield Maccabi. Later she usually stayed at my brother Irvine's house.

We got engaged in March 1966. I bought a ring from Billy Hill for £350. I had been saving to buy an MGB GT but that went by the way. Dad had a jeweller friend, Don Seldon, who came over from Leeds. To check the ring's value, dad put it among other jewellery, which he was showing to Don. The dealer immediately offered £395 for this one item. Dad explained it was mine, and handed it back to me.

Anne passed her driving test but unfortunately her first long journey became a rather hazardous adventure. One of her brothers was going away and said she could use his car provided she collected and returned it to Luton Airport. She enjoyed the use of the car but the time came to return it. I was drafted in to go to Leicester, follow her down to Luton, then bring her home.

It was a filthy night with the rain pouring down and visibility was poor. Unfortunately she took a wrong turning. I managed to stop her continuing and told her we needed to turn around. When we got to airport she told me that she'd bumped the car backing into a tree.

'Don't worry, I'll pay for it,' I said rather gallantly. What I didn't know was that it was a company car and the repairs would have been met by their own insurance. That was £200 wasted.

That mishap was nothing compared to the embarrassment we suffered on one of our regular journeys to and from Leicester. We'd stopped at a country pub for a comfort break and Anne used the bathroom whilst I bought two soft drinks from the bar. She was gone an age and I began to get concerned. I hovered outside the Ladies before plucking up courage to go inside to see if she was okay. I called out and sure enough Anne replied that the lock had jammed on the door and she was trapped inside. I managed to climb over and force the door, breaking the lock in the process. We both made a hasty retreat!

Her home proved a handy stop-off point to and from the FA Cup final. My team Sheffield Wednesday had made it through to play Everton at Wembley. Philip and I and two friends Brian and Leon decided we'd make a weekend of it.

We stayed the Friday night in a London hotel, visiting a casino. Leon and I decided we'd go partners and I watched as he played blackjack. At the end of each hand he was asked by the croupier what he had and Leon replied, 'The same as him,' pointing at a man in the first seat who was raking in the chips. They were both paid out without question. We won enough money to pay for both our visit to London and the tickets.

A win for Wednesday would have completed the weekend, but sadly they lost 3-2 after being two goals up.

Our wedding and honeymoon were eventful to say the least. The service was arranged for 31st August 1966, a Bank Holiday. It is of course custom that the bride's father pay for the reception, but this was out of the question. Anne's family business had been closed for many years. Her father was in a nursing home after suffering a serious stroke and her mother was the breadwinner, working in a dress shop.

Most times I visited Leicester we tried to visit Anne's father in his nursing home. I was unsure if he actually knew who I was but he seemed to enjoy seeing Anne. Her two older brothers were both married with young families and the youngest brother was completing his articles as an accountant.

Wedding day
31st August 1966

Dad said he would pay but only on the condition that no one must know. He also insisted on a tea dance and the date. Anne's mother, with the help of the gown shop, provided Anne's dress which was stunning.

He also booked three rooms at the Grand Hotel in Leicester, one for himself and mother, one for the bridesmaids, and one for the best man, groomsmen, and me to change in.

I travelled down with my best man and his wife on the morning by car. Jewish custom is that the groom fasts until after the ceremony which I did. We did stop on the way for refreshments but I had been told by mother that I wasn't to have anything until after the ceremony and I didn't. I didn't know at the time that Anne had endured a terrible pre-wedding night. All the lights had failed in the house, hampering her preparations.

The synagogue was very small with three clergy to take the service. First they wanted to know if my best man was Jewish. Luckily my own Rabbi arrived and assured them Brian indeed was. The reception and tea dance were held in the Communal Hall across the road from the synagogue. Dad gave Anne an envelope which contained a cheque for £200 made out to Anne Patnick along with a note saying every woman should be independent of her husband, which I found out recently he had done with both my sister-in-laws.

The service proceeded without a hitch. I wish I could say the same for the reception, though most people didn't realise that my mother was quite ill. She'd always suffered from diverticulitis, a condition that causes inflammation of the lining of the intestine. She didn't eat because of her tummy problem but drank the sparkling kosher wine and looked ghastly. Also I believe she had fasted and was drinking on an empty stomach.

I spent the entire time watching her at the table and wondering if she was all right each time she went to the lavatory. I was so worried I didn't eat myself, though I managed to reply to the toast. I repeated the joke that dad had been ill with a mystery rash which had been diagnosed by one of Irvine's friends as 'hacksawitis' which went down very well.

The honeymoon proved problematical. We'd booked a holiday in Tunisia but were forced to cancel because they brought the time of the flight forward to leave before the wedding itself! Then, after we rearranged the flights, the trip was cancelled on the advice of the Foreign Office who said that it was unwise for Jewish people to travel to an Arab country. In the end we settled on a small village on Majorca called Paguera. Brian and his wife Lynn drove us from the reception to Heathrow, getting lost on the way and having to ask a Chinese man for directions to the airport. On the plane Anne went straight to sleep but I found a drinking companion in a gentleman to my left. When the trolley came round he ordered a gin and tonic and I had a whiskey. I'm afraid that was just the start. Between us we downed roughly 11 drinks.

After landing I stood up and realised I was well and truly drunk. Fortunately the hotel sent a car to pick us up because I was in no fit state to drive. The hour-long journey was horrendous for me, asking the driver to slow down but to no avail.

Then at the hotel there was a note informing us our room wasn't ready until the next day. The receptionist didn't speak a word of English which, presumably in my state neither did I! I wasn't even incapable of signing the hotel register and Anne had to do it, signing in as Anne Green and Edward Patnick.

They provided an emergency room and we both collapsed on the bed not bothering to unpack or undress. The next day we were given our proper room and I ate for the first time in over 24 hours.

I also found out that Anne didn't like going to the beach, preferring sitting by the pool. I went to the beach everyday while Anne stayed by the pool. No one at the hotel realised we were a honeymoon couple for the first week until Anne told a couple who had taken pity on her since she was always alone by the pool.

The only other eventful event was our visit to a nightclub where I had a tummy upset and sent most of the time being sick, though there is a photo of us that evening where everyone says how well we both looked.

**Honeymoon and
an outing to Tito's**

And then, towards the end of the holiday, a surprise letter from my father. I would be taking over the business on 1st November. We came home full of the joys of Spring.

15

A close call

House-hunting began in earnest, but we suffered the usual frustrations of either not liking houses we could afford or not affording houses we liked. We fell in love with Den Bank House on Manchester Road, but since I was only on £15 a week there was no chance.

A solution arrived when Philip bought Den Bank House and we purchased his house in Whirlow Court Road for £6,500. Anne had started work as a hairdresser at Marjorie Dalton's salon in the Grand Hotel, Sheffield and was earning more than me, but I don't think on our combined wage we would have got a loan. However, Philip being an estate agent arranged a mortgage for us with a company for whom he was an agent.

Furnishing the house wasn't a problem since I could always buy or acquire some second-hand furniture. Through generous wedding presents we had a double bed and my brothers bought us a gas cooker. We were also promised a dining room suite by an aunt but the money never arrived. Unfortunately I had ordered a new one on the strength of her promises. I dreaded its arrival because I hadn't a clue how I would pay for it, but I was my father's son and wasn't going to cancel the order.

Dad also gave us, as wedding presents, two oil paintings which I liked, one had pride of place in our lounge, and the other adorned the dining room. I well remember a card night at my house. One of the visitors I wasn't particular friendly with but he played cards at the other houses I visited so I asked him to join us since it was my turn to play host. This man sat at the card table looking towards my oil painting, a Dutch oil still life of flowers on a wooden panel. He looked up and said, 'I'd get rid of that horrible painting.' I replied, 'I wouldn't swap that painting for your house.'

All of us were helped by my parents' generosity.

Anne often popped down to the auction room from her job for a chat or join me and dad for lunch in the Sunshine Café which was his regular venue on Thursdays. On one particular occasion there was a special sale of antiques and she had a look around during the lunch hour.

'Is there anything that you fancy, Anne?' dad enquired.

She pointed to a fruit bowl which was obviously continental. It had cross swords on the base which meant it was probably Dresden. Dad picked it up and examined it. 'You have good taste!' he said.

He then suggested I walk Anne back to her job. Later that day he handed me a small parcel wrapped in newspaper. 'Here, give this to Anne,' he said. I picked her up from work and handed her the package. Sure enough, she had acquired her first Dresden piece.

Working in the market, mother asked Anne to pick her up and take her to the furriers as she fancied a new mink coat. Mother was in her market clothes, plus her large leather market pocket. I said, 'Mum, you can't go like that, go another day when you are dressed properly.'

'Don't you worry, they will accept my money no matter how I'm dressed,' she replied. Anne was embarrassed, especially on entering the shop. Mother tried on many coats before buying a full-length black mink. Yes, she was right, they treated her like a lady from stepping into the shop until leaving with her new purchase. At the same time she bought Anne a mink jacket, and the same for her other two daughters-in-law, Lynda and Hazel.

I continued looking at furniture in houses while dad attended auction sales on my behalf if and when he fancied. One job will remain in my memory for the rest of my life. I was asked by Social Services to meet some people from out of town and look at the contents of a flat in Sheldon Road.

It was upstairs, consisting of two rooms, the hall plus an attic. A quick look told me there were three items worth moving or were saleable. The rest was rubbish. The attic was full but had to be cleared. It contained a load of mainly broken glass.

The two members of the family then informed me that they'd changed their minds and the three items that were saleable they were keeping. There was no way I would consider moving the rubbish unless the three items were included so I told them that and left.

I waited in the car for the man from Social Services who informed the two gentlemen they would have to move everything in the flat themselves so the keys could be handed to the landlord. After half an hour he arrived at the car to inform me the relatives had reconsidered and they would leave the three items for me if I would move the rest. This I agreed to do.

The next day I went with George to clear the flat. We started with the rubbish, leaving an oak chest, a hall table and an oak coffer until last. The bedroom, kitchen and hall didn't take long but the attic was a challenge. The broken glass had to be taken down two flights, making sure we didn't cut ourselves.

Then, at the back of the glass was a mirror which I hadn't seen until we removed the glass in the front of it. It was an oval convex mirror with a gilt frame and a bird on top. The chest, table and oak coffer and now the mirror we carefully loaded last.

The van was kept at dad's house, Wadsley Grove, so after we finished the job I dropped George off and made my way there with the evening paper of course. Dad had a visitor, Mr. Sheard. I said to dad that there were some things I would like him to have a look at. He couldn't wait and asked Mr. Sheard to come with him. Mr. Sheard was a book dealer but also dealt in antiques. Dad and Mr. Sheard joined me on the van and I showed them the items, but they were more excited by the mirror. Mr. Sheard said, 'I'd send that to Henry Spencer's Auction sale at Retford if I were you.'

A few days later I took all four items to Retford. I spoke with a young lad who told me he was an articled pupil and it was his job to receive furniture for sale and prepare the catalogue which was afterwards checked by one of the partners. I felt sorry for him, remembering my own days as an articled pupil. I gave him £5 to keep an eye on my goods.

To my surprise the mirror fetched £500. It was Georgian. The cheque arrived a few days before the 'wedding gift' dining room suite and luckily just paid for it.

I still can't help thinking had I walked away from that flat and if the two relatives hadn't changed their minds I don't know how I would have paid for the suite. Dad had told me a million times, 'Always check the attic, cellar and the dustbin, you never know what people throw away or forget.'

Anne and I settled into married life. She had her first car, a Sunbeam Imp Sport, which cost about £650, borrowed of course from dad, and we acquired a red setter called Chemi.

May 1968 saw the birth of our daughter Lisa Helen. The dog was wonderful with Lisa, guarding over her as she slept outside in the pram, not letting anyone except Anne and me near. When Lisa was six months old she sat on the floor playing with Chemi who let her do anything, even take bones from her mouth.

Unfortunately, Anne suffered from post-natal depression. Our daughter rarely cried, but if she did Anne couldn't stand it and I would take Lisa out in the car until she was asleep. I once took her to an automatic car wash and she screamed the entire time and has never been able to go in one since.

16

A new era

Yes, 1970 proved to be a very eventful year for my immediate family. Our son, Simon, was born in March and that same evening I became a freemason. Things were going smoothly, but we were in for a rude awakening.

Out of the blue, Sheffield City Council placed a compulsory purchase order on the Langsett Road shop. This was a real blow. Untidy it may have been, but the shop was well known as the place you could buy almost anything. We even had post from abroad addressed simply, Sheffield, England.

Once we had a request from overseas for a three-pronged fork. Dad duly sent one back free of charge along with a compliments slip. The shop was often quoted by parents to their children, 'Your room looks like Patnick's shop.' Even the leader of the city council, Alderman Ron Ironmonger, used the expression in a council meeting.

Langsett Road 'Closing Down Sale'

Dad consulted his solicitor who hired a barrister to represent us at the public hearing. This proved to be a waste of time. The council order was upheld. One of the problems was I didn't have anything in writing. Dad had given me the business and I paid £10 a week, £5 rent and the same for the stock, but this wasn't accepted by the hearing since I didn't have a formal lease.

Irvine, who'd been elected to the council the previous year, was an outspoken member of the Conservative opposition and managed to persuade the council to offer me a site in Holme Lane to build a new shop. Plans were submitted and agreed by the officers but the planning committee, made up mostly by the majority Labour councillors, refused permission. They said the piece of land should be used as a car park.

The decision amazed me because the land had been earmarked for commercial use and planning officials all thought the space was too small for a car park.

To rub it in further, at the time of writing, more than four decades later, the site has still not been developed. Irvine wasn't the least bit surprised at the decision. 'Unfortunately you are my brother and your name is Patnick,' he sighed.

We looked at a few shops but I set my heart on an old Co-Op in Page Hall Road. Including the basement, it had four floors with a large lift to them all plus an outside building. The only drawback was that the yard was too narrow at the front to allow a vehicle to get up the side to park.

Dad wasn't sure and said I should find out more about the district. This wasn't hard; there was a Weston's chemist across the road. I spoke to Ralph Weston who said it was the best shop in their chain. That was good enough for me.

The shop had two large display windows with a door in the middle, plus on either side of the door were large plate-glass windows that were curved, one of which was broken. The agents were J. J. Greaves. Dad said before buying it I had to see the partner in charge and get them to put a new window in for the broken one. This was done by altering the window to a straight piece of plain plate glass.

Dad duly bought the building, which was much bigger than Langsett Road, for £12,500. So began a new era.

Dad insisted the name remained the same, A. Patnick. I used a designer, David Barnes, to produce and print writing paper invoices and began to advertise the new premises. Patnick's of Page Hall, tripped nicely off the tongue, but David had other ideas.

He stressed we must have a corporate image and the name printed in such a way that it could be recognised by the first two letters; the logo as he put it. Therefore the A and P were joined together, along the lines of C & A. I explained we were a

The Page Hall store before we moved in

junk shop not a high street chain. David came back with, "Junkerama. It pays to visit our Junkerama". So "We Buy and Sell Almost Everything" was a thing of the past and the new slogan was to stay for over 40 years.

I don't believe anyone thought I would ever fill the large premises in Page Hall, but I decided that in future items from house clearances would all be taken to our new shop and sold from there.

I had to sort out staffing and contacted the foreman of J. J. Greaves who had recently retired to see if he would be interested in a job looking after the top floor, mostly antiques, plus the older bric–a–brac and collectables. He readily accepted.

The Page Hall store before (left) and after (right) David Barnes' 'Junkerama' make-over

Beryl, who had worked at the old shop, came with us, and two ladies who were Mormons, worked two days each. Mother also helped occasionally. In no time the shop was up and running.

Deliveries were a pain initially. They had to be fitted around other work and people had to be in to receive them. It soon became clear that a day or days had to be assigned. I decided on Tuesdays and Saturdays and employed two men, paying them for each delivery made. One of the men, George's wife, Dot, came to work for us part time and proved to be an excellent sales assistant for many years both in the shop and market.

We used the basement for beds, divans and bedsteads. Every house we cleared had beds, and any that were stained went to the destructor. The ground floor had normal household furniture: it also contained an office under the large central staircase. The first floor was mostly bric-a-brac with more office space; the third floor mainly curios and antiques.

One piece of fortune helped. Social Services had a new boss who insisted furniture from deceased estates, with no relatives had to be sold by auction. The first house load they sent for auction they received a bill for £150. My contact at the office told his boss they'd never received a bill from Mr Patnick, so nearly all future work came my way.

Soon after opening I had two Victorian drawing room suites, one a nine-piece, the other a seven-piece. We had them arranged in both windows and they certainly created a great deal of interest from dealers and the public. Indeed Anne's youngest brother and his wife bought one, at a discount of course. I never saw the suite in his house or ever again, though we did visit them quite often.

In the seventies I read that one of my friends, who had a large wholesale business, unfortunately had a fire at his warehouse. I happened to bump into him that evening, told him I was sorry, and asked if there was anything I could do to help.

'No, but thanks for your concern,' he said. I plucked up courage to ask if he would consider selling me the fire salvage. I received an answer I wasn't expecting. 'You can't afford it.'

I was quick to respond, 'Tell me how much you want and I'll tell you if I can afford it. You don't know what's in my pocket.'

The gentleman in question started to apologise but I walked away. The next day he phoned me saying I was quite right and he'd spoken to the assessors who had agreed £50,000 for the furniture and carpets. But he said there were other items that may interest me, such as underwear. Could I meet them at the premises at 2pm? I had no problem with that.

He was quite right, I couldn't have afforded the main stock. I walked around with the assessor and agreed £5,000 for what was left.

Near the entrance we passed the seat of the fire where rolls of cushion floor was kept. We had to be careful, there was only room for one person to edge along one side. The rolls didn't look too bad.

The assessor, a Mr. John Smith, hadn't mentioned this room at all and I asked what they were going to do with it. He said they'd have to pay for someone to take it to the tip. I had another quick look and said, 'I'll give you £10 and move it for you.' This was accepted with grateful thanks. It was probably the best £10 I have ever spent in my life.

The good stock was moved to Page Hall very quickly and I soon had my money back, then later we moved the cushion flooring. It was unloaded into the yard and the complete rolls taken into the shop. There, Beryl and Dot measured it and sold it at £1 a yard. It sold like hot cakes.

Meanwhile brother Irvine, with a circular saw, cut the bad ends off the burnt rolls and this also flew out at 50 pence a yard. Mother was on the scene too and nagged Irvine to cut the ends quicker. The customers were queuing! We sold out of the cushion floor on the Saturday – not bad going since it only arrived at the shop on Friday afternoon.

I was very pleased with my first fire salvage. The assessors suggested I pay direct to the people who had the fire, which gave me time to find the money to pay. It was arranged that my £5,000 would be deducted from their claim which suited me fine. The following week I went with my cheque book to pay my money. I was ushered into Eric's office which he shared with his elder brother, Dennis. Eric asked me how I'd gone on with the stock and I of course said I was delighted especially the cushion floor, explaining what a coup I had made with my £10 purchase.

This was a mistake. Dennis said they were entitled to 50% of my profit or least some more money than what I had agreed to pay. I ignored this and Eric never mentioned it again.

I did however receive a phone call from Dennis the next day asking if I could meet him at a fire damaged warehouse as they had some more fire salvage I might be interested in.

One of his employers, Merton, was with him and they took me to a part of the warehouse I had not seen before. I was shown a large quantity of flat-pack kitchen furniture. I made an offer which was readily accepted.

The next day I had it picked up and taken to the shop. I realised they would have to be assembled. This would mean finding someone to put them together. Irvine was available and very willing to carry out the task. He didn't find his job easy. All the boxes had pieces missing so it was a question of taking the missing bits from different items to make a complete article.

Irvine did his best and we managed to sell a few of his assembled kitchen units, but the majority were scrapped. I had bought a quantity of returns. It was a very good job I had bought the original fire damaged goods at a very good price otherwise I wouldn't have been able to stand the loss on the flat-pack furniture.

The next weekend I had a phone call from the assessor, John Smith, who enquired if I knew the people who had bought the large amount of the fire salvage, since I was a friend of Eric and so were they.

I replied I did, and he asked what kind of firm they were and I replied a large reputable furniture store. He said they would not be doing business with them again. In their advert for the fire salvage sale they'd used the name of the company that had the fire, which was against the ethics of selling fire savages.

And cheekily they'd demanded a refund because the goods didn't match the inventory. The son of the owners complained that one carpet was a 4 x 3 yards instead of 4 x 4, and a dining room suite had four chairs when it was down as having six.

I said I couldn't understand anyone complaining about such a minor discrepancy on a £50,000 purchase. He agreed, but again said we will not be dealing with that firm again.

I had been very lucky in more ways than one. First, I had advertised but didn't use the name of the firm who had the fire. And, I'd bought the salvage at the right price and finally I paid for the fire salvage, without having to borrow the money, even from my father.

The end of that month I received another phone call from John Smith informing me there had been a fire at a departmental store in Huddersfield and asking if I'd be interested in rolls of curtaining.

I knew nothing about curtaining but said I was interested, mainly because my first fire salvage had been so lucrative. Dad suggested I take mother with me.

The store smelt of smoke but the curtaining seemed untouched. After consulting mother I made an offer of half the cost price. This was accepted and a list of the stock was produced that had been verified by the assessor.

Mr. Smith then said there was some furniture available on the mezzanine floor. I had a good look around and said I would give them £5,000 for everything. His assistant, Andrew, said they were looking for double that sum. I walked around the floor another couple of times but didn't alter my first impression.

Back we went to Mr. Smith. He said he was sorry, but they did expect an offer in the region of £10,000. This I wasn't prepared to pay, so all that remained was to pay for the curtaining and leave. I made out a cheque for £5,000 and then left for Sheffield, explaining we would move the stock the next day.

Driving back, I was worrying about not buying the furniture but pleased with my purchases. Just before we arrived in Sheffield I noticed a car going the other way. I said to mother, 'That's Clifford Spencer, the auctioneer. I bet he's going to look at that furniture.'

On arriving back in Sheffield I explained to dad my disappointment at not buying the furniture. He said I shouldn't worry, but to concentrate on the curtaining, handing me a cheque for the £5,000. I took it to the bank and explained to the manager it was to cover my purchase of a large fire salvage that afternoon. He said the cheque had already been presented and the bank had honoured it. I said, 'That's unusual isn't it?' He replied, 'I knew you'd be in to sort it out today.'

The stock arrived the next day and I had already organised an advert in the

Sheffield Telegraph for Saturday. 'Hundreds of fire salvage rolls of curtain to be sold at half price.' Next to this was a smaller advert for an auction of fire salvage furniture by Cooper Sons and Spencer. My worst fears had happened. I was sure this was the furniture I'd turned down. Dad again told me not to worry saying, 'I'd back your judgement anytime.'

The curtaining was selling well, but probably not as quickly as I'd liked. Then I received a visit from Syd, who owned a curtain stall in Sheffield Market. I was surprised to see him but delighted when he asked how much I would take for the remaining rolls. I explained we had been selling it for three days but would take 65% of cost for what was left, but that I couldn't guarantee each roll was the length on the original ticket. He said this wasn't a problem, he would come the next day with his wife and measure every roll.

Next morning Syd arrived with his wife Miriam. It was a pleasure to see them work, unrolling each roll, measuring it, and then rolling it back on the roll, while seeing we made a note of each length. Not like mother on the stall. A yard according to her was from the tip of her nose to the end of her fingers, not very precise but the customers never complained.

So, the curtaining had delivered a nice profit, but I was still upset with not buying the furniture. I decided to attend the auction to see how much it went for, secretly hoping that it would bomb.

Two days after the sale I was surprised to receive a phone call from Andrew, the assessor. Had I attended the sale? Would I trust the auctioneer? I replied yes to both questions. I told him Mr. Spencer wouldn't knock anything down to his own mother cheaply. In fact, I thought the furniture had fetched very good prices.

A couple of days later I received a call from Mr. Smith, the assessor in charge of the Huddersfield area. He understood I had been to the sale of the fire salvage furniture. What did I think? I said the goods had all fetched a good price, even though I had obviously not bid for any of the furniture myself.

He said there was £20,000 worth of furniture at cost, which included another area of furniture that wasn't salvage, that neither I or Mr. Smith had known of. I then said, 'My offer of £5,000 was way out then, you must be very pleased.' I wasn't expecting his reply, 'I wish we had taken your offer. The sale achieved just over £4,000.'

'That can't be right, the goods were fetching half cost in fact in some cases over,' I replied. Mr. Smith convinced me he was right adding, 'There are expenses to come off that too.' He said my valuation had been right and he apologised for doubting my offer.

This of course this placed me in good stead, with this firm of assessors. For nearly ten years I was given first chance of fire salvage taking in the whole of Yorkshire and some in the Midlands, I bought nearly every one. Several from the House of Holland, which all proved profitable, though I was very careful with their flat-pack goods, I had learnt my lesson the hard way. My wife, Anne, changed our garden furniture every time their fire salvage arrived!

17

The fire salvages

One interesting purchase was a load of wine and spirits from The Box Tree, a famous restaurant in Ilkley which had suffered a fire. As I was loading the bottles on the van I was wondering how on earth I could sell them, since I didn't have a licence to sell alcohol. In the end, I copied dad's example and kept the alcohol for myself!

One of my brother's friends, Alan, started his own business importing tubular steel tables and chairs. The manager was passing Page Hall and decided to stop and have a closer look at our enterprise. He asked if I'd be interested in glass tables and tubular chairs, particularly seconds.

I visited their premises and was surprised to discover they were the height of fashion. Selling just second-hand furniture, we were always behind the times. It didn't take me long to make an offer of £5 a chair and £20 a glass-top table. This was accepted provided I took the lot, good, bad and useless.

I was convinced we could sell them at £75 and stand any that had to be destroyed. I was surprised how few were unsaleable. Some tables just needed rubber suctions and chairs, the odd screw. The table tops were either clear or dark glass. Some were scratched or chipped.

They sold very well indeed. I couldn't believe my luck, every month I was contacted with more of the same, though the tables did vary in size and shape, some larger and oval, others oblong which cost the same but fetched more money and seated six.

But all good things come to an end.

One day I was shown stock that was simply unsaleable. The manager followed me to my car and said he was sorry but Alan had sold the seconds to another customer who was paying the same price as me, plus V.A.T whereas I was buying them with V.A.T included. This customer was picking out the good ones and leaving the bad ones for me. I didn't receive any more phone calls from them, but it had proved lucrative while it lasted.

I also bought off one of dad's regulars, a firm called T. C. Vere, they imported basket ware from the Far East and had the same problem with their damaged goods. The seconds were not worth sending back so dad bought them at ten shillings each item. Usually they were Ali Babar dirty linen baskets which dad sold for £2 or £1. Some were very bad and had to be destroyed but they all cost the same, since dad took the good with the bad.

One particular day I was with dad and he was shown a large quantity of children's chairs; he paid the same price for these no matter what condition. Back at the shop I unloaded the van and mother began selling them. They didn't fly out but we had a steady stream of customers.

An hour after mum's first sale an antique dealer, from lower down the road, arrived and asked mum how much she would take for the lot. Mother replied, 'they are £1 each, how many do you want?'

He spent another half hour sorting the best ones and mum took his money at £1 each. That evening every one had been sold. Some for what dad paid for them, but none were destroyed. Mother couldn't understand how an antique dealer could buy brand new chairs but the next day they were on sale in his shop at £2 each. Dad was satisfied with his deal. The dealer unfortunately died very young, leaving his wife with two young children, a boy and girl. His wife, however, managed to carry on his business, after his death, successfully.

On another occasion dad and I went to Vere's and his son met us in the showroom. Dad waited for his father to appear which he did apologising for keeping dad waiting but he didn't mind. The four of us made our way to the warehouse and dad looked at the varied articles which were to be disposed off, then counted them and worked out the price of ten shillings each, which Mr. Vere accepted. His son went into a paddy about wasting time for peanuts when they should get more for them or just not bother at all. Mr. Vere said to his son that my father was a very good customer and never complained and he would always insist on serving him himself.

Dad carried on dealing with the firm until he retired and even then I continued buying from them after Mr. Vere's death with his son, though the price fluctuated depending on what they were trying to unload. This association continued until they went out of business. I remember after my marriage changing our garden furniture at least twice, for cane furniture, Harold Needham making loose cushions, for the cane chairs and settees all slightly damaged. These items cost a lot more than the ten shillings dad used to pay Mr. Vere.

In 1973 I bought my first new car – a Jaguar. It had been on order for months and Philip came to the showroom with me to collect it. As you can imagine, I was quite excited. Until that is, Philip noticed a scratch on the boot. The salesman looked at it and said, 'If you don't want it, Mr Patnick, that's okay because people are queuing up to buy these. I can sell it for more than you are paying.'

In fact we wiped off the mark, paid for the car and left, much to the salesman's disappointment.

But my thrill didn't last long. Soon after, I attended my fourth and final Maccabiah as the team vice captain. We had decided it was too much effort for Anne, Lisa and Simon to accompany me. On my return to Heathrow Anne met me in a hire car. The Jag had broken down and was at a garage at Henley's Corner being repaired. Only a month old and it was off the road for nearly the same amount of time.

My next fire salvage nearly got us into trouble with the law. I met Mr. Smith at a chemist in Halifax.

The fire had been at the rear and I began counting the goods in the main part of the shop, converting them into lots of £10 each. I thought of a ridiculous figure and began to talk to the owner and Mr. Smith, informing them that it was very difficult to work out what might sell and what would have to be destroyed. Also they would have to remove any items that could only be sold by a qualified chemist, which I certainly wasn't. The owner said not to worry because the only stuff I wasn't qualified to sell was out the back where the fire had been.

Finally Mr. Smith said, 'Well Mr. Patnick, how much for the lot without the back room and remember you move everything.' I replied £500. To my surprise he said that was fine.

All the way back to Sheffield I worried that I hadn't got a clue if I'd paid too much, if a fire salvage chemist stock would sell, and if so, how much to charge for each item.

I stopped and phoned the shop, telling the two lads to go to the market and get as many small cardboard boxes as they could. I also phoned Anne to ask her to make arrangements to come with me in the morning to help move the contents and record every item.

The next day we met at Dot's house and the van followed me to Halifax and the chemist shop. The lads had done a good job so we had plenty of boxes to fill. Each item was placed in a box and counted. Anne gave me the final count. I soon worked out that the stock was very cheap, nothing costing me more than a penny.

All I had to worry about now was would it sell? This was nothing unusual since I always had this worry until I retired. The next day the van was unloaded and I informed the two girls who would be serving that everything had cost sixpence and they would have to bear this in mind.

Anne also came at first just to pick out things for home. Then the word spread that Patnick had cheap chemist shop goods. The shop was packed in no time. The boys were unpacking boxes and filling shelves behind the counter. Beryl, Dot and Anne were serving, I began to help the lads unpack. Anne arranged the items into different areas, such as soap, plaster, toothpaste etc.

After two days I had my money back, so it was indeed a good deal. The shop was packed for days. Then I was upstairs in my office when Anne phoned from downstairs saying there was a problem would I come down. There was quite a crowd in the shop, with Beryl, Dot and Anne all serving. Anne said 'this gentleman wants to see you.'

I politely said, 'Yes sir what can I do for you?'

He replied that he was from a government department and that we were selling some poisons. I said that was impossible since the chemist had removed everything that we were not allowed to sell.

The gentleman then pointed at Beryl and said, 'I bought this from that lady,' I quickly said, 'Oh no you didn't, you bought it from that lady,' pointing at Anne, adding that there were three of us who would swear to that and maybe some of the customers too. I certainly didn't want Beryl getting into trouble for something that wasn't her fault.

He said he wanted to know from whom and where I had bought the goods. I informed him that I couldn't give him either, as it was unethical to disclose where the fire salvage had come from. I assured him that I had asked that anything I wasn't allowed to sell be removed.

He replied that he had purchased a 'part two' poison which would mean I and the lady who sold it would be prosecuted. I asked to look at the article and it turned out to be a hair colour which I had no idea was classed as a poison.

I phoned Mr. Smith who was very apologetic and said he was sorry I had been put in this position, particularly after asking that anything that wasn't allowed to be sold by me be removed. He also said I could give him his particulars to the government official concerned. Weeks later, we were informed that no action would be taken against us, but we were warned not to transgress again.

I was learning all the time. If poison was hazardous then electrical goods were too. I was called to see hundreds of fridges, electric heaters and other appliances following a flood in a basement of a warehouse in Sheffield. I knew of course, that electricity and water don't mix, but these appeared fine.

There was no way I could test them, so had to take a gamble. Moving the goods was easy – the basement had a trap door opening onto the pavement – but every appliance had to be tested which was a pain. Lo and behold, every one worked. I was delighted and also surprised. I knew how much second-hand fridges were worth, and could obviously charge more for new ones. In the end I decided on £30 for a small fridge.

A Jewish gentleman arrived in the shop and enquired how much I would take for 25 fridges.

'You can have them for £625.' I said. He offered me £600. 'You can have 24 for that,' I said and walked away. He took the 25 and paid the full asking price.

Two days later he was back, demanding I replace one of the fridges which had a small dent in the door. I could hardly get my breath. These were probably half the retail price but he wanted it changed. We had none left so I told the girls to give him £5 back and he was happy.

From that deal I learned that most electrical goods were sealed units so water didn't necessarily damage them. But I also had to take the rough with the smooth. I was expected to take small damaged items as well as large stocks.

For instance, water-damaged second-hand carpets from private homes were more trouble than they were worth. You could only sell them if they were very cheap and usually cost more to fetch and deliver than they were worth. But I never refused a call from an assessor, knowing that a large stock helped pay for the losses on items like carpets.

I went to see a fire salvage in Hull which consisted of tools, but not hand tools. There were large generators and many tools, mostly electrical and certainly not for home use, but I bought them anyway.

How they would sell was going to be awkward as people couldn't use them at home. I remember vividly collecting them from Hull and after picking them up, the lads needed lunch so we stopped at a fish and chip shop. I decided to join them so asked them to get me some too, paying for all three.

I didn't realise the shop cooked in dripping. Being Jewish meant I had never eaten anything cooked in dripping as it wasn't Kosher[1]. The smell was enough for me and they went straight in the bin. I managed with an apple.

On our return I contacted an acquaintance who dealt with this type of equipment and sold the lot to him.

---

[1] *Anything that isn't approved by Jewish Law*

18

Home is where the heart is

That summer Anne fell in love with a large five-bedroom house – 154 Millhouses Lane – which was coming up for auction. I took brother Philip, an estate agent who knew his job inside out, and we both agreed with her. It was lovely. I got my solicitor Nick Waite to check the deeds prior to the auction and he pointed out a potential snag. There was a covenant preventing any future building on the site. Also, of course, if we went ahead we would need to pay ten per cent of the purchase price as soon as the hammer went down.

154 Millhouses Lane

Financially we were doing well and I didn't see any problems with the deposit. But I would obviously need to sell our home in Whirlow Court Road. Buying a house at auction is exciting but stressful and we were happy when the gavel came down in our favour for £32,500.

But nothing is easy. Our old house didn't sell which meant a bridging loan from the bank, a mistake that could have ruined me. It was 12 months before it sold and a reduction of £10,000. Luckily I bought the carpets, curtains and light fittings for £500 with the help of the auctioneer Michael Haigh instead of the £5,000 they asked. Michael just told them they were worth £500 to me or they could remove them and sell them but he doubted they would get that amount for them if they did.

We moved in and everything appeared to be rosy. Lisa celebrated her sixth birthday and Simon was a lively four-year-old. I was nearly 38 years old with a thriving business and a loving family when disaster struck. I had a heart attack.

I wasn't feeling very well on the Monday and thought I'd pop in and see my friend David Barnett at his home in Lodge Moor after calling at Wadsley Grove to see my parents and drop off an evening paper.

David was a doctor at Sheffield Royal Infirmary and I wanted an informal check out to save seeing my own doctor. Unfortunately he wasn't at home, so after a chat with his wife Sharon I made my way home. I did in fact see David driving in the opposite direction, obviously on his way home, but decided against turning around.

The next day I went to work as usual, never giving my health a second thought. Wednesday lunch time I felt none too good and left work early, thinking I'd pick the kids up from school and drop the evening paper into mother and dad. But I began to feel worse. I parked the car and looked at my watch. It said 3.45pm. Anne would already have collected the children, so I drove home. I told Anne I had pains in my chest and arm. She took one look at me and rang the doctor.

Dr. Collins arrived and examined me then called for an ambulance, waiting with me until it came. I was admitted to Sheffield Royal Infirmary, the consultant being David Barnett's boss, Professor Kilpatrick.

David was at my bedside the next morning with the registrar. I was informed I had had a heart attack. I don't think David could believe it either, but the doctor said I would be fine provided I did as they instructed.

I remember saying, 'If you tell me to take rat poison I will,' David replying that was possible because sometimes they prescribed Warfarin.

Every day I was in hospital (I was there for a week) David found time to pop in to see me, often accompanied by one of the two registrars or the Professor. I didn't realise I was getting special treatment but I was. The registrars would check me out on their own before leaving for the day. On the eve of my discharge, one of them said, 'You'll be fine in six months, playing squash.'

'Good,' I replied, 'I couldn't play before my heart attack.'

David gave me strict instructions after I went home. I had to give up smoking, lose three-and-a-half stone and not drive for six weeks. I managed all three, reaching my weight goal of 11 stone 2 pounds.

One day he arrived at my home and asked if I'd like to go and see mother and dad to which I said yes.

'Good,' he said, 'We'll take your car.'

David drove me to Wadsley Grove and as we left he said, 'You drive.' On our way back to Millhouses Lane we passed brother Irvine, who couldn't wait to tell everyone not only was I driving a Jaguar with personalised number plates, 1 EKP, but I had a heart consultant as my passenger, just in case.

Back home, I learned certain things had happened while I was in hospital.

Irvine had decided to mow the lawns at Wadsley Grove, quite a hard and long job. The mower stopped rotating, so he decided to remove the obstruction without tuning the engine off which resulted in him almost losing one of his fingers.

More worryingly, the police had been tipped off that a criminal gang from Manchester were planning a raid on mum and dad's house. The police examined the house and found proof that the information was correct. They decided that valuables should be removed and while this was being done, by Irvine and some of his friends, the police would stay at the house and leak that all the valuables had been moved or sold.

Mother had a saying, 'Everything happens in threes.' They certainly did to our family in 1974. Everything turned out for the best and it wasn't long before the police packed up and left.

The first time I drove on my own was to fetch some potatoes. Anne said I wouldn't be able to carry the 5lb bag, so Lisa who was six, offered to come with me to carry them. I parked right outside the shop. The assistant said to me, 'You're not going to let that little girl carry that bag are you?' To which Lisa replied, 'Yes, that's the reason I'm here, mind your own business.'

The assistant replied, 'I think I've said the wrong thing.' Lisa replied, 'Yes you have.' I found the entire episode very embarrassing, but it wouldn't be the last.

I returned to work which meant more fire salvages. Mr. Smith asked if I'd be interested in a large carpet salvage with a cost value of £150,000. I said I thought it was out of my league, since I knew that I couldn't raise that amount of money. He said I should remember that money was an easy commodity to acquire but goods were not that easy. He said I should I take a look at least and so I made an appointment.

My next port of call was to the brothers whose fire led to my first fire salvage, since they had a large carpet department. They indeed were interested. The next day I arrived at their warehouse but was told by their secretary they had someone with them.

I was introduced to two gentlemen from Great Universal Stores, commonly known as GUS. I was no fool and realised they were working out a deal. In other words they were arranging how much they would get for their introduction to me.

I drove the GUS men to view the carpet. Mr. Smith welcomed me and introduced me to the manager of the factory. I introduced the GUS men to Mr. Smith who was polite but afterwards ignored them: he didn't even introduce the manager to them.

We proceeded to the large hangar-type warehouse. I have never seen such a large amount of carpet under one roof before or since. Mr. Smith then inquired, 'Which carpet would you like to see Mr. Patnick?' completely ignoring the men from GUS who had presented him with their card.

A forklift truck was at my disposal. I pointed at a roll on the top level that was brought down for our inspection. I looked at it, smelt it, and could see nothing wrong. I examined six more from different places and every one seemed perfect. The men from GUS tried to ask Mr. Smith to look at different carpets or just talk to him but he ignored them, saying, 'I'm dealing with Mr. Patnick. If you wish to know anything ask him.'

Mr. Smith then turned to me and asked if I wished to wash my hands. This seemed more like a command than a question, so I replied, 'Yes.' Off we went to the bathroom. Inside Mr Smith said, 'What do you think, Edward?.'

'I'd make you an offer of £80,000, but I haven't got that type of money.'

'What about them?' meaning the men from GUS.

I said, 'They think they can steal it and want to pay £20,000 or £25,000.'

Mr. Smith said, 'Fine, let's go back.' Back in the warehouse he asked, 'Is there anything else you wish to see Mr. Patnick? To which I replied, 'No.'

But the men from GUS started to ask about how much he was expecting to receive. Mr. Smith again informed then that he was dealing with me and if they needed any further information I would provide it. I spoke with them and they said they would make an offer of £25,000.

The journey back was very quiet. A few days later Mr. Smith told me the carpets had gone to a company in Europe for £100,000. Also that my offer of £80,000 was a good offer but they knew I would have had trouble funding it.

I began looking in auction rooms for articles for our new home. I was in no hurry, as things seemed to come my way. I did however see a corner cupboard I liked at Ellis Willis and Becket auction sale and Anne liked it too. It was bow-fronted with glass doors.

I left a bid of £135 with another dealer who helped them out on sale days, acting as the foreman, showing the goods or items the auctioneer was selling. Later that day I phoned the auction room to ask how much the cupboard had fetched. The clerk told me £85, so I believed it was mine. I arranged for the lads to meet me at the saleroom and phoned Anne to tell her we'd been successful. I went to the offices to settle but was amazed to be told I hadn't bought anything and it had gone to another dealer.

I explained to the woman I had left a bid with Robinson. I was very annoyed and confronted him near the cupboard in question. He said that another dealer had left a higher bid and he'd therefore bought it on her behalf.

I couldn't believe my ears but managed to track down the woman and asked if I could buy it from her. She agreed, but insisted I pay the £135 I had left originally. This I did, but I never left another commission with Robinson again and didn't do business knowingly with the lady either. If I hadn't phoned Anne prematurely to tell her I'd bought the cupboard I probably wouldn't have paid the extra £50, so it was an expensive phone call.

We had much better luck at a salvage sale in Leicester where I'd bought many items of furniture that had been in a fire at a warehouse belonging to a removal firm. Most of it seemed to have escaped any effects of the heat or smoke. Anne picked out a mahogany reproduction dining suite and a side table and coffee table both made of walnut. The suite replaced the one we'd had since our marriage which sold in the shop very quickly. The tables still grace our bungalow today.

Timing is everything in our business. For weeks Anne had been driving me mad about having a new fridge-freezer and we duly bought one for £350. Two days later I viewed a quantity of electrical goods at a warehouse in a fire salvage sale and couldn't believe my eyes. There, in the middle, was the identical appliance.

I ended up buying the stock, including the fridge which went on sale in my shop for just £175. My brother-in-law David supervised the sale, including the pricing, and we sold out within a week.

This fire salvage was the first one that I actually dealt with the partner in charge of the Sheffield office, a Mr. Ashton. The day after my purchase I received a phone call from John Smith, my original contact with this firm of assessors. He said, 'I understand you bought the contents of a warehouse yesterday of mainly electrical goods from my partner John Ashton?'

'Yes,' I replied.

He then asked if I had been shown two double divans.

'No.'

He then said, 'Be careful, they have nothing to do with the fire salvage claim.'

I said I was collecting exactly what Mr. Ashton showed me.

The next day I went with the lads to collect the goods and was met by the manager. 'There are a few more items that you didn't see yesterday that have to be moved,' he said.

Sure enough, I was shown two double divan beds, plus a quantity of glass holders for the garden. They were green with a spike to stick in the lawn and held two glasses.

I was shown the invoice for the two beds, £2,200 for the pair at cost. They were in a completely separate building and were never affected by the fire. I understand why they tried to include them, they just wouldn't sell at that price, and no one would buy a metal drinks holder for the garden either.

I just said I could only move goods showed me the day before by Mr. Ashton and went to supervise the loading of our van.

My confidence was growing by the week – enough even to take a family holiday. Two days before leaving I bought some carpets from a fire salvage sale and spent the eve of my vacation measuring and pricing them up.

Irvine and Philip looked after the shop whilst I was away along with mother who liked to keep her hand in. I thought I was well covered, provided I had bought the carpet right. My calculations were that each piece cost me a pound a yard and I arranged an advert in the local press.

I left on the Friday believing I had sorted everything. I phoned on the Monday to ask how the carpet was doing and mother reported I not only had my money back but was well into profit. In fact the Saturday was the best day we'd ever had.

On my return I discovered that Irvine and Philip had fallen out and left the shop leaving mother and the two girls serving. Mother didn't have the night safe facilities so had to take the entire takings home with her. She, however, didn't think it was such a dangerous thing to do.

We usually advertised special sales in the local print media. But one time David Barnes suggested we advertise it on television, since Yorkshire Television was doing a special promotion. I looked at the pricing and it didn't seem much dearer that the local paper. Unbelievably, the TV ad for our next carpet sale went out in the middle of Coronation Street, ITV's most watched programme. The next day our first customers, a local family, bought enough carpet to cover the cost of the whole consignment and the TV adverts!

Carpets always went well, unlike beds which customers were wary of buying second-hand. Every deceased estate seemed to have at least two beds which we had to take if we agreed to clear the whole house. Old and stained mattresses went straight to the destructor and the best bases kept in the basement at Page Hall.

One day Philip was helping out at the shop when an Irishman came in, saying he wanted to look around. He asked if there were more goods downstairs. The girls said only beds. Philip went down with him and a few minutes later arrived at my office upstairs saying he had a customer wanting to know how much the beds were.

I went quickly downstairs and asked the man how many he wanted and to point out which ones he had in mind. He said he'd take the lot at the right price. I had to explain that some were just head and foots, some with bases, and some mattresses. I would take £10 for a head and foot with side rails and £20 for a complete bed.

There were a vast quantity and I was amazed when he said he'd take the lot. He became a regular customer. We naturally called him Paddy and his items Paddy Beds. He was a godsend because no one else wanted them.

One day he arrived and asked if I wished to buy a van full of wallpaper. When I said no, he asked if he could store the paper so he would have room on the van for the beds. I agreed, naturally wanting to sell the beds. He unloaded all these rolls of wallpaper into the basement and said he had a call to make. He would return later for the beds and somehow fit the paper in too.

We are still waiting for that return visit. Just as suddenly as he appeared in our lives, he disappeared. In fact, when I later sold Page Hall I had to get rid of the wallpaper which was still there.

We certainly had some unusual customers. An American arrived one day and enquired how much I wanted for the panelling on the walls – an unusual request and one that wasn't easy to answer. The wood I hadn't bought, it came with the property, so it was money found, whatever I received. It was just a question of thinking of a figure and seeing what the reply would be. Yes, I sold the wood off the wall of the shop.

I was then asked how much I wanted for my office. This was a large room on the second floor, probably used as a fitting room originally. I just thought of a price but also said they would have to replace the wall with boards as I needed it as an office. This they agreed without any bartering.

Another American arrived saying he was interested in antiques. We really didn't specialise in this field, but upstairs we had a room full of small bits and bobs, things like pots and pans we acquired from houses, though probably too good for the market. Brother Philip was trying to interest him in anything. Suddenly he asked how much I wanted for everything on that floor. Again it was a very good question and I quickly totted up in my head anything worth £10, just like my father taught me when I was buying.

I came up with a figure which he accepted provided we packed everything in boxes. That wasn't a problem, I just sent the lads to collect empty cardboard boxes from the fruit market.

Philip named him Uncle Sam and while we packed the boxes he went off to visit other shops. He wasn't a nice man, but Anne invited him to our home for a meal. I quickly suggested we go out to a restaurant instead. I am pleased we did. His manners were appalling and he looked more a junk dealer than me.

Philip said he would take him to the antique shops in Sheffield the next day, which he did, hoping to earn some money through his introductions. He introduced him to almost every so-called antique dealer in Sheffield, but alas Philip didn't earn a penny. Uncle Sam sent for his goods and the Sheffield Star ran a front page picture and article on the American who bought the lot. He came to Sheffield on many more occasions and was taken everywhere by another antique dealer but never bought another thing from us. Maybe 'he got his leg in' with the floor of goods he bought but he never complained and no one forced him to buy.

The author in his shop after 'Uncle Sam's' visit

While at Page Hall I did receive a visit from the V. A. T. inspectors. They, unlike the Inland Revenue that had visited my mother and father, made an appointment to inspect our books. I wasn't really worried as I employed a bookkeeper who came every two weeks and wrote up my books. He would spend a couple of hours and always fill in the V. A. T. returns. He happened to be my accountant working for a large accountancy firm but did bookkeeping work during his weekends.

Until we moved to Page Hall I used to take all my bills and receipts with my bank stubs to the accountants once a year and they would produce accounts for me. Now we had tills and every day the till would be cashed up and the total entered on a weekly cash sheet that had every days takings and outgoing entered. This made it easy for my bookkeeper to transfer them into the books as well as being easier for the yearly accounts. All I had to do was add the market takings and leave my cheque book with the weekly sheets and the bookkeeper did the rest.

The V. A. T. inspectors arrived, there were two of them, one young and the other much older. I took them to my office where I had laid out all the papers they may need with the yearly book and weekly sheets. I asked if they needed anything else, which they said they didn't think so. I then said, 'well I have no intention of staying to hold your hands, you will need paying at the end of the month so I had better try and earn some money to pay you', and left. I returned four hours later and after chatting to the girls made my way to my office.

I did expect the worst.

On entering I asked if I was needed me for anything. The older man was sat away from the desk with the young one behind it. The young one asked me what I did with the market takings. Before I could reply or think of one, the older one said, 'He puts them in his pocket'. I just stood there and much to my relief the older one said, 'We've finished thank you'. They then packed up and left.

19

Trouble sleeping

You have to think on your feet in this business. I was delighted with the result of a bit of quick-thinking whilst looking around a fire salvage at a large bed manufacturers.

This was my first venture into new beds. There were about a dozen complete beds, the rest were just bases, hundreds of them, always difficult to sell without the mattresses. Then it suddenly dawned. Here I was at one of the largest bed manufacturers in the country: why not ask them how much they would charge for the equivalent number of mattresses for the unmatched bases!

I told the assessor the bases were worthless and asked if he would mind me talking to the manager so that I could buy extra mattresses.

'What you do Edward after you've bought the salvage is up to you,' he said.

I agreed to pay £20 for any new mattress provided I accepted they'd be made from the cheapest material in the range. They even agreed to deliver them free, on days they were in the area anyway. For me, it was just a matter of arranging the hiring of a 7.5 ton van to fetch the bases back.

An advertisement was placed in the local paper, 'New double divan beds from £35.' The shop was packed and they were selling, but we did have people asking for headboards. The stock reply was, 'You don't sleep on a headboard,' but some wouldn't buy the bed without a headboard. A quick phone call soon fixed that. For a fiver we could buy headboards from the same firm.

We required customers to pay upfront, informing them that delivery would take a couple of days to give us time to order and receive the mattresses and headboards.

However, one lady, who ordered a bed one Friday, arrived the following Tuesday saying she'd changed her mind and wanted her money back. I was upstairs and Dot phoned up asking what she should do. I explained that the bed was not ours, but now belonged to the lady. She could either have it delivered or when we sold it we would give her the money we received for it. Dot said the lady was adamant she wanted her money back. I said I'd come down and speak to her.

As I walked down the stairs I received a torrent of abuse. 'You cheating Jewish bastard, I want my money back. Hitler should have killed you all.' I was about to turn round and walk back upstairs. When the lady repeated her anti-Semitic rant, I told her calmly to leave the shop informing her she would receive her bed on the next delivery or we would sell it for her, less storage charge and delivery charge to her address. I also informed her that the storage charge was one pound a day.

A couple of days later she came back, accompanied by a woman from some local or government authority which meant nothing to me. The woman asked me out of the goodness of my heart to give the lady her money back. I just asked her whether or not if she'd been subject to such racist abuse would she give the money back? I never heard a word from either again.

The business can be very cutthroat. We were once asked by Sheffield City Council to furnish student accommodation. Each flat needed a bed, a bedside cupboard, a chest of drawers, a table and two chairs, plus two rugs and two sets of curtains. We had plenty of furniture; the only problem was the beds and curtains.

I decided to order a vanload of new single beds and the curtains could be obtained from Eversure Textiles. I put a small profit on the beds and curtains and priced the rest accordingly. Everything was fine until a new lady was put in charge of the contract. She phoned the bed manufacturer direct and also Eversure Textiles, so I lost the job completely. I never thought to remove the labelling on the goods.

In some areas I was proving to be better than the experts. I bought a quantity of three-piece suites which had been near a fire, but again were not smelling of smoke. They were perfect and filled a large space of the shop. I obviously wanted to sell them as soon as possible and asked my best friend Brian, whose father had a furniture shop in Attercliffe, if he was interested.

Dot was dying to start selling but I asked her to wait. I left Brian and his father to it, convinced they would purchase the suites, but they declined saying there were too many. I put an advert in the paper and sold all 50 in a fortnight. So, the furniture man couldn't sell them but the junk dealer could! It was the same with upholstery material to calico.

During this time I had a phone call from John Smith asking how well I knew the elder of the two brothers which I bought the first fire salvage from. I replied that I knew him very well but not as well as his younger brother. Mr. Smith then told me the older had a friend who was an auctioneer who would give him more than I paid for any salvage they had. All they had to do was tell them how much I was willing to pay and they would make a better offer.

I was worried that Mr. Smith would accept this but wondered why he was telling me and what he wanted me to do? It could mean he expected me to make better offers for any future fire salvages. I just didn't know what to say. I knew that Mr. Smith wouldn't accept anything for himself without paying for it and definitely wouldn't accept "a back-hander"[2]. I had heard him say 'I could do with a new duvet', when I was looking at the very first fire salvage and after I bought the stock I suggested he took the duvet which he refused, saying he didn't accept bribes. I was quick to point out that I would charge him the exact price I paid for the article. He accepted and when I worked out the price told him and received a cheque for the amount with a request for a receipt which I supplied.

I did think I had lost the chance of any more salvage when Mr. Smith said, 'I told him we are quite satisfied with Mr. Patnick and will continue to use him.' The following week I received a phone call from the auctioneer in question, who informed me he would buy off me any fire salvage I acquired and give me a profit on the price I paid. I informed him I could handle any salvage I bought without any help from anyone.

Around this time, my friend David Barnett, the doctor, was going to San Francisco to take his doctorate and wanted to store his furniture until his return and maybe sell his house. I suggested he speak with Patrick Crapper since he was an estate agent and whom he knew quite well.

I rang Patrick who suggested I bring David round. We had a coffee and chatted generally. Patrick suddenly changed the subject to ask about circumcision. He explained that he had a problem while away on holiday with a zip and was told that he now needed circumcision.

He asked what it entailed and if it would hurt.

David was quick to say, 'I didn't feel a thing, did you Edward when you had yours done?' Since we were both circumcised at eight days old, according to Jewish custom, I replied, 'No I didn't, but I don't remember it was so long ago.' I failed to add that I couldn't walk for 12 months afterwards for obvious reasons!

Patrick then advised David to let his house until his return, leaving the fridge and deep freeze in the property as they could deteriorate while in store. This was news to me but Patrick said that they would be much better being used while they were away. So it was decided to let the house furnished and just move personal things, plus ornaments and anything that he wouldn't want strangers to use. This they did. On his return after two years away he was appointed to a job in Leicester under his old boss Professor Kilpatrick.

[2] *Slang for a bribe*

While in Sheffield, David visited our shop, of course, and fell in love with a piano. It was a figured walnut piano with fret front, brass sconces and candlesticks. He asked how much it would cost, bearing in mind it would have to be delivered to Leicester.

I did explain it wasn't a good instrument, since it was a wooden frame but he insisted he wanted it. The lads delivered it to Leicester and I charged him £45, which paid for the delivery, plus they put on other things that needed to be taken from their home in Sheffield. Their daughter learned to play the piano on this instrument.

David and his wife Sharon also collected Goss china miniature ornaments which helped Anne and me a lot because I often came across them in house clearances. The ordinary ones were not expensive so I would put them away and give to them whenever we needed a present for them; to me they were cheaper than a box of chocolates and much more appreciated.

These miniature ornaments were really souvenirs for tourists. Many had a coat of arms of cities, or were set in famous landmarks and even army equipment. There were also cheaper versions such as Arcadia ware. David had one of the largest collections I have ever seen, filling a very large china cabinet. He bought many from antique fairs and finished with some expensive pieces.

I had acquired what I believed to be a set of Royal Doulton character plates in the late sixties. Since we had nowhere to display them at Whirlow Court Road, I allowed my brother Philip to use them in his home. The plates I had bought along with the contents of a deceased estate and they didn't really cost me anything. After we moved to Millhouses Lane we decided they would look nice round the small sitting room. David always admired the plates.

On one occasion we gave him a Royal Doulton plate I had acquired of a doctor, since I already had that character. He had begun to collect figures of doctors because of his profession.

David and Sharon soon had a collection of Royal Doulton character plates, including one called the 'Book Worm', which wasn't in my so called set.

When we first met David he was a lowly-paid junior doctor working all hours at the Sheffield Royal Infirmary. He supplemented his income by what he called 'ash cash,' money received from signing the death certificate for someone about to be cremated.

I believe it was £10, a lot of money for a young doctor. This usually meant he could go out for a meal with us with the money from this venture. As he progressed up the ladder to become Professor of Medicine he was able to afford the luxuries that were unavailable in his earlier career and he bought the Royal Doulton plates.

He often took delight in informing me that while he had a full set, I still needed the rare 'Book Worm.' This I acquired at a price, £240, at Newark near the end of my working life. Yes, I paid far too much for it but it completed my set.

David and Sharon were divorced before I managed to acquire it and I don't believe he ever saw it in our house or knew I had bought it.

When we moved to our present bungalow, Anne and I didn't believe they would fit in, so they went to be sold by John Walsh in Wakefield but they didn't sell, so we still have them packed away in a box.

Another friend also collected the same Goss figures so we would donate one on occasions we were invited to her home, again instead of a box of chocolates.

On one occasion she popped into an antique shop on Ecclesall Road in Sheffield to enquire how much a piece of Goss was in the window. Whether or not she was enquiring to buy it I don't know.

However, she told the owner she acquired most of her Goss from Edward Patnick. The shopkeeper told her not to trust me as I would charge her too much for them. I can honestly say I never charged her for any Goss piece that came from me; they were all gifts, so really expensive.

Some friends moved into a house on our road and, since I had known both of them most of my life, I was quite pleased. The wife came to the shop to look for things for her new home. I naturally asked what she was looking for and she said just odd bits but old.

I said, 'we have plenty, if you spot anything let me know and I'll sort it out for you.'

She employed a lady who was an interior designer, buying most of the things needed for her new home, but who wasn't with her when she visited our shop.

She picked out two chairs, one a rocking chair with a matching footstool, the other a gents chair, both Victorian. She asked how much they were and I being a fool said, 'I'll charge you £25 for the rocker and give you the Gents chair as a house warming present.'

The £25, I believed, would also have to pay for the delivery as she would never get them in her car. I was amazed to hear that her interior designer said, 'You shouldn't have gone there, he will have charged you too much.'

I certainly didn't charge her too much or anywhere near what she paid the interior designer for far inferior goods.

I saw the chairs in her original house after they had been re-covered and in her bungalow in London and recently in her new flat in Sheffield after they moved back to their home city.

I wonder whether the furniture provided by her interior designer has lasted as long and cost as much as my 'expensive' chairs. I did see the interior designer in the most expensive furniture shop in Sheffield and wondered if she was buying for my friends and how much on top of the price my friends would have to pay.

I saw other home interiors she had designed and to me, a junk dealer, they all looked the same. I am very pleased my wife has taste and didn't resort to using this lady. Though we have had rooms designed, they always had Anne's input.

Sometimes ignorance can cost you a packet – or provide an unexpected windfall. At one fire salvage in Bradford I bought hundreds of lengths of material, each about six feet long. Ideal for curtains, I thought. I never stopped to ask what type of shop sold so many pieces of silk and since the front of the shop was badly burned, I couldn't even see the name of the store.

Back at our shop I showed the girls some samples. Beryl measured one length and said, 'These won't sell because they won't make two curtains.'

I was a bit downcast but decided to give them a go at the market just to see, assigning one of the four stalls to this fabric. The response was amazing. I returned from the car park to find the stall encircled by people, some ten deep. I couldn't get near and shouted to Beryl and Dot that I would stay at the back but they must make sure every piece of material was wrapped up on payment.

We were so overwhelmed I stayed with the two van boys to ensure nobody took stuff without paying. The next week our stall was again surrounded by hundreds of Asian men and women and we sold out. No, the cloth couldn't be sold for curtains, but it certainly sold for what it was made for – saris!

That year brought more health problems. I had regular appointments with my consultant since I'd been admitted to the Royal Infirmary on several occasions with heart attack symptoms.

Each time I was released without them being to diagnose anything wrong. Then one young doctor said, 'Since you put on such a good act, I suppose we'd better keep you in.' After one of my two-day stays I attended Lodge the following day, actually performing quite a bit of ritual.

Friends said I was looking well and the consultant said I had nothing to worry about. However, late the next night I was taken ill and rushed by ambulance to the Northern General.

Professor Smith was waiting for me with a technician and a nurse and I was taken straight into theatre where a balloon was inserted into my left groin with just a local anaesthetic and a nurse holding my hand for reassurance. It was rather a worrying time because unusually, the balloon didn't work for a few days. Work however it did and I was back on the road in no time.

While I was in hospital Anne tried to run home and the business, not an easy task.

One afternoon she arrived saying she didn't know what to do about some furniture she'd been offered by one of the partners of an estate agency. She was very sorry to worry me but couldn't possibly make an offer without some guidance. She had a list. After reading out the first item I said, 'Don't bother telling me the rest I have seen them all over the last couple of years,' and proceeded to reel off the list.

Anne was amazed. 'How do you know what he's shown me?'

I told her that every house of furniture I bought from this source always had one piece that would not be for sale, but had to be kept back for relatives and should be delivered to his house.

She ended up buying the items.

I didn't always take things as carefully as I should. I stupidly tried to help the lads shift a pianola and came over all funny.

20

Driving me mad

By 1978 and my health wasn't my only concern. I've always felt I was a good employer and had some loyal staff, but drivers in particular gave me problems over the years. I probably made a mistake allowing them to take the van home after dropping other staff off en-route.

One driver brought along an ex-professional footballer who was an alcoholic and asked if I would employ him to act as his mate to work with him on the van. Of course I didn't know he had a drink problem until it was too late. Like a fool, I employed him.

One day, without my permission, the driver loaned the van to the ex-footballer to do some removal job. I didn't even know he had a licence. That evening he ended up going to the Fiesta Nightclub in Sheffield in my van.

The club had an underground car park with only a six-foot six-inch headroom. Our van was ten feet high. The idiot tried to drive in, destroying half the top of the van. Muggins here had to pay for the damage to the van and the sign which was destroyed.

When the actual driver left my employ, he simply parked the van outside the shop and I never heard from him again. Except I received a solicitor's letter informing me I owed him severance pay! Yes, I had to pay, despite the fact he left on his own accord without notice.

We did manage to employ two drivers who were normal. The first was a lad called Steve who worked for us in the eighties and another Jonathan, during the late nineties. I also employed Mark, Dot's nephew, who started out as a driver's mate and I paid for him to have driving lessons.

Harold Needham, a great friend, introduced me to a lady who worked for 'Mencap' who was trying to place some of their people under a work scheme. She brought along Michael Monks whom we employed, paying just 40 per cent of his wages. He was a big strong lad who stayed with me until I was eventually forced to retire on health grounds.

We had only one blip, in his first week. I noticed him putting something under the blankets on the van. It was a tray of correction fluid. I informed the Mencap lady and she came to talk to him. I explained to him that what he had done was theft. All he had to do was to have asked and I would have put a price on it or given it to him. He said he was taking it for his sister and was sorry.

I never had another problem with Michael. In fact he proved to be the most loyal and trustworthy employee I ever had, which proves that everyone deserves a second chance in life.

After making Mark redundant, I tried to work on the van but it was too much. I went back to Mencap who provided Andrew whom I took to the Lightwood driving area for tuition and after a few hours I trusted him to drive back to the warehouse.

The problem with Andrew was he couldn't find his way anywhere. Michael was the opposite. Once he had been somewhere he would find the place again. This was illustrated when they had taken some household goods that needed throwing away to a council dump near Holmfirth. Another visit was required, and Michael said, 'It's a waste of time two of us going for this little bit of rubbish. Let Andrew go on his own and I can get everything ready to go back to Sheffield.'

I quickly reminded Michael that Andrew wouldn't be able to find the place.

'But we've just been,' said a frustrated Michael.

I suggested we test Andrew who said, 'You turn left where the horse is nodding its head.' We decided Philip should go with him just in case the horse had stopped nodding!

The two never got on, which didn't help. I pulled up on the road one day to find Michael threatening to hit Andrew because they were lost. Andrew reported the incident to his father who was naturally concerned. I assured him it was a storm in a teacup because of their frustrations with not being able to read a map.

Unfortunately the same week Andrew fell off the tailboard and hurt his ankle. I had to phone his father again. Of course he wanted to know if Michael had caused the accident. I assured him this wasn't the case but I would take his son to hospital to be checked. His father said he would come to the warehouse and take him himself. This he did, and again asked if Michael was involved. I stressed again that he wasn't. It proved to be a bad sprain and he was off work for two weeks.

One time Andrew drove me to deliver some benches to an address in Cambridge when the van suddenly veered off the road. I thought we'd had a puncture and instinctively grabbed the wheel. To my horror I saw that Andrew's eyes were closed. I screamed at him, 'Stop the van!' and he woke up. Fortunately we escaped a crash, and we swapped over.

I shouted at him that he could have killed both of us and others too. His excuse was that he'd been up all night babysitting for his sister. I must admit I never stopped rollicking him all the way there and back and he never uttered a word. My final remark was, 'Never come to work again if you're unfit to work or drive.'

I had issues with a number of drivers over the years. Once at 6.30am the van didn't turn up. After many phone calls the driver finally answered to inform me he'd left my employ and I could find the van outside the warehouse with the keys in!

In 2002 my daughter Lisa had a stillborn child, a very distressing time for everyone involved. My driver at the time quit whilst I was staying with my daughter. I later phoned him to ask what the problem was. His mother answered and said that he didn't work for me anymore. I said I'd been away at my daughter's home because she'd had a stillborn baby. The lady said, 'That's not my fault,' and I put the phone down.

Another time I was at a wedding in London when a driver left a message on my mobile saying he'd found another job and wouldn't be at work in the morning. We had intended to stay, but had to come home at midnight to be at work at 6.30am the next day, again finding the keys in the van outside the warehouse. I gave another driver time off one lunchtime only to discover he was taking the van for a job interview, spending my diesel in the process!

One day we finished work very late so I lent a lad called Nick my Escort to take Michael and himself home. At a crossroads, Michael said he was clear, meaning there was no traffic coming from the passenger side, so Nick proceeded without checking the driver's side. He therefore hit a car coming from his side. Of course it cost me money.

On another occasion I left a driver in the car with the keys in the ignition at the market while I checked to see if I was wanted for anything. On my return to the car it had been clamped by the market patrolmen.

I couldn't believe that he had just sat there and let them do it, but he did. One of the market stallholders was walking past and said 'I'll take it off for you, just give me your jack and tools for the wheel'.

He removed the wheel and took the clamp off, without damaging it or the wheel. As I was about to leave a patrolman arrived and said I would be prosecuted for removing the clamp. I just said, 'I have never touched it'. He enquired, 'Who did then?' to which I answered, 'A man that was passing.' I never heard another word about the incident.

My last driver lived at Parsons Cross, not far from where my grandfather Levine and Aunt Leah lived. As usual, I allowed him to take the vehicle home at night but got a call saying it had been stolen from outside his home. This was a real blow, just a week before Christmas, a bumper time in the market. I reported the theft to the police but was merely given a crime number and told to inform my insurance company.

I needed to hire a replacement urgently and told my driver to make sure he brought his driving licence into work the next day. True to form, he turned up without it. When I questioned him he said he had no intention of hiring a van. In fact he wanted his wages because he was leaving.

I scraped together some cash which I gave him, less £20 because he hadn't worked a full week. Suddenly he shouted that I hadn't paid him his bonus. I told him he wasn't entitled and received a volley of abuse – the usual stuff, 'You dirty Jewish cheating bastard etc.'

I was quite upset and Philip asked him to leave the building. Michael, my trusted driver's mate, kindly came up to make sure I was all right saying, 'There was no need for that.'

I went home and told Anne. Philip was with me and said, 'Did you get the warehouse keys from him?' I must admit it never crossed my mind.

Anne had a phone call from Simon, my son, who said I should report the racial abuse to the police. I didn't really want to involve them but was persuaded and two policemen arrived to take a statement.

A couple of hours later they returned with the keys and asked if I wished to press charges. I said I wasn't really bothered and had received racial abuse all my life. As mother said, 'They are just ignorant people who don't know any better.' At least I had the keys back. I must admit I didn't have the same trouble with the girls who worked in the shop and market.

21

A well-earned break

Holidays were always an escape from the pressures of buying and selling and my underlying health issues, although I could sense what people were thinking while I stood and watched Anne, Lisa and Simon struggle with all the luggage.

It didn't help when we arrived at one foreign destination to be informed we had to collect our luggage from the plane because of a strike by handlers and porters. Anne just about blew a gasket, refusing to leave the aircraft until someone was found to carry our bags. Thankfully, arrangements were made.

There were added stresses too one year in Sardinia when one minute Simon was playing happily on the beach, the next he was gone. I raced up and down the sand but couldn't find him, my pulse racing dangerously high. All sorts of things were going through our minds. Then we discovered him playing contentedly with another boy behind an upturned boat just a few yards away.

Another time he was bitten by a dog in Rimini, Italy. Blind panic set in with the word 'rabies' on everyone's lips. We were staying at the Grand Hotel and the manager was marvellous, taking us all to the hospital and making enquiries about the dog. He informed us that the dog had been caught and since it had a collar it was unlikely to have the disease, sparing Simon an injection.

One year we decided to visit my Aunt Esther in Los Angeles, a place called Thousand Oaks, as part of a wider tour of the West Coast and Las Vegas. We heard that some of our friends from London would be there at the same time and arranged to meet up. They had a boy and a girl like us and we had a wonderful couple of days at Disneyland and arranged to meet them again in Vegas.

We wanted to take Simon and Lisa but my cousin Judy persuaded us to leave our children at Thousand Oaks with Aunt Esther and asked if she and her husband, Bill, could come with us. It's a shame we agreed because we were booked in what was the world's largest hotel, the MGM Grand, and our suite could easily have slept six.

We met our friends at their hotel and took in two shows. One was just a pre-dinner show the other was a dinner show. Judy came to the first but our friends had booked just the four of us for the second. We had a great time, walking the Strip playing the slot machines and so forth. Very early in the morning we returned to our hotels. After our two-day stay I went to the reception to pay for any extras and was shocked to find we had been charged for meals and room service, on the night we had gone to the dinner show. Yes, that was my cousin Judy.

Another blow was that I'd hoped to declare the American holiday as a business trip but on return my accountant said we couldn't justify it. I should have asked before the trip although we probably wouldn't have gone.

One journey that will stay in the memory forever is a trip on the Orient Express to celebrate our silver wedding. Luckily an insurance policy matured about the same time and we could afford the luxury of the Pullman from Victoria to Dover, a first-class ferry to Calais, the Orient Express to Venice, and then a cruise which took in Egypt.

I will never forget our dinner on the train: I spoke to the head waiter telling him we would like second sitting and explaining being Jewish what foods we didn't eat. Before dinner we went to the cocktail bar where a gentleman played a grand piano and sang popular songs which everyone enjoyed.

We were called to our table which was right at the far end just for two. Anne had a twenties cocktail dress and I was in a dress suit. The first course was fish which looked delicious with a wonderful pink sauce. But before we could tuck in, the head waiter removed our plates!

He returned with the fish which now had a lemon dressing. He apologised, explaining that the first dish had a seafood dressing. Yes, on a train chefs can produce an alternative but I have found most restaurants on land can't!

I had arranged a one-night stay at the Cipriani Hotel on an island across from St Mark's Square in Venice. This meant a short boat hop. I must admit it was very luxurious and expensive. In fact while waiting for Anne I looked at the menu and the only dish we could afford was plain spaghetti.

Checking out, I wondered about the backgrounds of the people arriving and departing. As a junk dealer I felt completely out of my comfort zone. One lady paying her bill said she wouldn't be staying there again as the clientele had gone down so much. I didn't have time to think if she was talking about me, when she added, 'I can't believe you have people like Fergie to stay here.' She was of course referring to the Duchess of York! I realised I was definitely staying at the wrong hotel, but as mother used to say, 'My money's as good as anyone's.'

The two-week cruise was originally to be on the Orient Express ship but unfortunately it had a fire so we had to travel on another liner.

From my childhood I'd dreamed of seeing the Pyramids of Giza and the Sphinx. After a very long coach journey we arrived thirsty and tired. The local hawkers were waiting to pounce with expensive water and tut.

I was told that no one with heart trouble should enter the pyramids, but I was determined. Going all that way and not going in wasn't an option.

A young doctor on the trip convinced Anne he would take care of me, though she refused to go in, as did the doctor's wife. So the pair of them waited while we ventured into the pyramid.

It was all a bit disappointing. We paid to get in and had to bend nearly double to reach our destination which was merely an empty place with nothing but bare walls. Then, returning to the exit, our guide stationed himself where we had to crouch and demanded money for us to get out!

My American doctor friend refused to pay, so I was stranded behind him stooping and uncomfortable. I thrust some money in the guide's hand and shouted, 'Let us through.' I've never been so pleased to see daylight.

The Sphinx was equally disappointing, covered in scaffolding and tarpaulins. I assumed it was being repaired or restored.

22

End of an era

In the autumn of 1977, mum and dad decided to sell the family home, Wadsley Grove.

They'd found a lovely bungalow on Psalter Lane, Sheffield with two bedrooms, plus two reception rooms, a large hall and kitchen. Outside there was a useful garage and a very pretty garden which wasn't overlooked.

They'd collected every conceivable thing over 56 years of marriage and business together and only a fraction could be taken with them (dad's pictures and mother's beloved bric-a-brac did survive) and an auction was arranged to sell the surplus, including large pieces of furniture and dad's collection of books.

They asked each of us if there was anything we wanted. Anne had fallen in love with the large chandelier for our dining room despite my assurances that it was far

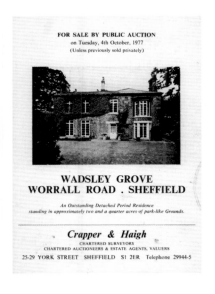

FOR SALE BY PUBLIC AUCTION
on Tuesday, 4th October, 1977
(Unless previously sold privately)

**WADSLEY GROVE
WORRALL ROAD . SHEFFIELD**

*An Outstanding Detached Period Residence
standing in approximately two and a quarter acres of park-like Grounds.*

Crapper & Haigh
CHARTERED SURVEYORS
CHARTERED AUCTIONEERS & ESTATE AGENTS, VALUERS
25-29 YORK STREET SHEFFIELD S1 2ER Telephone 29944-5

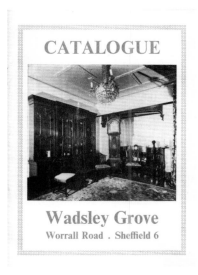

CATALOGUE

Wadsley Grove
Worrall Road . Sheffield 6

**Michael Haigh before commencing the auction in the ballroom.
Anne is seated on the front row on his right**

too big. Sure enough, I measured and confirmed it would only be six inches off the floor when erected!

We did acquire two Windsor-type children's chairs and two glass shepherd sticks which mum said kept colds away. Mother, wherever you are, they don't work!

Everything was sold through Michael Haigh of Crapper and Haigh who dad trusted and believed was the best auctioneer in the city.

Me and the lads sorted through all the effects and prepared them for sale. They took piles of stuff from me, either putting them on the van to go to Psalter Lane, or in the ballroom to be sold, or in the bin.

Dad didn't interfere but mother occasionally checked to see what I was doing as I worked myself around the house going through every drawer. She seemed to be spending an awful lot of time in her bedroom looking through a very large linen press after I had finished sorting it. After two days of this I asked, 'What are you looking for mum?.'

'Nothing,' she replied. Finally I sat her down and said, 'Mum, you obviously are looking for something, just tell me what and I'll tell you what I've done with it.'

Mum was in tears and replied, 'A baby's bootee. It was Norman's, G-d rest his soul. It was the only thing I kept of his, dad got rid of everything else.'

I was filled with sadness and horror. I had indeed found the little shoe earlier and thrown it in the bin. It had gone to the tip to be destroyed. There are things in life that are simply beyond value.

The sale took place in the ballroom and was well attended. Myself and Philip plus the two lads showing potential bidders the various items. We were quite surprised at the prices raised; the contents of the cellar fetched £400, ten times the original price and that was after all the parties. The chandelier that Anne loved went for £475.

A few days after they moved into the bungalow a young man rang the bell and introduced himself as the next-door neighbour. Mother invited him for a cup of tea.

During their conversation he admitted he didn't have many friends, as he was 'gay.' Mother said, 'You pop in for a chat anytime you like, I like a good time too.' Mother just hadn't got a clue what he actually meant. Even if she did, she certainly had no prejudices.

23

Dad's passing

The summer of 1979 was one of the saddest of my life. My father died on 29th July at the age of 82. He'd been in a nursing home for six months suffering from dementia. It had been a distressing time for all the family. Dad's memory was deteriorating and it was proving too much for mother to cope with him at home.

His condition got so bad a number of homes rejected him as a fire risk. He imagined he was back in the shop at Langsett Road sitting smoking his pipe tossing lighted matches onto an imaginary fire. Finally he was accepted in a home in Broomhall Place where they put him in the kitchen with a concrete floor where they were happy to let him sit and smoke his pipe. Occasionally he dropped a lighted match on himself but there was always someone around to make sure he didn't harm himself.

It certainly wasn't ideal, but it suited dad and gave mother an extra eight years of life. Irvine, and maybe Philip, weren't pleased to have him there, but I took the decision and I still believe it was the right one for mother's sake.

She insisted on visiting twice a day every day. On the Sunday morning dad died I decided to visit him without mum but took Lisa. For some reason I told her to stay in the car while I popped in to see her grandpa. This was a blessing as the Sister informed me dad had died a few minutes before I arrived.

I then had to take Lisa home and go to tell mother the sad news.

There had already been complications over his resting place even before he died as the old cemetery at Ecclesfield was full. This was the one used by members of the Central synagogue which dad belonged to and where my brother Norman was buried. A president of the Jewish congregation had taken me to see where dad would be buried. They intended to dig up the path at the end of the cemetery and bury him there, if I agreed – on the same row as Norman's grave. As mother often said, 'Your father will come back to haunt me if he's buried on the English side.' This was the opposite side of the road that was used by the members of Wilson Road synagogue at first but was now and then used for either members.

Mother was shocked at the news of dad's passing but took it quite well, although even after the funeral she couldn't get used to not visiting him. Luckily Aunt Leah had moved into sheltered accommodation just one bus stop above mother's bungalow, so most afternoons she would visit her sister, catching the bus just for one stop. I would pick her up on my way home because the bus stop back was quite a way down the road.

After dad's death mother gave me the key to his very large safe. I couldn't wait to open it and see what treasures he'd locked away. I opened the door to find a solitary cardboard box and opened it expectantly. Inside were small bars of Cadbury's Dairy Milk chocolate.

Dad had been a great influence on my life, indeed my whole family. Being articled to him meant I had to serve five years as his pupil, so if we had a disagreement I couldn't leave and he couldn't sack me! Irvine always said that dad and I made Steptoe and Son look normal.

He had a very bad temperament but never bore any grudges. He could lose his temper but all I did as a teenager was to walk out for a few minutes and he would have forgotten why he had shouted at me in the first place.

Although I never inherited his love of books and auction rooms, I knew I would miss his advice – maybe I should have listened to him more. As a dealer, he had a knack of buying things that would appreciate in value, become fashionable later and had a wonderful appreciation of art.

Dad always said, 'There's a sale for anything, including horse shit, but can you afford the time and space to wait for that one customer?' His theory was, 'Something bought right is half sold.' He certainly didn't believe mother needed all her sales pitch to sell the goods.

He was a self-educated man, who always shared his knowledge – if only I'd taken the time to listen and learn. He was extremely generous – a quality I'm pleased I inherited and so have my children.

He was afflicted with bouts of depression, often staying in bed for days at a time, but never receiving any treatment. I consider he was a hypochondriac, taking all kinds of potions and medicines. Many times I heard him say, 'Bessie, I'm not well, just today.' As children we were often told by mother not to make a noise because he was in bed and we weren't to wake him.

He had his faults – but don't we all!

He was particularly scruffy, wearing very old clothes. Shirts with no collars, an old Crombie overcoat and a trilby hat, which was as old as his coat. He rarely wore a tie. His shirts needed studs to accommodate his collar, which he couldn't spare the time to put on.

March 1960: Mum and dad in their finery at Irvine and Lynda's wedding

He always used to say that people could always tell his status by looking at his wife. The rare occasions he did dress up, he always looked smart but they were indeed rare. My sister-in-laws would cross the street to avoid him, but I'm pleased to say that Anne never did.

Characters like him don't seem to exist any more. I reacted against his clothing style by going to the other extreme. I never wore a shirt twice, always showered on returning from work, and until recently, always wore a tie socially.

One of his traits was to buy the first lot of any new auctioneer on the scene.

The foremen of the auction rooms all knew this and would make the first lot something that was normally almost unsaleable or of very little value. The few first lots he didn't manage to buy, dad always said, 'They'll never make a decent auctioneer.'

I'm not sure how or why the habit developed. Perhaps he thought it might prove a lucky omen, or maybe it was out of respect to newcomers.

I remember one such occasion involved Patrick Crapper, who was articled elsewhere in Derbyshire, but took his first job with Ellis, Willis and Becket and was selling for the first time. His first lot was in the cellar, impossible to see from the rostrum. Patrick walked down to this area and dad stood immediately behind him.

The lot was offered with dad continually poking poor Patrick in the back during the sale. This was ignored by the raw auctioneer. He repeated this until finally Patrick knocked the lot down to another dealer and swivelled around, about to respond to this person hitting him in the back. He was quite surprised to see dad and refrained, but looked very embarrassed.

Patrick went on to have a very successful career as an estate agent, but dad was proved right because he never was a particularly good chattels auctioneer. He didn't have to be because his partner Michael Haigh was probably the best of his generation.

When Clifford Spencer retired at his last sale and the last lot had been sold for £5, he said, 'Since that was the last lot I will ever sell by auction, I remember Mr. Patnick always bought the first lot of a new auctioneer, so I have decided to give this lot away. It will not appear on your bill sir, this is a tribute to Mr. Patnick and I hope it may set a new precedent to other auctioneers.'

Aunt Leah had a handbag stall in Sheffield Castle Market and after she retired came to work for me in the market. Some time later Uncle Morris, one of dad's brothers, joined the staff too, occasionally helping after doing shopping in the fruit market. Each week he came earlier so in the end, except for doing his shopping, he worked a full day and I paid him just like Aunt Leah and Beryl.

From left: George, Uncle Morris, Aunt Leah and maybe my wife, Anne, serving in the market when we were moved into the small shed that housed the animals or pet market, before moving to the Setts Market. Mr. Lee is in the foreground lighting George's cigarette

He certainly had a lucky touch. We were sorting through some 'pudding bundles' – items of bedding and clothing – we'd purchased at an auction. Mostly it was old stuff but Uncle Morris opened one bundle which was surprisingly good.

'We could take these pillowslips off and get as much for them as the pillows,' he said. After taking off the first one, he discovered something in the bottom of the pillowcase. I felt inside and pulled out a bundle of bank notes!

But it wasn't all plain sailing. I bought a quantity of seconds; mostly stretch covers, from Eversure Textiles. Whilst I was in hospital we had a complaint from a customer that a cover for a driving seat wouldn't fit. Philip, who had been helping out, said Beryl had served the man and both he and the van driver had offered to put it on the car for him, saying it was plenty big enough. So when he complained they refused to give him his money back.

The man, who happened to be a lawyer, took us to the Small Claims Court. Philip, Anne, Beryl, the driver and me, all turned up at court for the hearing. I couldn't believe that such a fuss was being made over something which cost £2.50. Halfway through I wanted to give the man his money back there and then, but Philip said, 'You can't do that in court.'

Philip told the court that if the man had allowed him to fit it on the car, we could have avoided the hearing. Then out of the blue the judge said: 'Will you do that now?' To which Philip said, 'With pleasure.' The judge asked where the car was and since it was only in the car park next door said, 'Right, we'll go and see if it fits.'

I stayed where I was while the others proceeded to the car park. I must admit I feared the worst. Philip's beaming face told me all I needed to know. The judge then dismissed the case, saying he couldn't understand why it had ever been brought to court in the first place, wasting everyone's time.

He added that he had done business over a number of years with the Patnicks, especially my father, and had always been very satisfied with his purchases.

My 12 years at Page Hall were about to end. The man who owned a DIY shop next door made me an offer I couldn't refuse. It was nine times more than I had paid and it also gave me a chance to reduce my overheads by downsizing to smaller premises in Abbeydale Road. With hindsight I would have been better off retiring from the junk business and investing in property, but I carried on as before.

I bought a large stock of salvage three-piece suites from a manufacturer, needing to hire premises from Sheffield Corporation to house them. There was no electric light in the building but I decided it would do for a short-term let of one month.

The first load had filled the shop and the rest went into the warehouse. I had examined some of the suites but not every one. Mr. Smith showed me the inventory and I only paid a percentage of that for the lot. I didn't think I could possibly lose.

The first load sold quickly, making a good profit too. The other two loads were in the warehouse. I went with the lads to pick up a few suites for the shop.

After the first one went on the van one of the lads asked me to come and look at it. I was surprised to see it looked worn. On closer examination I realised it was second-hand. Every suite that has been used has bits down the sides of the cushions and this one did. I examined other suites under torchlight and feeling down the sides. Sure enough there were coins and pieces of paper.

Mr. Smith said he would come to Sheffield the next day and examine the suites himself. This he did, taking away debris from the sofas to confront the manufacturers. He even managed to find a couple of envelopes with addresses on them.

A couple of days later he phoned to say he had been in touch with a person in Liverpool who said. 'Yes, I bought a suite but had returned it because it was faulty.' Mr Smith had the lot picked up by the manufacturers and my price was adjusted appropriately. It wasn't the only time firms tried to pass off faulty goods as fire salvage.

I bought a large stock of water-damaged table lamps from a store in Leeds who had a branch in Sheffield too. Beryl sold them in the market with my daughter, Lisa. I made sure every lamp was marked with the original price and instructed the girls to sell them at half the marked price. Simple.

I returned to the stall after lunch and was pleased to see they'd sold out. Lisa and Beryl were pleased to see me – they'd had a visit from a gentleman and a policeman who claimed the lamps were stolen. They'd been forced to withdraw them.

The man was the manager of the branch in Sheffield. He said they must have been stolen because they were the only store in the city that sold these goods and had their price tags on them.

I was livid and marched into West Bar Police station. I asked to see the person in charge. The answer is always the same, 'That's me.'

'I'm sorry, but I demand to see whoever's in charge and that's certainly not you.'

'Tell me why you want to see him and I'll decide.'

'Sorry, you fetch whoever's in charge and I'll tell him,' I demanded. Finally an Inspector arrived. 'Can I help you?' he said. 'Yes, I'm Edward Patnick. Have you had any notice that a large quantity of table lamps has been stolen?'

'No,' came the reply.

'Well why have you told my staff to stop selling them?'

'A member of the public informed one of our constables that stolen goods were being sold in Sheffield Market.'

'Since you've no report of the goods having been stolen, would it have been sensible to ask the person who reported the offence where they had been stolen from? I bought and paid for every lamp from a store in Leeds yesterday and have a receipt that confirms my purchase. I therefore require an apology from whoever authorised the terrorising of my staff. I will carry on selling the lamps today no matter what you or the man who reported me to your police officer says. Do you understand? I will provide you with my name and address and you can visit me at anytime and I will produce the receipt when you visit my premises.'

That week I received an apology from the Chief Constable, though I later found out it had been sent by one of his Chief Superintendents. I knew him socially and he asked me if I had received his letter. Since I had no idea he had sent the letter I said no. Then he explained that the Inspector who authorised the constable to have the lamps removed from sale had been reprimanded.

24

Where there's muck there's money

They say that money makes the world go round. It certainly does in the junk business. And where there's muck, there's definitely brass. So many times I stumbled across cash or valuables amid the remnants of peoples' belongings.

For example, I was asked by estate agents Crapper and Haigh to look at a house in Dobcroft Road, Sheffield. They warned me it was in a state and that my staff would need protective clothing.

The kitchen floor was actually rotten and dangerous. There was dog excrement everywhere and a quantity of silver coins that needed picking up so that they could be deposited at the bank.

They added there was only one item of furniture worth removing, a large chest of drawers in the back bedroom. Money was no object, as the estate had plenty of funds to meet any costs incurred.

On collecting the keys they informed me that the chest had a drawer missing which they had at the office. If I accepted the clearance I could burn everything, including the carpets in the back garden. The only key was for the back door and we had to be careful where we trod because of the rotten floorboards.

The large chest was obviously Victorian, a nice piece too. I stood wondering why the drawer was missing and decided to have closer look. I was staggered to find two five-pound notes in the drawer space.

On returning the key I told the agent we would undertake the job, provided the kitchen floor was repaired and my lads were suitably rewarded. I also informed him about the two fivers.

A week or so later I received a call to collect the key and to speak with Mr. Crapper to collect the drawer. On arriving at Patrick's office he said he needed to ask me about the money. Had I left the cash where I'd found it? I assured him that

I had. He said the money had gone missing. We could only assume it was the workmen who'd done the repairs.

He then revealed why he had the drawer in his office. On viewing the property they'd found £20,000 in the chest! That was why we would be paid handsomely for the clean-up including purchasing protective clothing and disinfectant.

The first task was to get the lads overalls, gloves and rubber shoes that could be disposed of afterwards. We put disinfectant down everywhere and they started picking up the coins. The rubbish and carpets were carried into the garden and burned. This wouldn't be allowed today because of health and safety laws. I'm not even sure we would be allowed to do the job.

Mentioning that cash windfall put me in good stead with the estate agent. We had a long and fruitful relationship until my retirement. In fact Patrick handled few assignments, leaving these to his partner Michael Haigh where possible. Patrick was more on the property side and his reasoning was to get the place emptied as soon as possible because the house would look better, bigger and would be worth much more emptied, a logic that can't be faulted.

This wasn't the only time I benefited by handing back money. Some years later I found a bankbook in a wardrobe. As well as showing a healthy balance there was £400 in cash. I handed it over to the man from Social Services who had taken me to the flat.

After that I got quite a few clearances from him and I'm sure this helped. It was swings and roundabouts. Some jobs they gave me were good, others worth nothing. Sometimes a particular estate had money to spare but another had no money at all and they needed every penny to help to pay funeral costs.

We had to move everything. Carpets in particular could be a nuisance. There was usually underlay too and nine times out of ten they had to be destroyed which cost time and money. When I started we could leave anything we wanted in a council property but later they imposed a charge. I remember once receiving a bill for £35 for goods left in a house. After that I even picked up scraps of paper off the floor!

Moving carpets sometimes had its perks. I remember vividly clearing a flat in Tenter Street in Sheffield, watching the lads lift the carpets and underlay before returning the key to the council. The carpets were horrid things that needed to go to the destructor with the underlay. But lo and behold I found two £20 notes. They helped with the destruction charges.

The majority of houses were filthy, and a few were a pleasure to move because they were clean and tidy. But these tended to be predictable. The dirty houses certainly produced the biggest challenge and reward but the clean ones, since they were fewer, easier to appraise and move.

I loved to discover unexpected valuable items I hadn't originally seen when viewing the contents of a house or flat.

I'd agreed a deal with the relatives of a deceased home owner in Woodseats, only to find well-meaning neighbours had a key and removed some of the bedding and clothing before I could clear the house.

I threatened to cancel the job, but the clients apologised and I carried on. In the living room there was a cabinet with a dozen or so pieces of china. I boxed them up and took them home for Anne to wash, ready for me to price and take to market. The next day, I noticed that a large jug was missing.

Anne said, 'Oh, it's in the lounge. I thought we'd keep it. You don't mind, do you? By the way, you do know it's Clarice Cliff.'

No, I didn't! Clarice Cliff was the most prolific and important Art Deco ceramics designer in the 20th century. It was a good job those neighbours didn't know their stuff. We still have that jug today.

On the top of a wardrobe I once found a beautiful Royal Dux figure of a donkey and cart. We still have that but unfortunately a cleaning lady damaged an ear and we never got round to having it mended.

Another time I discovered a quantity of paste jewellery, again in a wardrobe, in a cupboard at the back.

In a flat near my home I came across a blue jewellery box left out on the side. I guessed it has been made to house a special item. Beside it was a photo of a lady, presumably the deceased, in full elegant dress including a tri-corn hat which led me to speculate she had held some important office, maybe Lady Mayor, or some such.

The two men who met me didn't open the blue box and I certainly didn't. I bought the flat contents for £475 and it was only after they left that I opened it. Inside was a tiny gold item the shape of a bracelet but so small in diameter that I couldn't see how it could fit on anyone's wrist, except maybe a baby. Attached to the safety chain was a gold pencil held in place by two gold rings.

Anne confirmed it was indeed a bracelet and showed me how to open it. I never did find out anything about the lady but I did keep the pencil.

You can't imagine the mess that some people live in. Families with money too. I remember the late Rev. Frank Thewlis, a Methodist Minister, saying that in some homes he needed to put on bicycle clips before entering. Often I would stand at the door wondering how on earth we would tackle the job.

At one property I cleared on Chesterfield Road environmental health officers had been in and fumigated the place and removed the carpets. I feared the worst but was quite surprised to find the furniture was saleable, though everything, including me, stank of disinfectant.

Then, on a window sill, I found a purse full of money. It was indeed a bonus, but I still needed a hot shower.

In another house I found silver coins on the top of every door. It made my mind up to take on the job and it had a favourable outcome by making a profit on the contents. I always allowed the lads to keep any coins they found, telling them to spit on them for good luck.

A large house in Crookes stays in my memory because of the smell. I was packing in another room and suddenly heard a scream from George in the kitchen. 'Look, there's a body in that pan,' he yelled.

I said, 'Don't be silly. It's a large pan but you can't get a body in that.'

George said, 'Have a look then.'

There on the hob was an uncooked skinned rabbit. I went outside and was sick as usual. I said to George, 'Throw the pan and the contents in the bin.' The wretched smell disappeared after we left the windows and doors open.

Even in some of Sheffield's poshest neighbourhoods I stumbled on squalor.

I was asked to move a large house at Sandygate. The keys were next door with an antique dealer. I couldn't believe the state of the place. I was informed that the owner lived in the house but only used the front room which we were not to touch. I was also told he was an alcoholic, had a cat, and we were not to move the pet food or bowl.

It didn't matter what time we arrived or left, none of us saw the cat or the man who lived there. I did venture into the room once and was amazed how anyone could live in such squalor in what was, or should have been, a beautiful house in one of the best areas.

The man obviously slept on a settee which needed to go on the skip. I can only assume that whoever moved him into his nursing home had another skip for the rubbish in that front room.

After moving the large house at Sandygate I was amazed to be asked by the antique dealer who lived next door if we would just take a fitted wardrobe away from a property she owned. I said I would look and see if it was worth moving. I thought it would be easy to move so I arranged to remove it. It took half a day to dismantle and the same amount of time to reassemble and after it was sold it had to be dismantled and then reassembled at the house of the person who bought it. Not one of my better decisions to take it away even for nothing.

One house in Gleadless Valley was crammed with milk bottles – in the sink, drawers, wardrobes. Everywhere, empty bottles, all washed nicely. I thought I was doing the local dairy a favour by going there and obtaining 50 crates to collect them in. I went back to the depot and gave them the address to pick them up. I never expected the reply. 'We can't do that, you'll just have to deliver them here.' I told them I had no intention of doing that. They would be left on the grass verge and it was up to them to pick them up. I have no idea if they ever did.

I always expected solicitors, estate agents and Social Services to have carried out a search before allowing me even to look round the premises. These are professional people who have been entrusted to look after the owner's interest and are well paid for their efforts. Social Services always carried out searches before allowing me to even look at any house contents.

In one house in Nether Edge I found a quantity of share certificates which I took back to the estate agent. He said if I found anything else of value to let him know!

Remember, these people were entrusted with disposing of an estate yet couldn't be bothered to do a basic search. I also found there a Dresden monkey band. I wanted to keep it but Anne thought it was horrendous. When I took the keys back I mentioned it to the agent who said, 'Yes, I saw that. It's no good, that's why I left it for you.' It did very well in an antique sale, thank you.

Social Services nearly always carried out a proper search on estates that they dealt with usually having two employees on the case. Very occasionally they would say they couldn't find something they thought should be on the premises.

Once I was asked to keep my eyes open for the deeds of a house, which I found in a wardrobe, but they had been well hidden.

Dad told me he once found a will that no one knew about. He immediately phoned the Social Services. He was asked to bring it to their office and not move the contents until they had read it. Even though dad had made on offer for the contents which had been accepted he had the lads put back everything from the van. He never heard anything about that clearance again.

I was asked to clear a flat by Social Services on a council estate. I am always amazed what people collect or save. The flat had a walk-in wardrobe full of handbags, all brand new. Every one had been opened by the men from Social Services and all were left open and completely empty.

Most had a small zip pocket which contained a mirror. None of these had been opened I guess, since they all contained either a silver or pound coin. Mother always made sure if she gave anyone a purse or wallet that she placed a coin in it for luck. This lady had the same belief.

On moving the contents of a converted flat near Bramall Lane I was given the key by Social Services and told just clear it and don't worry about any payment as there was nothing of value in the place. They also informed me they had removed £20,000 from the sleeves of an anorak behind the door. The occupant was Chinese and they were unable to find any relations but were continuing to make enquiries. I was amazed seeing the anorak but it proved that they had done their job which is more than can be said for other professional bodies I have dealt with.

At one house in Stannington, north of Sheffield, the solicitor involved said he would be very surprised if I accepted the job. It was indeed filthy, but packed with saleable furniture and everything else under the sun, including clothes, hundreds of pairs of shoes, ornaments, pots and pans, and bags of rubbish and clutter everywhere.

I could see a good profit since I had been told that they did not require anything for the house contents but everything had to be moved. In what I supposed was the living room, I had to climb over chairs, furniture and bags of rubbish to look at the furniture. A bureau bookcase had caught my eye on the far side but it was difficult to assess without getting close. Often the top didn't match the bottom or the piece had woodworm.

The one thing I didn't expect was to find money, but I did in every drawer and cupboard, even inside shoes. There was enough to pay for Simon's Bar Mitzvah, celebrating his passage into manhood.

It is usual for the parents to throw a party after the ritual in the synagogue. Anne had decided the dinner would be an elaborate affair with 230 of our friends, plus about half a dozen of Simon's.

How I was expected to find the money had worried me. But the answer came from this one house in Stannington with money over too. The lads also had a treat, spitting on coins as they removed the things I had sorted.

Under a mattress in another house I found a wallet containing £2,500 in old £5 notes, which were no longer legal tender. I was unable to give the money back, even if I'd have wanted to, as the people left after I had paid them for the furniture and I didn't have their name.

I didn't like finding money because it caused a problem. Whose was it? And if you handed it over with the keys would the owners receive it? It was always a deceased estate and usually I bought all the contents and had to move them or pay to have them moved, so was it technically mine.

Once at a flat in Crookes, under the sink drainer was a cutlery drawer containing a yellow plastic cutlery holder inside a brown container. I put the drawer on the pile to sort out later. Beryl was going through it and asked me to lift up the cutlery. Inside was a large quantity of bank notes. I stuffed them in my pocket and counted them later at home. There was £2,000 – yes, a very good day's work.

I've been to at least two flats where the person showing me around said they were sure there was cash in the place. It didn't take me long to point out where it would be. The first time the money was in a locked bedside cupboard, the second in a shopping bag next to a comfy chair. Each time I pointed to the place and both times I was right and watched as the money was taken away. I would have made a great detective!

Another time I was moving the contents of a house which was pretty straightforward. While the lads cleared the room downstairs I used the bathroom upstairs. Some are to be avoided but this one was quite clean.

I used the toilet and noticed an airing cupboard. On opening it there was nothing in it to move but I did notice a piece of string tied around a pipe. My curiosity made me look closer. It seemed to dangle down the back of the cistern. I pulled it and it was quite heavy. On the end was a small red bag containing a couple of gold chains and a charm bracelet. I avoided many toilets but I was pleased I used this one.

At a flat clearing in Lowedges, a council estate in the south of the city, whilst waiting for the lads to come with the van I spent the time filling the dustbin with discarded food, wastepaper, old receipts, newspapers, magazines etc.

On the kitchen table was a small plastic soapbox with a small hole in the top. As I threw it in the bin I heard a rattle so decided to see what it was. I gingerly opened the container to discover a half-set of false teeth.

The palate was warmish and I was sure it had to be gold. I later checked it by placing some acid on the metal and since it didn't turn green I was obviously right. I still have the dentures and use them as a prop in my various talks. They always produce a laugh.

Once at the Dore Probus organisation I said, 'This palate is nine carat gold.' A man near the back shouted, 'No it isn't. It's 18 ct. I used to make them.'

I just never knew what I would find, sometimes obviously personal mementoes. In one house in Nether Edge I paid quite a lot for the contents, more than £400, expecting to come across something of value among a lot of old furniture. Sure enough in a dressing table inside a small plastic box I found a 1914 farthing, a Victorian Jubilee gold sovereign and a small gold coin which turned out to be an 1852 American dollar.

I still have them and the box and wonder how they were acquired and what significance they held.

On another occasion I was asked by one of the partners of Eadon, Lockwood and Riddle to look at a house in Parsons Cross. The partner said that the furniture wasn't good enough for their saleroom but I may be interested.

Author with the above mentioned mahogany box

The house had little of value in it – a table and chair downstairs, plus a few kitchen sundries; upstairs a double bed, a dressing table and wardrobe, plus a few clothes and bedding. I couldn't see how I could pay for moving the furniture.

As I returned to the estate agent downstairs, I glanced back and saw a mahogany box under the bed. After a proper look, without moving the box, I agreed to move the furniture but explained that I couldn't make a profit but it would just pay for moving. The agent agreed. So I had bought the contents for the price of moving it. Everything went to the destructor except the mahogany box and a small desk, which I have kept.

One day I had been asked to look at the contents of house by an estate agent which I did while the lads were having lunch. I picked the key up and proceeded to the property. I stopped at a fruit shop and bought an apple and an orange. I gave the assistant a £20 note which was all I had.

I proceeded to eat my purchases while looking around. I realised I had put the change in my pocket all together, notes and coins, and took out the £5 and £10 notes and stuffed them into my back pocket.

Going back and forth in the house I found a £5 note then a tenner on the floor. I picked them up and put them into my back pocket. After having a quick look around in the first room I made my way back to the hall. There I found £15 again.

I again picked the money up and put it into my back pocket. This happened every time I left one room to go back out. On leaving I decided to count the money I had picked up. My pocket was empty but on the floor were two notes, one £10 and one £5.

Before picking them up I decided to check my back pocket again and to my surprise there was no lining to the pocket. All I'd been doing was picking up my own £15.

One peculiar thing about clearances – the number of people who left tins of food behind. We never went without red salmon or sugar, throughout our married life. We weren't allowed to sell food or drink either in the shop or market. We used to give most of the tinned food to St. Luke's Hospice for their summer fete.

One solicitor was so determined not to leave any valuables behind he prised open the left-hand drawers of a Victorian Davenport desk, not realising they were false! Everyone to their own expertise, he certainly wasn't going to leave anything for the junk dealer to find.

Luckily all the main pieces were there, they just needed a good joiner to put them back which I arranged. Mother said she could do with something like it to keep her correspondence in, so I gave it to her. It is still in the family.

My dad always impressed upon me to check everything people had discarded, including the dustbin, and to pay particular attention to cellars and attics.

One house comes to mind in Sandygate. I was rooting around hoping to find some hidden treasures and decided to start in the attic. Getting up wasn't easy but I commandeered a chair and put a stool on top.

I was rewarded straight away by finding a miniature sterling silver bullock with a mother of pearl cart. One of the handles to the cart needed soldering but that wouldn't be a problem. However getting down from the attic was. As I put my weight on the stool both it and the chair collapsed and I finished in a heap on the floor.

I really hurt myself and lay there for ages until the lads came and helped me to my feet. I suffered a few bruises and dented pride and needed a hot bath with plenty of Epsom Salt. I still have the bullock and cart and the painful memories of that house.

You'll be amazed at what I found, deeds to property, wills, false limbs, bank books. In fact I was once interviewed on the radio about my weird and wonderful discoveries in wardrobes!

On another occasion I was asked to look at a house contents, but I was also informed that the only thing worth moving was a modern brand new iron bedstead. The lads went with me and the place was full of rubbish, bags full, plus all the furniture which was also rubbish, but there was this modern, unassembled, iron bedstead. The lads brought it down stairs and Michael suddenly said, 'There's only one side rail, it's useless'. The lads spent hours looking for the other rail but to no avail. We left the bedstead with the rest of the rubbish; another wasted afternoon.

25

Well and truly rolled over!

In 1974 Sheffield market had moved to new stalls on what was the car park. It became known as the Setts Market. The Sheaf Market was accommodated in a new building opposite Castle Market on Exchange Street.

The stalls were smaller and the rents higher, but we had no choice. When the Sheaf Market was first mooted dad was chairman of the Sheffield branch of the National Market Traders Association and put his name down for a shop. I was not even offered a stall in that market, let alone a shop. Some people never took up their option, selling the rights at inflated prices.

As always, no one who'd ever stood in the market was involved in the design and it had many shortcomings. I was stopped one day by Alderman Dyson, chairman of the council's market committee, who asked what I thought.

'The stalls are smaller and the rents have nearly doubled,' I moaned.

'Son, you'll just have to bring more stuff and sell it cheaper,' he replied. No wonder the council was almost bankrupt.

One of my early touches was a large stock of chocolates still in their cellophane. However, as I said before, market rules forbade us selling anything classed as food. I arranged a meeting with Mr. Ellis, the market superintendent, and took a box of the chocolates with me. I asked if there was any reason I couldn't sell them in Sheffield. If so, I'd have to take them to other markets elsewhere. To his credit he agreed. We sold out in a day at a pound a box, making a 100 per cent profit.

I did find problems with the market near the end of my career but I never managed to see or meet another superintendent, only the 'Tobymen' who collected the rent. In fact for the last 20 years or so I never even knew who the superintendent was.

On another occasion I was approached by a new fire salvage assessor to ask if I would be interested in a stock of toys, a large quantity of battery powered monkeys. Of course I was, and arranged to meet him to look at them. I made an offer and was surprised when he asked what was in it for him.

In all the dealings I'd had with fire salvages I was never asked this before. I was rather taken aback but said he could have £100 in cash which would be included in the total price. I would leave the money as a deposit and pay the balance by cheque on collection.

The stock arrived just before Christmas and was a godsend. We sold them all in Sheffield market in one day, with four of us serving. One put the batteries in, the next caught the monkey and proved to the customers it worked before taking the batteries out, the third bagged up, and the fourth collected the money. Yes, another good deal but I still wonder what happened to the £100 in cash.

A fire assessor called Andrew cost me dearly. I'd first met him when he was learning the ropes under John Smith. Now he was in charge of the Huddersfield branch. I was asked to meet him at a large factory near the town. You don't know what to expect in this business, but he showed me 100,000 paint rollers, plus a small quantity of the materials used in making them.

I made an offer for the rollers and after consulting the directors of the firm involved it was accepted. I took some samples away with me to show Anne but she wasn't at the shop. However, my brothers thought they were ridiculously cheap and would sell easily at a pound each.

'But there are 100,000,' I said.

Irvine said I should pop to the warehouse next door and show them to the two brothers I did business with on my first salvage. To my delight they agreed to buy the lot from me at a handsome profit. I was pleased with myself and waited until the shop closed to show Anne my day's work.

Before going home I arranged for two 7.5 ton vehicles to accompany our van to Huddersfield to fetch the stock. They would leave at eight the next morning, an early start for me and the lads.

We arrived at the factory at about 9.30am. Andrew greeted me and said there was a slight problem. Could I wait until he sorted it out? We must have waited an hour before he reappeared, informing me the directors had changed their minds and were going to keep the rollers after all.

I was distraught but there was nothing I could do. Until I paid and moved them, they didn't belong to me. The hired vans returned to Sheffield empty. I suppose you could say I'd been well and truly rolled over! Another lesson – never sell something before you have it in your possession and paid for.

Believe it or not, another time I bought some water-damaged rice from an insurance assessor. The rice was only slightly damaged, but the whole stock was blighted.

The lads arrived back with these large sacks covering the whole of the van. I'd already lined up a newly-opened Chinese restaurant near the shop. I took the load there and the owner examined the stock. He said the rice was fine. But it was for rice puddings, not for Chinese food.

The entire lot finished at the destructors, leaving a trail of grains all the way from the shop to its destination and another loss to me.

Some years later, just before Simon's Bar Mitzvah, Anne decided to redesign our bedroom and the lounge. I had met a friend, Laurence, who I had been friendly with in my teens. He owned quite a number of flats. I said I was looking for an old wooden fireplace to replace our plaster one in the lounge. He told me he had one which I could have if I wanted it. All I needed to do was to remove it and replace it, with bricks and plaster.

Since I didn't have anyone to undertake such a task I suggested his men could remove it, which I would pay for and also make good the hole that was left. So the wooden surround cost me £200. That was cheap at the side of the rest. Cream carpet, new wallpaper, curtains, new fire insert with reproduction tiles, plus a marble hearth, and the Italian suite which needed recovering.

I had a friend, Ike, who had a small upholstery company and whom I had played football and cricket with for Maccabi, though he was a much better player than me and much older, he being near the end of his sporting career, while I was starting mine. He was delighted to carry out the job. Anne picked the new fabric, which was really a curtain material in very light beige. Ike couldn't believe the price we paid for it. Since this was what Anne had decided on, as most men will agree, we can't win, our wives know best and they nearly always get their way.

Mum used to come for lunch, with Aunt Leah, most Sundays. After the bedroom was finished mum and Aunt Leah ventured upstairs to see it. The room had been transformed from an en-suite double bedroom into the entire length of the building talking in two double bedrooms. The door to the second bedroom was dispensed with and an alcove made from our original room through to what became a dressing room. This was fitted with mahogany robes that had mirrored doors on two walls. The en-suite was also transformed and modernised.

The king size bed had sheer curtains which were draped down, about two-and-a-half feet, from the head on each side. Mum look round in amazement and said, 'Where does Edward sleep?'

Anne jokingly pointed to the dressing room where there was no bed.

Mother then said, 'I've never seen anything like this, have you Leah?'

All Aunt Leah could say was, 'Beautiful! I've never seen anything like it, Bessie.'

The lounge was transformed in colour, with the new carpet, wallpaper, fireplace and glass shelves in the alcove and the finished suite. We only used the room on special occasions so everything looked pristine, right up to the time we left in November 2010.

Not long after I was offered salvage that contained un-upholstered cushions. They were cheap but as usual I panicked wondering if they would sell. I contacted Ike, who after consulting his business partner, decided to purchase the whole lot – three loads of our Luton van. We delivered the first load and agreed to take them the second consignment early next day.

I arrived at the premises with the van at 8.30am but there was no one around. The loading bay was open and the shutters up, so I naturally walked into the building looking for staff. Soon after, the partner who agreed on the purchase arrived, informing me that I had triggered their alarm and what did I think I was playing at.

He said I had no right to enter their building and would have to pay the hundred-odd pounds it would cost to reset the alarm.

I pointed out that the door was already open and was fulfilling my appointment with him to deliver the cushions. I was furious but he insisted I was to blame. He wasn't interested in the fact that the building hadn't been locked the night before.

I just told him to pay me for what we had delivered, which he did, less the money for resetting the alarm. We left with the cushions still on the van. My friend Ike just shrugged his shoulders. I needn't have worried. The two remaining vanloads sold very well in the market and we made a profit even having paid for the resetting of the alarm.

The firm eventually went into liquidation but some time later we were moving the contents of a high-rise flat. I was about to leave when a van arrived with a sign that advertised beds direct to the public. I was amazed to see getting out of the van the man who had made me pay for the resetting of his alarm. He was with another man, obviously delivering to the flats. I said as loud as I could, 'Who are you conning today? Anyone who buys anything from you needs their head examining. I can't believe anyone would buy anything from a rogue like you.'

All he said was 'Don't be like that, Mr. Patnick,' and I left.

One house of furniture I was unable to buy was a house on Ecclesall Road. The President of the Sheffield Jewish Community asked me to look at a house full of furniture that had been left to the synagogue by one of its members, plus another house next door that was empty. I looked at the furniture which was mostly 1920s style.

I was asked how much I was prepared to give for the contents. I gave a figure of £8,000, but added that it would fetch more by auction and members of the community would say I had not given enough for the contents. I suggested I would bring in a local auctioneer who would sell the contents and the houses if they wanted. This they advised me to do and I arranged to meet one of the partners together with the President the next day.

I walked around the house with the auctioneer pointing out different item which I believed to be of importance. One was a candelabra in the hall another was a very nice garden seat, emphasising they needed to be taken away to be sold. Some time after I went to view the sale and noticed that neither the seat nor candelabra were there. I enquired about the two items and I was told it was nothing to do with me, they had been given the job and I should mind my own business.

I spoke with the President and explained that two items of value were not at the saleroom. They appeared in the next sale and together made over a £1,000. The garden seat, alone, was sold for over £500. The sale grossed £15,000, but I don't know how much they were charged for expenses including removal, destructor charges and commission.

I, of course, was never thanked for my help.

Another time, I was in the shop one day and an antique dealer came in and said, 'I've a present for you.'

'What is it?' I enquired.

'A Jewish emblem,' he said.

He handed over a red box. It contained a magnificent Masonic jewel.

'Peter, this isn't a Jewish emblem.' I then told him what it was.

'Well, it's no good to me. You can have it,' he said.

It must have been one of the few real antiques in his shop, yet he gave it to the junk dealer down the road, simply because he didn't recognise what it was. In fact it was as a Georgian silver gilt Masonic Jewel from the Hallmarks and has been admired by masons and audiences in talks throughout the country.

The Georgian silver gilt Masonic Jewel from the Hallmarks.
From left to right: Chester Hallmark; Silver Hallmark; Makers Mark, Richard Lucas of
Liverpool; King's head replaced by the Queen's head in 1840; Letter Hallmark 1837

Information supplied by Timothy Kent (September 2004)

26

Master of my Masonic Lodge

Around 1974/75 I was asked if I was interested in some three-piece suites since a vehicle carrying them had been involved in an accident on the M1 near Sheffield. The large van carrying them had over-turned and the customer who they were to be delivered too had refused to accept them. They had been transferred to another vehicle, which meant they could instruct the driver to deliver them to me and agree a price afterwards. That was always a bonus as I didn't need to decide quickly what to offer and wonder if I given enough or too much. They were small two-seat settees on long legs in pink dralon, very dainty.

Anne liked them and kept two suites plus two extra chairs for our house. I suppose the room looked like an exclusive doctor's or dentist waiting room. The rest we sold very quickly, as usual at something like 50% of the normal retail price. We kept these suites until Anne decided to redecorate which meant we had to refurbish. This came about because of another fire salvage, which was two very large rolls of very top quality carpet. I couldn't believe why they were considered fire salvage. They neither looked as they had been in a fire or smelt of smoke. After Anne saw them she decided to have one of them for our house. This roll was laid in the lounge, hall, two flights of stairs and two landings, it was a patterned carpet. Since the carpet was fawn and brown Anne decided our pink suites didn't go with the carpet. I decided to keep the other roll, since it was the same pattern, colour and design as the other, just in case we ever needed to replace the carpet, since room wasn't a problem at Page Hall.

I asked Uncle Bernard if he could recommend some one to re-cover the suites, since he now only manufactured new suites and he didn't re-cover them anymore, this he did. I phoned the gentleman and asked if he would come and look at the suites and give me a quote for the job. This he agreed to, arriving one evening while our friends David and Sharon were visiting too. He glanced at the suites, but his eyes were all over the room. Then he said, 'Do people give you all these lovely things'. I couldn't believe what I was hearing. David of course took up his theme asking who had given me just about every item in the room. I tried to put him right by saying I have paid for every item in the room and then showed him the door, without asking him to send me a quote for the re-upholstery of the suites. David continued asking who had given me everything in the house for months afterwards.

I of course couldn't win. Anne still wanted to change the suite, either the colour or a new one altogether. Ralph the man who helped me to move Rev. Khan's effects had acquired a shop on Abbeydale Road which sold reproduction furniture. Anne decided to look and see if there was anything that could be used in our lounge. She told me there was an Italian suite that would look nice in the lounge, would I meet her and see what I thought; this I did.

I asked Ralph how much it was and he replied that, 'I could have it for £500'. This I agreed too and the lads took it home and brought the two suites back to Page Hall which we sold and this meant the new suite only cost £200, after taking this into account.

We were unlucky to have a burst pipe in the hall. It was a very slow leak from a radiator which none of us noticed for some time but the hall carpet was rotten. We decided to claim on the insurance. After showing the insurance people the carpet and pointing out it needed all replacing which to my surprise they agreed to, providing we couldn't buy the same carpet to patch it.

I asked a large carpet warehouse to look at the carpet, asking them if they could acquire some carpet to replace our hall, or if not, how much it would cost for the whole to be replaced. They couldn't replace the hall so quoted for the lot to be replaced. I then informed the insurance company of this and their quote to replace the entire carpet. I also informed them that I had a roll of carpet at our shop that would do the job, all they had to do was to pay the price I'd paid for it plus the fitting, but I insisted they should see the carpet first.

The same gentleman arrived at Page Hall who had inspected the damage carpet at our house. He looked at the carpet which I produced the invoice for, from their own insurance company, and he agreed to pay just what it cost me. This I accepted since there was no mention of two rolls of carpet so I was pleased with the deal.

In 1985 I became the Master of Hadassah Lodge in Sheffield. Being Master of Hadassah Lodge meant I had to learn the ritual for each candidate that joins the lodge during that year. I was lucky to have three candidates and each one had to go through three ceremonies, which meant a lot of hard work in memorising the ritual.

I didn't listen to the radio in my car for 12 months; I just repeated the ritual to myself. I also attended 24 Installations of new Masters in the other lodges at Tapton Hall, the Sheffield Masonic Hall, plus having to learn the ritual to install my successor. I also attended an Installation at Grand Lodge, Freemasons Hall in Great Queen Street, London.

David Lewis was a member of Hadassah Lodge but after his marriage and setting up home in London he joined a lodge there and became its Master the same year as myself and invited me to the ceremony, which I was delighted to accept. I also visited lodges throughout West Yorkshire which meant quite a lot of travelling to the 100 plus visits and countless speeches responding to toast to the visitors.

I was helped with my speeches by Irvine's advice to always be prepared to speak at every lodge I attended. This meant I would be preparing my response during the ceremony though there were times my preparation was wasted. But the preparation stood me in good stead on many occasions.

The author wearing the jewel in Masonic regalia

Irvine said I had the advantage on many people by not being afraid to stand up and speak. I was also told by him not to drink alcohol before I spoke as drink plus the adrenaline could cause trouble with my delivery. I was very grateful for his advice and still heed it to this day.

It was a very difficult year for me health wise. I was suffering bad angina even when I stood up to speak. Dr. Fleming suggested whiskey might help, so, before I spoke, I would buy a glass to drink after I'd finished. I must say, it worked!

I began having angina attacks whilst resting, even in my sleep. I also developed extreme back pain from a slipped disk. Anne insisted I go to hospital to have my back sorted. She sent first for my friend Nat Elston to take me to hospital. Anne, Lisa, Simon and Nat attempted to get me to the car but this proved impossible.

I got halfway between the front door and the gate but just couldn't take another step. Anne went to phone an ambulance and Simon brought a high stool for me to perch on. This I did until the ambulance arrived, with everyone, including me, in hysterics, which didn't help the pain in my back. The slipped disk needed rest and I spent two weeks on my back in the Hallamshire Hospital.

The following year proved to be even more eventful. The angina got worse and I was finally rushed to hospital, this time the Northern General. Dr. Fleming had always said I would be fine because Professor Smith knew exactly what needed doing.

I was admitted just before the August Bank Holiday weekend. Everyone was wonderful, but Professor Smith was on holiday. The ward thought he was just away for the weekend but by the following Friday things hadn't improved so I was taken to have an angiogram.

On the way I had a major angina attack. They had to stop wheeling me to administer pain relief. A whiskey would have worked quicker! On the Saturday morning I received a visit from Mr. Goitte, a Spanish surgeon, who informed me that I couldn't possibly wait for Professor Smith's return and he needed to operate.

The operation was a complete success. On the Monday night Anne stayed at the hospital and our friends Caroline and Harold Needham kept her company until I regained consciousness. I remember waking with a nurse at the foot of the bed and Anne at the side. I believed it was a brightly lit room, though Anne told me afterwards it was dim.

The surgeon asked me how I was feeling. I just said, 'My chest hurts.' He replied, 'I'm not surprised, I've been jumping up and down on it for four-and-a-half hours, and it will get worse.' I'd had a triple bypass and eight days later was on my way home.

While waiting for Anne I overheard a nurse explaining to a new patient the procedure and the risks involved. I was pleased no one explained this to me as I don't think I would have let them go ahead!

I certainly wasn't pleased with the odds she quoted to the new patient. The nurses informed Anne I'd been a model patient, Anne remarking she didn't believe them. They smiled and said I'd done everything they'd asked. It was nice to be home but I still needed to take things easy.

It was two months before I went to the lodge. As I walked towards the dining room a gentleman asked me to reply on behalf of the visitors. I didn't get the chance to say 'No I've been ill.' I bought myself a whiskey and when I actually spoke it was the first time, for some two years, I didn't have any angina pain. I certainly didn't need the scotch afterwards or since.

While I was recovering in hospital Lisa was due to go to Israel, taking a year out before starting university. She opted to take a youth leadership course in Jerusalem. I persuaded her that I would be fine and she should definitely go and enjoy the experience and she did.

Later, Anne, Simon and myself went to see her. We toured Israel for the first ten days which Anne and Simon had never done, then we spent a week in Eilat where Lisa joined us. I was again pleasantly surprised that neither the journey nor the touring had any effect on my health.

My public speaking began to take off. I'd started several years before, to a church group in Hutcliffe Wood Road. I was, I suppose, following the family tradition. Mother used to give talks to organisations such as the Women's Institute or church groups about her life. She also belonged to the Business and Professional Women's Federation as well as being, with dad, an executive member of the National Market Traders Association.

One speech she gave was well reported. They were trying to bring in six days opening for shops. In Sheffield, most shops were closed Thursday afternoon, though dad closed all day on Thursday, saying it wasn't worth opening for half a day.

The proposal was opposed by mother. She was quoted as saying, 'I don't mind being a servant of the public, but I object to being a slave to them.' What she would have said about Sunday opening, I dread to think. When she stopped public speaking she suggested they contact me instead. Never once did she consult me. It was difficult to refuse as they always said 'Your mother said you would speak to our group.'

After my heart bypass I insisted on a donation to heart research at the Northern General Hospital. It is amazing how many organisations expect you to do talks for nothing. Even though the money went straight to charity, I am sure some believed that the money would just go into my pocket.

The majority of talks were pleasant experiences but two less favourable events spring to mind. The first was at Sheffield Cathedral Hall. I had to take the afternoon off to attend. I mentioned I'd had a triple bypass and so any donation would be going towards heart research.

Someone decided on a collection. I was busy putting my junk away when a lady gave me the basket containing a lot of coins. I poured them in my pocket and thought I would count the money at the shop, exchange the coins for notes, and send a cheque to the charity.

A couple of days later I received a letter from a lady saying how surprised she was that I had taken a collection. I showed the letter to brother Irvine who said, 'They think you've kept the money for yourself.'

The collection had raised £33 plus some change which I made up to £33.50, and asked the Northern General to send me a receipt which I forwarded to the lady who had sent me the letter. I never received an apology or acknowledgement.

The second less savoury occasion was a talk I gave to Stocksbridge Probus Club. It was held in the lecture theatre of Stocksbridge College commencing at 10am. This meant a morning off work.

While I was preparing to talk, putting my junk on the table and waiting for the chairman to introduce me, I counted how many people were there and was surprised there were over a hundred. I always make sure during my talks that everyone knows that I am Jewish and also a freemason.

I spoke for over an hour and answered questions. As I finished the chairman handed me a £5 note for my charity. I was annoyed, but there was nothing I could do.

Then a member of the audience made some remark that he didn't understand how I could possibly be a freemason. I said if I had spoken to an audience of freemasons I would have received more then £5 for charity and left. I have spoken to only one Probus club since.

27

Mother's passing

My time at Abbeydale Road wasn't happy. Patnick's of Page Hall had a ring to it and our new base was small compared. Typical of the attitude was when a very wealthy Jewish gentleman with many properties in the city, popped in to buy furniture for his flats.

He looked around, picked out a number of pieces, and said he would only pay just over half of the price on the ticket. We could take it or leave it. Dot told him that I would need to authorise such a deal and we'd get back to him. It was late when I got back and I said, 'No way.'

Dot said she wasn't surprised and had offered the goods at a discount which I thought was fair, taking into account it would only be one delivery. Since it was Friday I said, 'Let him stew until Monday.'

The next day I went with Lisa and Simon to the synagogue. The customer arrived as Lisa was chatting to me. I said, 'Lisa and Simon, this gentleman owns the shop you were showing me the other day near Cole Brothers. If you go in there pick what you want, say a couple of pairs of jeans and tops, and however much they are marked give the assistant half the price and tell them this gentleman said it's all right.'

The Jewish gentleman said, 'You can't do that.'

'Why not? You did at my shop yesterday,' I said.

'But your shop is different.'

'Why? Am I not allowed to make a living or is it only you?' I replied. Needless to say I told the kids never to go into his shop no matter what they saw in the windows. I probably lost a good customer but I don't believe any person should dictate prices just because I'm a junk dealer.

The fire salvages seemed to be drying up and it became obvious that we were not making enough to keep the business afloat, never mind pay our living bills. We decided to put our house up for sale. The bank was pressing for me to lower my overdraft and even suggested I should not issue any more cheques.

We lost mother in May 1987. It was all very strange. I had given a talk to a women's group and showed them a photograph of her holding Norman, my eldest brother who died so young.

As I mentioned earlier in the book, a woman said that she'd held him and that he was too beautiful to live. I'd made a mental note to mention this to mother the next day. I was then junior warden of the synagogue, so I went there in the morning and popped in to see mother on my way home, walking there and back for the exercise. I rang the bell but there was no reply.

Mother examining a vase before trying to sell it

Although I had a key, I couldn't get in because the security chain was across the door. I walked around the back and peered through the window. There she was in her recliner, her legs on the footrest with a cup of tea beside her.

I decided she was asleep and banged on the window, but she didn't respond. I managed to find a phone box and asked Anne to collect me but to first phone Irvine and ask him to bring something to cut or remove the chain.

I walked back to mother's and Anne arrived with Irvine and sister-in-law Lynda. Irvine made short work of removing the chain. Mother looked very peaceful and then I realised she was dead and not asleep as I had convinced myself.

Under Jewish faith the burial should take place as soon as possible after the death. This being a Saturday, nothing could happen because it was the Sabbath.

The next day was the start of a Jewish two-day festival, Shavuot[3]. This meant mum would have to wait until the Tuesday to be buried because no manual labour can be carried out at this time.

I was a little annoyed with the Reverend at the synagogue. I expected him to have a chat with me about the implications of her death on my role as junior warden of the synagogue. All he said as I entered the synagogue was, 'I've heard the news, but I can't speak to you about it.'

He left me standing by the door not even knowing if I could carry out my duties that day or the next two. I decided to take my seat as a warden but ask the President to carry out my duties. I still don't know if that was right or not.

This wasn't the only reason for my anger. The Jewish custom on death of a parent are strict, though not everyone carries them out.

I decided prayers would be held at mother's bungalow, morning and night, for a week which is exactly what tradition expects. This means you are in full mourning for seven days which also entails not working. The Reverend said this couldn't happen because it would interfere with the reading of the Torah, the books of Jewish scriptures and other sacred texts, so prayers were arranged for the evening only.

Simon led the evening prayers all week. After the service on the first night, the reverend informed me he was going away the next morning so wouldn't be attending prayers again. That was fine as we could manage quite easily without him.

The next morning, Wednesday, Nat Elston picked me up to take me to the synagogue. We passed the Reverend's house and his car was parked outside and was still there later. In fact he was stood on the path. So he could have attended prayers that morning. I was annoyed at his lack of respect.

[3] *Shavuot celebrates the giving of the Torah*

Our next duty was sorting mother's will; dad's had been easy – everything was left to mum. My first shock was that the family solicitor had not been used, but Irvine's, who was an old customer of dad's. He had recently started his own business and unknown to me was now mother's solicitor and had drawn up her will.

Dad had purchased many freeholds around our old Langsett Road shop. Beryl used to collect mother's ground rents long after we left and she used to pay her. I kept the master book and the solicitor asked me to deliver it. He greeted me on the stairs and I handed it over. In his final bill one item read, '…to receiving ground rent book, £60.' Nice work if you can get it!

Mother gave us equal shares of her estate except for certain bequests. Philip had to have his money put in trust so he was only allowed the interest raised with three named trustees looking after the investment.

I did ask if I could have one ornament which was a Churchill toby jug. I was told to go to the auction sale and buy it there. Mother had asked me to take the jug on many occasions and this was the only reason I asked for it, so I certainly had no interest in going to an auction to buy it.

Mum had three modern semis in the Newlands area and I thought it would be a good idea to have one each but this was rejected too. Philip and I were left two pictures each, and Irvine the pick of the rest. Much to my surprise and Philip's anger he picked the lot.

I have often wondered what happened to dad's very large drawing room watercolour. None of his pictures have been seen again after mother's death except the two Philip acquired and the pair left to me. I did acquire a Churchill Toby jug some years later from one of my house clearances, which reminds me of mother whenever I look at it.

Mother's death took time for me to accept. I suppose everyone believes their parents will be around forever and when the inevitable happens we still think they are just sleeping and will wake and everything will be back to normal.

It was only at the funeral that I realised mother wouldn't be there with her advice and guidance. She had been a constant pillar in my life from infancy to my business which she helped whenever needed.

She was a larger than life figure who didn't like just being a housekeeper and mother, but we wanted for little. Yes we had clothes and were well fed but she wasn't a conventional mother.

On one occasion I was about to have lunch at the Langsett Road shop which mother was preparing for me when a gentleman came into the shop. I went into see if I could help. He enquired if he could speak to either Mr. or Mrs. Patnick. I asked who he was and he replied he was from the Inland Revenue. I went into the kitchen and told mum who said, 'Bring him in here'.

She looked at the man and said, 'You are the Inland Revenue, I've always wanted to meet you, yes you are my silent partner, sit down here,' which he did. Mother continued, 'And have my son's lunch, you may as well have that, you take almost everything else we have'.

The man went red and didn't know what to say, as mother put my lunch in front of him. He suddenly got up and said, 'I think I'll return on a more convenient occasion', and left. I never saw this man again and neither mother nor dad ever referred to him returning to the see them.

From an early age we all had bank accounts, whether it was the school bank or saving certificates or saving stamps. On many occasions, she said, 'Your meal's in the oven, help yourselves, I've a customer to attend to.' Customers came first because they put food on our table and money into our bank accounts.

Mother never drove a car but had a full driving licence. She sat with each one of her boys as they learned to drive.

One of mother's sayings was, 'What you can see, they've got, and half of that is probably not paid for.' She couldn't stand snobs and made sure we were brought up as normal children. We also were taught the value of money and to help people who were less fortunate than ourselves. Mother did bear a grudge and would go weeks without speaking to anyone she had words with.

The shop was closed on a Thursday so that was the day mother went to the Turkish Baths. First she would go to Glossop Road Baths then, when it closed, to Heeley Baths. We, her three sons, were designated to drive her there and of course collect her after she had finished. Since I was the youngest I had the job from the age of 21 to her death. What she enjoyed was 'Big Ada' giving her a massage. Anne once told mother her back was hurting and mother suggested Anne should visit Big Ada. I believe she only went once and me simply saying you should visit Big Ada seemed to cure her back.

Mother used to often shout 'Irvine, Philip, Edward' and whoever answered first got the job of whatever was required.

I never enjoyed selling like mother but it was a necessity, though I never mastered her art. She had a saying, which she used when something went wrong either in business or our private lives, 'What's for you doesn't go by you.' I often quoted this and thought about that saying during my life, because I believe it is very true.

I was having a really bad time in business with the bank on my back, but the money mother left paid off my overdraft. I considered buying her bungalow and selling Millhouses Lane but I foolishly decided against it.

I never had any luck with properties. Usually the sale only paid off my debts. However I did move business premises. My friend Harold Needham had bought a large warehouse in Norton Lees, Sheffield and offered me a similar one which backed on to it. He only wanted £5,000 which I thought was very reasonable.

Luckily we found a buyer for our shop and moved to Derbyshire Lane. It was much larger premises but very cold and impossible to heat. I had fitted, on advice, a very large gas blow-heater which was suspended from the ceiling. This proved expensive and noisy, so was used sparingly.

Our move coincided with the retirement of the partners in the fire salvage assessors. In fact I bought two loads just before they said farewell. The first was a quantity of gardening goods which didn't sell well.

Luckily I had an acquaintance that had a DIY and gardening store who bought the lot which got me out of trouble. Just. The other one was a quantity of paper, large rolls of sticky labels and other paper goods.

Simon wasn't working at the time and I wasn't available to go with the lads to collect it. Like my father, I had done my job buying it cheaply. I didn't realise how heavy paper was. Simon made sure every item went on the van. They were stopped by police on the return journey and taken to a weighbridge. The van was completely over the legal load limit. They then had to unload the paper leaving half on the van. The rest was stored until we were able to pick it up.

I was fined £2,000 for carrying goods over the 3.5 ton maximum weight as well as paying a storage charge for half the load. It proved to be very expensive paper and no way was I going to make a profit. Years later when we moved to our present home we were still using sticky labels from that stock.

The assessor Mr. Smith went to great pains to thank me for the service I had given him over the years. Remember, we'd first met in the early seventies and he was sure I would be contacted by the new people in charge, particularly Andrew who would now be working in head office.

I never heard from Andrew or anyone else until months later when the other partner arrived at Derbyshire Lane to thank me for all the help I had given him in buying and moving salvages. I was pleased he'd called, but of course it didn't put food on the table. And that was it on the salvage front.

28

Unusual purchases

Putting a price on the contents of a property can be straightforward but also quite a challenge. One of the first clearances I did after moving to Derbyshire Lane was one of the most extraordinary I ever came across.

At first it was quite straightforward: meet the agent at the property – a nice bungalow in Holmesfield on the outskirts of Sheffield – and have a look around. Inside it was all well kept and normally furnished, except for several freezers at various points plus a mass of pots and pans. It seemed more like a catering establishment than someone's retirement home. It was the garden that proved the most interesting. Parked up were three Morris Minor shooting brakes, or station wagons. There were also the remains of a wall and a pile of gravel.

'Let's see what's in the shed,' said the agent.

I looked down the garden at what I can only describe as a cricket pavilion, which I honestly thought belonged to a house behind the bungalow. I followed the agent across the beautifully kept lawn. Inside, there was room to walk up one pathway and across the top and back down the other side.

The agent stayed near the door and I took my time walking around. He inquired if I had seen everything. I said, 'You mean the tools on the workbench; the garden tools; the thousand or so blocks of wood (which I later realised were parts for a parquet floor); the three lawn mowers, and the JCB digger.'

'You have a good eye,' he said.

'You have to in my business. Right, let's look in the garage'. We walked back across the lawn and on the left-hand side of the bungalow looking from the back garden was a small door into the garage. The first things we saw were two more shooting brakes parked in line. On the right were hundreds of small boxes stacked on top of each another. On inspection, they were all full of bits of glass.

The agent then said, 'Let's look upstairs in the bungalow.' I thought he was joking, but sure enough there was an outside staircase leading up to a door. It was definitely not a loft, but a large room that didn't have an entrance from the inside of the bungalow. There were tables and chairs stacked up plus… a fish and chip frying range.

He said, 'What do you make of that?'

'What, the tables and chairs, or the fish and chip range?'

'Oh, that's what it is,' he said.

I decided to have a quick look in the deep freezers whilst he locked up outside. I suppose I remembered the first stock I bought when all the food had gone off by the time I moved it. The two in the back bedroom were empty but the one in the hall seemed to be full of bags of frozen peas.

The estate agent joined me in the front room and sat down. 'Well what do you think, how much are you prepared to offer me?'

I looked him straight in the eye and said, 'What for, the furniture, three freezers, the kitchen equipment, five shooting brakes, half a stone wall, the pile of gravel, the hand-tools, thousand of pieces of wood, garden tools, three lawn mowers, a JCB, boxes of glass, tables and chairs, plus a chip shop range?'

He said with a straight face, 'Yes.'

I said, 'You realise you can't get the three cars or the JCB from the back of the house without demolishing at least the back wall of the garage.' He obviously hadn't and we had to go back outside for me to explain. He said, 'I'd better take instructions, but you are you interested?'

I replied in the affirmative. Some weeks later he rang asking to meet again at the bungalow. The cars and contents of the garden hut, plus the dismantled wall and gravel, had been removed. Someone had indeed knocked down the rear of the garage, as I had suggested, and removed everything. I was a little disappointed not to have bought the lot, but I had negotiated a good deal for everything that was left, particularly since I was unable in any case to dismantle and rebuild the garage.

The tables and chairs sold quickly as did the other items but the chip shop range was sticking and had to be moved to the back of the shop. One day I was doing some office work and Dot came into my office and said, 'Come quick, I've got a customer who's interested in the chip shop.' We agreed a price and he gave the delivery address – The Park Café, Millhouses Park, Sheffield.

A junk dealer is supposed to be able to buy and sell anything. Dad always said, 'Something bought right, is half sold.' To this day I don't know what or if I should have given a price for the whole lot without pointing out the pitfalls of moving the cars and the JCB from the back of that property.

There was no such worries about another house, actually near that bungalow. It was a large property and everything had to be moved. The only problem, there was a boat in the front garden. I had already booked a holiday over Christmas and New Year, the quietest time of the year in our game.

No one wants to buy second-hand at Christmas. I had to ensure the house was cleared and the keys handed back while I was away. Philip was out of work and agreed to oversee the whole operation.

I sorted the books and sundries on the day before I left and pointed out to the lads what could be sold while I was away and what could wait in the warehouse for my return. The boat was old in my opinion, worthless. Philip agreed and I suggested it could be taken to pieces and burnt in the back garden.

Philip walked into the warehouse and shouted, 'Michael, what a wonderful boss you've got. He bought you a boat for Christmas.'

This became a standing joke even after I returned from holiday but the house was cleared and I handed the keys back after my return. Philip kept telling everyone how I had bought Michael a boat for Christmas. I must admit I did worry that the neighbours would complain about the fire but we got away with it.

Sometimes you wonder about pricing – if you've been fair both to yourself and the client. I was once asked to submit a written tender for a job because they needed two quotes. I picked up the keys and took Philip with me to offer a second opinion. I had a quick look around and left Philip to do his own thing.

He said, 'There is a picking in the outhouses that will go to Newark along with quite a bit of the furniture. Dot's husband George will move the coke, coal and wood which wouldn't leave much, if any, rubbish in the outhouses to be moved by you.' He then passed me a piece of paper with his estimate - £150.

'I've made it a bit more, about £225,' I said.

'You may be right, but there's a lot of work involved, and you will have to wait till Newark to get your money back,' he warned.

I pointed out there was a lot of enamelware and zinc items that were in the outhouses - buckets, a bath, tubs – plus an old-fashioned wooden dolly agitator used in hand-washing clothes. I decided to compromise and wrote a tender of £200 for the contents.

A week later the partner in charge rang asking if I had made a mistake with my offer. He said the other party wanted £200 to move it all. We did move everything and did very well out of the deal.

I still can't believe that anyone would have the nerve to ask £200 to move such a very profitable clearance. I wonder how many more people paid to have estates cleared.

Memories of dad came flooding back when I was asked to look at a flat in the Shirecliffe Estate, Sheffield. The furniture and contents were very poor and of little value.

Also in the flat were hundreds of virtually brand new books, all on American forces aeroplanes. I was looking at them wishing I could ask dad's advice when the person who was dealing with the estate said, 'I believe they are book club books and have little value.'

I bought and paid for the contents and began to move everything, leaving the books until last. I began to worry, as usual about the books, if they would sell. On the way back to the warehouse I decided to stop at three different bookdealers.

Each of the dealers bought a few, so I was left with hundreds. The lads were having lunch and I was trying to decide what would be my best way to sell them, when a dealer arrived, whom I didn't know. He said he'd been chasing me all across town.

'I've bought all the books you sold to the three bookshops, can I see the rest?

At this point Philip turned up and greeted him like a long lost brother. Philip then said, 'Leave him to me, do they stand to much?'

I replied, 'No.' Philip sold the lot to the dealer and I made a handsome profit even after Philip's usual commission.

Over the years we faced competition from car boot sales springing up all over the place. When I occasionally attended sales I often saw some of my customers – not dealers, but ordinary members of the public – looking for bargains to flog the following weekend.

I remember one lady, a regular market customer, telling Dot and Beryl that after her mother's death she had taken the contents of the house to a car boot sale and made £400. I wondered how much those things were actually worth. These sort of people thought it was such an easy way to make money, but the things they sold hadn't cost them anything. They needed no money for stock, wages, petrol, V.A.T, or income or corporation tax.

The days of cheap lots were fast disappearing although I occasionally had touches. One sale I attended was the stock of a printer who'd gone bankrupt. I did what dad before me had done and went early to look round.

I didn't really see much to interest me but since I had travelled out of Sheffield I decided to stay. Then the auctioneer offered two pallets of Christmas and birthday cards. I must admit I'd seen them but hadn't examined them since they were bound and covered with transparent paper. They certainly looked normal.

The auctioneer asked for £200 but didn't receive a bid until he came down to

£50 when I jumped in and bought them with my first bid. It was near the end and I waited in case there were any other bargains.

Like dad, I couldn't wait to examine my purchase. I couldn't believe the amount of cards there were, 5ft high and 5ft square, on each pallet. I went a day later with the van and two lads to bring them back to the warehouse. It was there I received a shock. The Christmas cards, except for the loose ones on the top, were blank. Dad would have said, 'They've been topped up,' meaning they were hiding the fact that they were blank by putting the good ones on top. I was worried I'd be stuck with them. Back at the warehouse I left the lads to unload and went to see my mate Harold Needham. He thought they would sell well.

I said, 'I have my doubts as the insides aren't printed.'

Good, that means people can put in their own messages,' he enthused.

Later I showed him a variety of the blank cards and he said right away, 'I'll take 200.'

I charged him 50p for the whole 200. I never liked to give away anything from any lot I bought until I had sold at least something. In the end I had 'Merry Christmas and a Happy New Year' printed on them and we sold out well before the holiday.

The birthday cards weren't so easy as most were numbered or messaged for a particular relation, such as nephew and niece. I was however pleased with the deal.

At another sale in a Chesterfield club I was interested in some personal weighing scales. There were hundreds, sold one at a time, with an option to then take as many as you wanted.

I started the first one and many more after that. Since no one else was bidding I thought I would buy the rest, but the auctioneer said, 'These are very cheap, I think I'll buy one myself.' He then bid and knocked it down to himself! This was against the law but showed, I suppose, that they were indeed value for money. I left and don't believe I ever went to one of their sales again.

The markets were changing too. As I explained earlier, we were moved onto a narrow road on the Setts Market between the Sheaf Market and the Castle Market.

The roofs weren't large enough to protect the customers, the goods or the stallholders. Many people retired and there was no atmosphere since food was no longer allowed to be sold on outside stalls. Plus the 'pitchers' were not allowed either. Shouting your wares was against market rules. Everything that markets were known for had been removed: even the market gardeners were put in another area, on King Street.

Michael Edwards, known as 'Potty Edwards,' (later the title of his memoirs) was one of the first to realise its downfall. He was in partnership with his brother Bill but the business couldn't support two families anymore. He moved to Germany for a while utilising his skills as a door-to-door salesman. How that worked I'll never know, but he came back to Sheffield and worked for himself, demonstrating items such as paint pads, car cleaning equipment and fruit juice squeezers amongst other things.

He also opened a kiosk in a little market on The Moor, one of the main shopping streets of Sheffield. So instead of one outside market area we finished with three. Not one of our council's great ideas. Michael started selling bunches of flowers which, as we say in the markets, he 'flashed up,' wrapping them in cheap but colourful paper and a fancy bow. However, Michael loved to work a crowd and use his patter. One day I arranged to meet Anne near The Moor and she said, 'Look what I've just bought, this wonderful orange juice squeezer. It was only a pound.'

'You've never bought one of those from Michael have you?' I asked.

'Yes I have, they are wonderful, and I've never seen so much juice come out of such a small orange.'

'Anne, Michael is a demonstrator. Come with me.' I took her back to Michael's pitch. He wasn't demonstrating and no one was near him. When he saw me, he pulled a pound out of his pocket and said, 'I did say "nish" but she insisted on buying one. I couldn't not take her money because of the large pitch I had and Anne was the first to put her hand up.' Michael then showed her how he got so much juice out of his oranges. He injected them with juice. We did keep the squeezer and yes it did do the job but we never got a glass and a half full of juice from a small orange!

29

Derbyshire Lane ablaze

Social Services were still sending me the odd jobs, although I could go weeks without a phone call. I was asked to move the contents of a flat on the Park Hill estate, the giant blocks that dominate the city centre.

Part of the clearance deal was that we had to return the television and video to the hire purchase (HP) company. We always made sure that we locked the van or left someone in the cab, otherwise goods would simply disappear. We left the TV and video until last, the plan being that the lads would drop them off to the HP offices on the way back. Later I got a phone call from Mark saying the set and the video had been stolen on the landing after they put them down to lock the flat!

Another notorious estate in Sheffield was Manor Park where we cleared quite a nice clean flat. Again, there was a TV – brand new – and a video player included in the clearance.

But when I sent the boys back the next day to collect the TV and video they said they were not in the flat and must have been stolen overnight. Whether someone had a spare key, I'll never know. I had to explain to Social Services that the best items in the flat had gone. It never occurred to me that any of my staff would steal stuff, but events like this made me wonder.

For years I had made good money from fire salvage work. But being on the other side of the fence wasn't so profitable.

One morning I got a call at 4.20am telling me my warehouse was on fire. I arrived at Derbyshire Lane just after 5am to be greeted by fire engines, police and flashing blue lights.

The blaze had started near our back door, probably by kids setting fire to cardboard boxes. My friend Harold Needham said there was little damage to my property but his stock was damaged by smoke. However checking through my warehouse it was clear a large part of my wares were wet through. This was mostly bundles of clothing and other rags. About 8am the assessors arrived. They first said, 'You'll not have a stock book, so you won't be able to make a claim.'

I said, 'Yes we do have a stock book. This is mandatory by law. But you'll find it difficult to identify goods by it. However, if you point out which article you want I will find it in the stock book.'

They were taken aback by this. They obviously thought I didn't have a legitimate business and could ride roughshod over me. I was then asked how much damage had occurred and what sort of claim would I be putting in. I said it was too early to say, but they insisted I give them a figure. 'Here's the stock book you go through it with me,' I said.

'This won't be necessary. We just need a figure.'

I looked at all the sodden goods and like a fool said £5,000. They left without argument saying, 'That's fine.' I then went about assessing the true cost. This involved cleaning up the warehouse, which took a week, numerous trips to the destructor, charges per load there, the lads' wages, my wages and so on. As dad always said, 'Whatever the lads receive in wages, you are worth double.'

I eventually arrived at a figure. The claim would be on Harold's insurance. All I had to do was to give them the invoices and the total. I believe it came to something like £6,500.

To my utter surprise they refused to pay, saying I had told them that the cost would be £5,000 and they wouldn't pay a penny more. I couldn't believe that a figure plucked out of the air at eight in the morning after arriving at the warehouse at 5am, would be accepted as a final figure but it was.

The assessors I had dealt with when buying fire salvage seemed very fair but when you are on the other side, it was a different approach.

I must be a very trusting person because every time I have had an insurance claim I have been left out of pocket. Once I claimed for a coat which received a cigarette burn at a football match. The insurance company took it away and returned it two weeks later having cut it down to a jacket!

My health insurance refused to pay for a follow-up scan which the specialist said was essential after my heart operation; and every time we claimed on our pet insurance for treatment to our dog it was refused.

Two claims on the van insurance – for an engine fire and when it was stolen – took ages to process and I waited more than two months to be paid. Yet they expect us to pay the yearly renewals on time.

I thought I'd need another claim after a burglary at Derbyshire Lane. The thieves

Brother Philip at his stall in the car park of Castle Market

gained access through the roof. The till contained a small float, which of course went. Beside the till was a glass display unit containing some small, more expensive items. The most valuable was an unusual clock. Every antique dealer that came to the warehouse enquired about it. Sure enough, that went too.

The police didn't hold out much luck in catching the perpetrators nor recovering the timepiece, advising me to keep an eye on local car boot sales. The following Monday I visited Sheffield's second-hand market, taking the dog with me for some exercise. The animal was perfect cover because I didn't want the dealers to think I was prying on their goods or prices. Brother Philip had a stall too but that was in the car park of Castle Market across the road.

I was amazed that the first stall I glanced at I spotted the clock. I phoned the police, keeping an eye out in case it was sold or moved. I didn't know the dealer concerned; in fact I'd never seen him before. I was surprised how quickly the police arrived but after questioning the stallholder the officers said he'd bought it legitimately. I was annoyed and insisted they remove it right away. The man informed the police he had bought the clock from his brother-in-law, an antique dealer.

By this time I was really angry and walked over and asked him who his brother-in-law was. It turned out his relative was a regular customer of ours whom I knew very well. I also knew his late father, an antique dealer, who had a shop not far from our old Langsett Road premises, the same antique dealer who bought the new children's cane chairs.

I was convinced the dealer must have seen the clock in Derbyshire Lane and since it was so unusual, have realised it must have been stolen. The brother-in-law was interviewed and was adamant that he had bought it legitimately. After a short time the police returned the clock saying the address that was given by the original seller was false. I had a verbal battle with the antique dealer but he was adamant that he'd never seen it in our warehouse. I told him never to visit our establishment again.

I didn't speak to him for years, but his mother always went out of her way to chat. When we did eventually speak years later I must admit he was always very nice but neither of us ever mentioned the clock incident.

30

Yet another move

Our time at Derbyshire Lane came to an end in the 1990s when my son Simon told me he had a friend who was interested in buying the premises. We were not doing the business to warrant keeping it going. I was pleasantly surprised at the offer, seven times more than I had paid.

I consulted Harold and he had no objection to my deal or my profit. An antique dealer rented us a container while we found new premises. Work was still coming in but the fire salvages were finished and it was just a matter of keeping our heads above water, if you'll forgive the pun.

Life as a junk dealer isn't always peace and love. We do run into some tricky situations. Two Social Services contracts spring to mind.

In Broomhall I was just putting the key in the lock when a man appeared out of nowhere threatening me with violence if I entered the flat. I told him I was only looking around to give a price but he wasn't having it and I went back to the car. I made sure I took the lads with me the next time but he never surfaced.

Near Crystal Peaks I had just started shifting furniture when a man appeared in the flat and started picking stuff up. I told him to back off but he pushed me over. I grabbed him as I fell and his coat came off in my hands. Michael beat a hasty retreat but our driver emerged and hit the man just as he had picked up a TV which of course he let go of.

The driver then put the intruder's arm up his back and frogmarched him out. I asked Michael why he hadn't helped since he was bigger than all of us, but he said he didn't want to get involved.

The police came and asked if we knew the intruder – which we didn't – but the first person I saw in the street told me who he was and said he would be drunk by now. The police took the jacket and we moved the furniture without further incident.

We also had to put up with nosey neighbours, interfering busybodies and people trying to con us out of goods. Once in an upstairs flat a lady appeared and said the wringer machine belonged to her. She lived on the floor above. How on earth anyone would borrow a thing that would take two men to carry down a flight of stairs is beyond me.

On another occasion I was told that the person whose contents I was moving had borrowed a quilt. I gave the lady the telephone number of the person who was in charge of the estate and told her to contact them.

The only quilt I could see was on the bed. I undid the cover to discover an almost new quilt. Later I found a receipt for a rather expensive duvet purchased in the last month. Needless to say the lady never phoned the phone number I gave her or came back to claim her quilt.

Social Services warned me about one maisonette on the Manor Park estate where the occupant had lay dead for over a month. They'd removed the carpet and sprayed the room. When we arrived the floor was littered with hundreds of dead flies. It made me wonder how someone could be dead for so long without any of the neighbours knowing. The buzzing from the flies should have been warning enough!

After a barren spell on the business front my luck was about to change by meeting a new contact. A neighbour of Michael Haigh's died and he recommended the sale of her contents be handled by an auctioneer from Wakefield.

Michael asked if I knew of a local hall for the sale and I was able to recommend Kingfield Hall. He also wanted my two lads and I to assist in the auction and to clear any bits from the house the auctioneer didn't want to take to the hall.

I enjoyed the sale but only bought one lot, a tray of figures. An antique dealer had missed this lot and approached me to buy just two figures. He said his wife collected them and offered me a profit on what I had paid for the lot and I agreed. I later discovered that they were Hummel figurines, very collectable and valuable. By this time I had sold him them. I never sold another Hummel without checking the price from a catalogue first. I also didn't trust that dealer again.

However, this auctioneer brought a new string to my bow. The fire salvages had dried up, but through this one event I started a new chapter in my business. I began to receive phone calls from him to clear houses.

I travelled all over West and South Yorkshire to move goods and each one was interesting and different. Some were small, others very large houses.

This new venture led to my sojourn to the Newark Antique Fair. The first time I ventured there was one Tuesday. Anne had started taking small interesting items I had picked out from house clearances to Doncaster Antique Fair held on weekends and occasional Bank Holidays. Some were antique, others looked too good to be sold in Sheffield Market.

Philip had been working for himself, doing the same as me, buying and selling second-hand goods. He did have a period with a shop selling imported reproduction items mainly china and pottery. He soon discovered that this wasn't paying, as others had the same items and there was always someone who would undercut you in price. Dad taught me was unless you could buy the entire stock someone would always undercut you.

Philip graduated into buying deceased estates just like me. I was slightly worried since he advertised for them locally and having the same name people might think it was me. I didn't take any action. He was entitled to make a living just like me. He began to stand in Sheffield Market on a Monday, mainly a second-hand market.

Dot had left my employment when I sold Derbyshire Lane. She then later started working for Philip on a Monday. This I didn't have a problem with since I didn't have enough work for two girls.

Anne in the meantime began standing at the market in Chesterfield on a Monday with the goods I had picked out from houses as too good for Sheffield market.

It was ridiculous taking them to Doncaster once every two months and the rest of the time them staying in the warehouse. We too, tried to supplement our stock with repro goods from warehouses but encountered the same problems as Philip. There was always someone willing to undercut the price.

We soon realised Chesterfield wasn't paying. I used to go with Anne in our Ford Escort help to unload and then park the car and have breakfast while she set out her stall. On returning to Sheffield I would check on the lads, take the dog for a walk and go to see Philip for a chat. One day he told me about a stall to rent near him and suggested I take it for Anne.

At first it was very good: dealers would arrive at just after 6am eager to snap up early bargains. Anne washed every item before packing it away in paper and into boxes. The dealers always noticed when Anne had new stock by the new paper the goods were wrapped in and waited eagerly for her to unpack them and then pounce. She insisted every article be numbered and marked and entered in her stock book.

I had the job of pricing each item which wasn't easy. Mistakes can be costly. It's obvious that if you price too cheaply they will sell quickly, whilst if you go the other way, stuff just won't sell.

Philip had persuaded me to attend the Doncaster antique fairs and also suggested Newark, reputed to be the largest antique fair in Europe. We went there on Tuesdays with leftovers from the Monday market, including Anne's better quality sundries.

The first time we were quite busy but it began to rain and I decided we might as well pack up and go home.

The hour's journey certainly appeared to be a worthwhile and the takings were good too. So began my career at Newark. At first it was just Newark but then Swinderby came into the equation nearby. The problem was the weather. The market stall we used was far from adequate for Newark but this was all we had.

I also had to rethink the sorting of each house of contents that I bought. Goods had to be clearly marked either for Sheffield market, Doncaster, Newark or Swinderby. By now we were in a wooden building behind a car sales pitch near the top of Woodseats Road. Philip had more or less given up working for himself and worked for me if and when needed plus the various antique fairs.

About this time a woman called Dolly who was mother's and then my oldest customer, died. She used to visit our stall in the market every week before opening her own bookstall in the Castle Market. She would buy items for her children or herself, especially good quality linen.

I was asked by one of her sons if I would buy the contents of her home. I was very sorry to hear of her death but quite willing. I had been there many times and it was a treasure trove. Sure enough, most of the articles bought from mother or myself were still as they were.

The linen was in the bundles as they had been delivered. The cellar was full of ornaments and trinkets. It had a large stone table and shelves packed full of items. I had once been shown the cellar by a cleaning lady when I delivered something bought that day in the market, with the jibe, 'I don't know where these will be put.'

I was also shown outhouses full of linen. I was asked how much I would pay for everything. Plucking a figure out of the air, '£10,000.'

I wasn't expecting his comeback. 'Make it £15,000 and it's yours.'

Then I gave it some more thought. 'Wait a minute Terry. You're not doing yourself or the family any favours. I believe it should go to auction and I know the man to sell it for you. If you hang on I will phone him and see if he will come and see the estate.'

I talked to John Walsh, the auctioneer in Wakefield, arranging to meet him at the house with Terry, the next day. I was surprised how knowledgeable he was plus his understanding of linen, and believe me there was a lot. The outhouses were large and were packed full. Much of it still in its wrapper. I had never seen such a quantity of plated goods in one house plus every type of ornament all kept clean and polished.

The auctioneer explained the procedure to Terry. The family should not be allowed to have anything from the house. Everything would be sold and any beneficiaries could bid for what they wanted and this would be taken off their final inheritance.

He said occasionally more than one person would want the same article and it was always difficult deciding who should have it. This way the highest bidder in the family would acquire it. I must admit I hadn't thought about this and it would have caused me problems if I had given the asking price. Yes I did have regrets not paying the £15,000 for the contents, then and afterwards, but I had to do the best for the family who I had known all my life.

Both Terry and John, the auctioneer, trusted me to sort what needed to go to Wakefield to be sold and what would be left for me to clear. It was a mammoth task, but I went through every bundle. All the pristine linen went for auction, the stained material in my pile.

Weeks went by and every spare moment was spent sorting Dolly's goods. Everything went smoothly until the removal firm came. We cleared a box room of bundles of linen which revealed an opening to another small room. Yet more linen!

John rightly said there was so much linen it couldn't possibly be sold in one day and I attended every sale of the estate. Terry and his family were there, occasionally buying goods for themselves. I calculated that the linen alone fetched £35,000.

In a business sense I was wrong not giving the £15,000 for all the contents but my conscience is clear and I had done the right thing.

There's a saying, 'Never introduce your best friend to your girlfriend.' Some time later John asked me to look at some furniture at a house just outside Sheffield. I was miffed when I discovered the identity of the deceased – a relative of Terry. After all the money I'd saved them with Dolly's estate, they by-passed me and had gone to John. Why, is a mystery to me. Maybe they weren't satisfied.

I must admit I did well out of the deal, making new customers especially at Newark.

One man in particular specialised in linen. I was surprised how much he spent and suggested he should go to the sales at Wakefield. This he did and he proved to be a good buyer from them and me. This again enhanced my standing with John, the auctioneer.

I started receiving regular phone calls to look at furniture or clear houses across the region, with Newark a good outlet for my wares. I remember a blue leather three-piece suite and a pair of Smelter figurines. As we unpacked I couldn't believe the interest. One young attractive girl jumped a fence to examine the figures while the suite people were clamouring to buy it. Yes this was my first real experience of Newark and it certainly had a buzz.

The one thing I stressed. I sold junk, though people bought antiques. In other words, my signs on the stall said 'A. Patnick. Junkerama.' I never claimed to sell antiques and never commented or mentioned what period anything was. That was up to the purchasers to decide.

31

Happy hour at Patnick's

I was still receiving calls from private individuals. One asked if I could meet him at his late mother's house. I was met by an immaculately dressed gentleman, smelling of cologne. He showed me round and asked if we could guarantee to move everything from the house that day.

I arranged the clearance there and then. I asked how much he expected for the contents and was surprised to be told, 'Give me anything and it's yours but it must be cleared today. All the good items will be on the Antiques Roadshow in a month, at Chatsworth, so there is nothing of value here.'

I wish I could buy the same clearance once a month now. I remember keeping one large tablecloth that would have fetched the price I paid. The majority went straight to Newark, the rest for Sheffield market.

One time someone bought an item from a stall next to us at 10am and came back with a film crew from Bargain Hunt at 2pm. The show had done their homework on the article and they were able to speak on it in depth.

One of the show's presenters once accused us of smashing up good furniture. I had to explain these were bits that had broken in transit or things that were unsaleable. There was no point in taking them back so we left them. He obviously had more knowledge than the junk dealer who was supervising the act.

Dad's saying, 'There's a customer for everything, but do you need the time and room to wait for that person?' was illustrated by a story about Henry Wigfall who had bicycles and electrical stores all over Sheffield.

One day dad visited the head office in Rutland Road. In the warehouse a man was sorting through a box of old metal nuts and Mr Wigfall asked him what he was doing. He replied he was looking for a nut to fit a particular bolt. Mr Wigfall pulled a shilling out of his pocket and said, 'Go to an ironmonger and buy one, it's costing me your wages to find one in that box, it's cheaper to buy a new one.' If we couldn't sell it at Newark was it worth keeping? Some things, maybe but others would never sell, so they needed destroying.

When we first stood with furniture a young man from Bournemouth used to arrive most Tuesdays and more or less bought anything we had left that was cheap. He was always accompanied by an attractive young lady who wrote down everything he bought, from buckets to bedroom suites, as well as labelling each item.

After a couple of years the young lady arrived without the man and had a quick look around and was about to leave when I asked if there was a problem. She said they hadn't much money to spend because the cheque from their main buyer hadn't arrived.

I asked if we could help in any way. She replied that until the cheque arrived they couldn't buy much, though we had plenty that would be of interest, but no money. I said, 'Surely we can work something out.' She then said, 'I could give you a post-dated cheque.'

'That'll be fine,' I replied.

She said she would be back in ten minutes with, whom we found out, was her boyfriend. Sure enough ten minutes later she returned and they more or less cleared everything worth buying.

I received a phone call from the young girl six days later to present the cheque since their customer's cheque had arrived and had been cleared. I presented the cheque which went through without a problem. Unfortunately we didn't see him at many more fairs again.

My dad had told me, 'Remember two things, you can only get cheated by a customer once and if they are regular customers, think how much money you have made out of them over the years, usually you will have made enough to stand the loss'.

I had had a similar case at our Page Hall shop where we had a customer who came once a month from Hull to buy furniture for export to America. Sometimes he would have quite a bit, other times only a few pieces, but he always managed to buy something.

After a couple of years of always paying cash he asked if we would accept a cheque. I said I didn't have a problem with that, so the next few times he paid by cheque. He bought some furniture which came to £175 and he produced his cheque and left with the goods.

A week later I was informed by the bank the cheque had bounced. I was most surprised since I thought he was one of our better customers. I also thought we'd lost a very good customer. I regretted he hadn't told me he had difficulties, maybe we could have worked something out.

Two years later he walked in and straightaway said, 'I owe you £175,' and handed over the money. We found out he'd been inside for drugs offences.

Genuine mishaps do happen. One of our regulars paid a bill by cheque but the bank refused to honour it, saying it needed two signatures. We weren't to know that when we accepted it. Anyway, I left the cheque in the till hoping he'd be in.

A few months later he appeared. I told him about the problem and he said, 'I was wondering why it hadn't been presented.' It turned out he was a schoolteacher and didn't live in Sheffield. He came during school holidays to see his parents who lived nearby.

The market was an obvious place to pass on forged notes. We unknowingly took one or two in our time at Newark.

Newark was proving interesting, profitable and hard work. We hired more vans and a marquee, but even that wasn't big enough. We graduated to two purpose-built, lightweight tents which we practised erecting in the garden before exposing our skills to the fair. They proved a godsend.

Having a cup of tea in one of the new tents at Swinderby

Later Anne discovered that a lady hired out caravans, which she left next to the stall at Swinderby and then on Sunday afternoon transferred it to Newark. This made our lives a little easier, not having to travel back and forth to Sheffield.

One clearance agreed with John turned into quite an adventure. He'd asked me to meet the son of the deceased at the property between New Mills and Huddersfield. It didn't appear to be a difficult job; Michael, bless him, managed most of it with just a sack barrow, although I needed to give him a hand with the three-piece suite which needed to be delivered next door. I was about to shake hands when the client said, 'Fantastic, thank you. Have you cleared the cellar kitchen?' I looked at him in amazement. I didn't know there was one!

There was no entrance from the house and we were taken down the drive to a back door that took us into a very large room, a typical cellar kitchen. It had a large stone table, a sink, fire range and stone shelves all around. There were a very large quantity of bottles full of liquid, plus a few tubs and a locked safe.

I asked if there was a key to the safe. The reply was, 'Yes, but I've left it at home. Give me your card and I'll send it to you.' I certainly didn't expect that to happen but I did say without the key I could not make him an offer that included the safe and it wasn't worth me taking it back to Sheffield. The man said he would definitely forward it.

I asked if he wanted all the bottles to go. 'Yes, the auctioneer said you would move everything.' We then got on with the task. We filled six crates with the bottles, using blankets to protect them and even found room for the safe.

The lads unloaded the van in the warehouse. Michael was experienced enough to know where each item I had indicated needed to be put, either for Sheffield market, Doncaster or Newark, each having its own area.

I phoned John to inform him about everything – the furniture, delivery of the settee next door, hidden cellar, the bottles, the safe – and that the executor had been satisfied with our work and happy with the price agreed. A few days after, I received the key for the safe without a note or return address. The safe was empty because the family had done their job.

One month later was Newark Antique Fair. We went with two vans, a large 7.5 tonner plus our own van. We erected our tents as usual, which took up three normal pitches, then unloaded the vans.

The lads then returned with the vans to Sheffield and loaded early the next morning for the market, Philip deciding to sleep in the tent. Anne and I had the caravan, not luxurious, in fact quite old, but we had a TV run from a generator. The tables were usually erected outside the tents and the smalls were put out on them. They were quite full when Philip began to shout, 'It's happy hour at Patnick's Junkerama.'

Philip liked a drink, but 6.30am was even early for him and he never drank while working for me except after we had finished for the day. To my surprise he was unpacking bottles of wine and beer from the tea chests. All I could say was, 'How have they got here?'

Philip's sarcastic reply was, 'On the van.' I didn't remember telling Michael they were for Newark.

Suddenly a man asked how much they were. Philip looked at me. I shrugged my shoulders. Philip replied, '£7.50.' The man handed Philip £75, since there were ten bottles. Philip came over with the money and said, 'I don't believe this. I meant for all ten! We'd better have a look at what's here.'

Neither of us really had a clue about either the contents of the bottles or how much to charge. They stood to nothing, except for labour and petrol. Philip soon had a crowd around and doubled the price, charging £15 a bottle. As I gave them carrier bags and paper to wrap them in, I asked customers what they thought they were buying. 'The labels are very old but perfect,' was the reply.

Another lesson learned and money found by mistake. We also sold the safe for £45.

I could always find a picking in every house I cleared for John. And Newark was an excellent outlet.

Once I arrived at a house in Wakefield that was in such poor condition it had a tree growing through the middle of it and branches protruding through the roof! The place was wet-through. The bedroom suite was in poor condition and would need a lot of repair. Philip came with me as I valued his opinion. He believed it would sell at Newark as it was. He thought someone would restore it or have it done. That was good enough for me.

Dad often said, 'Whatever you value pieces of furniture at, the contents are often worth more.' It certainly was the case here. The bedroom suite was full of beautiful linen, although it was wet or damp. Again it would be gamble if it sold.

On the landing was the another safe with no key. I began moving a few things into piles either for the destructor or to be kept when I came across the key plus a purse. The safe contained lots of papers, old passports, birth certificates, bills, etc plus a couple of inexpensive rings which was a bonus.

The purse did contain money which helped to pay the destructor charges which were quite costly at Wakefield but cheaper than bringing it back to Sheffield. The linen, bedroom suite, plus other items were all to be kept for the next Newark.

The linen and other items sold well but the bedroom suite was not as easy to move. Lots of people looked but decided it was a major restoration job. We were about to close when a stallholder from lower down our row began to look at the suite. We left him alone at first but soon it became clear that he was interested Philip decided to speak with him.

How much did we want for it?

I said, '£450, but you could make me an offer. You will not insult me by offering me money.'

'How about £250?'

I shook his hand and the deal was done. I was pleased to see the back of the suite and certainly didn't want to take it back to Sheffield and we didn't have to deliver it either. The deal turned out all right. The safe sold for £45, but it wasn't easy. Certainly our business can be hard work but every day brings a different challenge.

I was still receiving a few phone calls from private individuals, one to look at a house near our old shop in Abbeydale. It was bad, full of rubbish and loads of unsaleable furniture plus a lot of smalls.

I did point out that most would have to go to the destructor which would be expensive. I was then told that an auctioneer had valued a chest at £200. Yes, the same one that tried to muscle in on my fire salvages and also tendered for the contents of the house I bought for £200; they wanted to be paid the same amount to clear it. I said, 'Well let him move it all and he can sell the chest for you.' The man explained that the auctioneer would not move the rest.

Philip saw my car and stopped to see what I was doing. I explained about the auctioneer saying a chest was worth £200, but wouldn't take the rest. Philip followed me upstairs to look at the chest. It was impossible to examine it with only the top visible. I managed to bang the top and said to Philip, 'It's plywood.'

The owner said, 'You put the rubbish in the front room and I'll move it each evening, with my son and a trailer, will that help?' It certainly did. We had almost finished when the landlord arrived to inform me that the auctioneer had been and didn't now want the chest. I wasn't surprised. We took if off his hands for nothing. We sold it for £20 even though it was all plywood.

Among the contents were three cases of Beezer comics I didn't even know were there. I took them to Swinderby but didn't put them out, as I believed they were too modern and no one had asked or showed any interest in comics.

One day at Newark Philip suddenly revealed a customer had enquired about comics. 'What happened to those comics you took to Swinderby?' I managed to find them and in no time the customer was studying them.

The man asked Philip how much he wanted. 'Make me an offer,' was his reply.

I was amazed when his offer was £200. Philip looked casually at the cases and said, 'I was expecting £300.' There was a short pause and the customer said, 'I can go to £285.' Philip said, 'I'll ask my brother.' It was hard to keep a straight face but I managed to accept.

You got all sorts at Newark. One couple used to pester us for anything from ships. We did come across menu cards from cruises, but they didn't want those. I used to say loudly to Anne and Philip, 'We sold those things from the Titanic, didn't we?' or 'Have we still got those dinner plates from the QE2?' They soon got the message.

Another man had a notice around his neck saying, 'I buy bus tickets.' This always had me wondering what anyone could do with used bus tickets. We found quite a collection of them in the attic of a house it Huddersfield. Sure enough he came to Newark and bought them but we didn't get a fortune for them. You need more than one person to show interest in anything before a high price can be obtained.

In that house the attic was also crammed with thousands of postcards from around the world with weather reports all kept in cardboard boxes. All I could say it's a pity they were not picture postcards.

We moved all the goods from that house over the next couple of weeks filling some ten or 12 skips of rubbish. Every house has goods that people keep but this one they hoarded everything. Philip and I had to check every piece of paper to ensure we didn't miss anything of value.

Sometimes he would find something and ask me what I thought about it; other times I would ask him. It was a tedious job. We both did different rooms in the attic, making three piles. One was for rubbish, one not sure, and one to take to Newark.

The 'not sure' mound was scrutinised again and a consultation had between the two of us. The postcards I didn't think would sell, Philip thought they would so we kept them. Luckily they were already boxed, so didn't need to be examined individually.

I took them first to Swinderby but I didn't sell many, if any. I did phone Philip and said, 'No one is interested in the cards, don't bother bringing any more to Newark'. Philip came back with, 'Remember the comics didn't sell at Swinderby but I did well with them at Newark.'

Laurence, the Irishman, went through every postcard at Newark and bought quite a few. I sold some to a friend of Philip's at £10 a box but they were very slow sellers. I can't say we made much on them because of the time and labour involved, but the clearance was an unusual experience.

I moved the contents of a house in the Wakefield area for John, the auctioneer. It was a normal terraced house with some old furniture but very little of value as any antiques had already been removed, but as usual there was pickings in the sundries.

I heeded my father's advice; always check the bin, the cellar and the attic. The first two revealed nothing, but in the attic I found a teddy bear. It had been wrapped in a piece of linen for years. There was something about this teddy that made me put it in the boot of my car. It had a slightly humped back and its head nodded.

I called in at Philip's home on my way back and showed him the teddy. He said he would phone a toy dealer he knew. Philip described the teddy then said, 'Well it's my brother's, not mine. I'll ask him and come back to you.'

Philip then told me it was a 'Yes, No,' teddy and said the dealer had offered £400 for it. I was amazed, even though I realised it was worth doing research on and maybe old and probably German. I said I would think about it.

My first thoughts were, if it's worth that to him, how much it is really worth? I left Philip's and went home. Anne said, 'I wouldn't like to think I was giving £400 for that old thing.' The next morning I put teddy back in the boot and went to the warehouse. Harold Needham popped in and I couldn't resist teasing him about how much he thought it was worth.

'I've been offered £400 for it from a dealer on the phone, without him even seeing it,' I said. Harold then said, 'Why not try it on eBay? It's marvellous, I use it all the time.' The Internet age had just begun but I hadn't used the auction site before.

Harold said, 'If you bring the teddy to our house I will put it on the site for you.'

I didn't think I could lose anything, so I took the bear to Harold's that evening. He stood teddy up and put a ruler next to it, taking three pictures, in different positions. He then proceeded to transfer the images to his computer and onto the eBay site.

I decided that I would put a reserve on the bear of £300. Over the time teddy was on the site we received one enquiry and not one bid. I thanked Harold for his effort and asked how much I owed him, but Harold wouldn't take a penny saying, 'It's not worth worrying about. I use it all the time so its swings and roundabouts. It's the only thing I failed to sell.'

Some time later Philip asked about the bear. I said, 'I've still got it in the car.' Philip suggested he phone the toy dealer again. The dealer wasn't far away and said he would pop over. Sure enough, within half an hour he was there and after one look confirmed the toy's origin. He said '£400. Is that acceptable?'

I was again surprised but accepted. He paid me in cash then chatted for a bit. Philip asked him what he was going to do with it. I wasn't interested because I was very pleased with the deal.

He said, 'I'll keep it for myself in my collection,' and left. I gave Philip £50 for selling it which he was pleased with, and I couldn't believe anyone would pay that sort of money for an old teddy bear.

I think after a month I would have said I wasn't interested. I wondered if he had seen the bear on eBay since so many dealers scroll these sites especially when they specialise in one area, like toys.

I must admit I have never used eBay since. I suppose it's like me and car boot sales, I just don't do them. I leave them to amateurs but many dealers make a good living out of them. So do the dealers who trade with charity shops, picking up bargains before the general public have a chance to see the goods.

Another thing I have never done is go to jumble sales, though I was once asked to price goods up at a boys' club. I was asked to attend a jumble sale of an organisation I belonged to ensure they were doing the right thing. I observed from a distance a lady worker putting some very nice linen under the stall and this never appeared again. This wasn't my style and I never went to another one.

At a charity group I noticed tins were sorted by the staff and put under the counter before being sold to the public. When I asked why, I was told that certain doctors wanted first pick. I never asked if the doctors paid for these tins.

I was asked by an acquaintance if I would look at the part contents of his house as he was going to live in London in a flat and wouldn't be able to accommodate all his and his wife's possessions. I was quite surprised to see the items he was getting rid of.

After a quick look I phoned John in Wakefield and asked if he would look at the items that I believed would sell very well in one of his sales. This he was delighted to do; there was furniture, silver, some interesting paintings and old prints. I also recommended a removal firm to transport their furniture to London. Though this was the last time I recommended this particular firm as they refused to move me when I moved or made an excuse when I called to confirm my booking two days later, that they had a firm booking the next morning for the same day. I was furious as I had used their father and grandfather to do all my fire salvages plus a few private jobs like two grand pianos and had recommended them to countless people. I had never received one job from them but other removal firms gave me jobs to do or recommended me for surplus furniture or items they had in storage but they hadn't received payment for two years or more.

The furniture and effects I bought from these firms never amounted to much for them, but were useful to me. I was asked if I would pop up to the house in the afternoon of their move to London and see what was left for me to clear. This I did and was surprised to receive a bottle of malt whiskey for all the help I had given them.

The removal firm were just putting the last bits on the van to go to London from the garage so it was easy for me to assess what I had to move. I was surprised to be shown a large quantity of English copper coins with a note saying a firm in Chesterfield, with their name and address, would buy them for scrap. I walked round with a daughter and her father to see what was left, really it was mainly rubbish but again there was paper that maybe of interest. They were very pleased with the auctioneer and the removal firm I had recommended.

We moved all the rubbish and the interesting paper, saleable goods plus the copper coins. I was surprised that the coins were accepted by the firm in Chesterfield, who weighed them and paid me cash for them. I was also surprised to receive a phone call from them in London asking what had happened to two prints which were in the hall. I knew exactly where the paintings were and I had no hesitation in informing them, that they went to be sold by auction in Wakefield. I was asked if I could get them back as a son-in-law liked them. All I could do was ring John and ask him if they could be withdrawn from the sale and if this was the case, someone would have to collect them or arrange delivery. I was told this wouldn't be a problem as the son-in-law had to go occasionally to Leeds for his work so he would collect them. Luckily the prints hadn't been catalogued as they were to be included in a special sale at a later date. The prints were duly collected and taken to be reframed.

The person who reframed them enquired, when he phoned to arrange the collection, what the person wanted to do with the pair of watercolours under the prints. I never heard anymore about them, but I did find out later how pleased they were with my clearance and the auction results, especially the silver, which had fetched much more than they expected. I was also pleased with my clearance, which showed a worthwhile profit.

32

Cash in the Attic

My German teddy bear experience proved one thing. You can find 'Cash in the Attic.' I was doing maybe one house clearance a month or so for John Walsh, the auctioneer. I always seemed to find a picking even though the best had been removed for his auction first.

In the loft of one house I found a large electroplated nickel silver tray with two handles and beautifully chased or engraved. This had been put away and forgotten for the junk dealer to find. The £100 it fetched certainly paid for clearing the rubbish that was with it.

In another attic wrapped in an old blanket I found a very large four-fold, hand-painted screen which sold for £85.

I didn't always come up smelling of roses. In a bungalow there was a pianola with hundreds of rolls that could be played on it. I thought it would be a doddle to sell, but we couldn't give it away in either Sheffield, Swinderby or Newark. We finished smashing it up the second time it went to Newark.

I was asked to look at some surplus goods at the Rising Sun public house at Bamford following a refit. Philip knew the owner and said he would like to come with me to see what they'd done. In the car park was a helicopter! Philip commented the son ran a 'taxi in the air' business.

We were ushered to a large ballroom where the owner joined us. Lined up like a jumble sale were pictures, prints, decorative pottery and other small items. I was asked to make an offer which was accepted.

Even though they were mainly modern prints and pottery, I decided to take everything to Swinderby. We had our best day ever, taking £1,750. As we finished loading up to go to Newark, Anne decided to use the ladies. Just as we were leaving the site she remembered she'd taken off her market pocket in the toilet cubicle. She ran back but it had gone, never to be seen again. Another costly mistake. The pub's goods proved to be expensive because the returns were nil.

We also had bad luck at some of the venues. My friend Harold suggested we try Thoresby Market on a Sunday. We arrived quite early and since no pitches were marked out, we started to erect our market stall on the first available space. We had just about finished when we were informed we were in someone else's pitch. We moved twice more, for the same reason. By this time the only place left was in a very large puddle, though some would say a small lake. We stood but our feet were very wet and we soon realised strangers were not welcome. We persevered for a few weeks but our takings didn't warrant the time and effort.

And then Swinderby Fair was cancelled unexpectedly because the people running it discovered they only had planning permission for five fairs a year, not six. They decided to move the February sale to a quarry. We were assured there would be no problem erecting our stall on the site. I would take the goods in the van with the lads but Anne and Philip would actually stand at the fair, returning home on each of the three nights.

Despite the assurances of the organisers, erecting our tents was impossible. The fair was on concrete and our pegs just wouldn't penetrate the surface. We found stones to try to keep the stall firm.

However after I left, the wind got up. Anne rang me in Sheffield saying the stall looked like blowing away and could we come and try to secure it. We were in the middle of moving the contents of a flat so I said I would pop over as soon as possible. I then received another call to come quick or we would lose everything.

We left our job unloaded and rushed to the quarry. On arrival the tent was down and most of the furniture broken. Even the tent was beyond repair. Philip did complain to the organisers but they insisted we had the wrong pegs and should have brought ones that went into concrete. These I have yet to find.

Philip tried to get the rental back but that proved impossible. Most of the stock we left on the site in pieces. The few buyers that had ventured there had a birthday buying goods for next to nothing. I don't believe we sold one item. Anne and Philip were pleased just to escape with their lives.

33

Modern marvel leads the way

Touring the north of England for years we relied on our nose and maps to find places. Until of course the advent of satnav which proved invaluable. I used it for the first time after being asked by John to look at the contents of a bungalow in a rural location in West Yorkshire. I didn't bother looking it up, just punched the address into the navigation device on the dashboard.

I followed the instructions to the letter and found myself on what can only be described as a dirt track. I kept going very slowly down this path. However the technology knew what it was doing because at the bottom I was pleased to be back on a normal road.

I was greeted by a relation who showed me around. Every nook and cranny had been emptied and placed either on the floor or on other furniture, so my first thoughts were that there were no hidden treasures here.

Lastly I was shown the garage which was crammed with rubbish of every kind. My question was, 'Has all this got to be moved?' and the unwanted answer came back, 'Yes.'

Back in the house all the linen and clothes were in pillow slips, bolster cases, or linen bags; the sundries were mostly left on the work surfaces in the kitchen or on sideboards, tables and other furniture which I would have to sort and pack for three different venues.

In the bedroom I found boxes of stockings. The pictures told me they were quite old and would no doubt sell at Newark just for the adverts on the front of each box.

But I was wrong to think there were no treasures. They were definitely a picking or two among the ornaments, china, glass, pottery and kitchen utensils. But the garage needed emptying and nearly all, if not all, would have to go to the destructor and that would cost time and money.

On my way back to Sheffield I ignored my satnav and carried on past the right turn that would have taken me up the dirt track.

I decided we would have at least two loads for different destinations. One would be for the destructor, plus one at least to bring back to Sheffield. I just had to work out which to do first. It was easier to bring back all the saleable goods to Sheffield leaving the rubbish in the garage along with any in the bungalow.

All the rooms were big. In the lounge was one of the largest settees I have ever seen in any clearance. It was in excellent condition, although reproduction in style. This would go to Newark along with the smalls, linen, boxes of stockings, some clothing plus fur coats that I had already earmarked for there.

Everything from that bungalow seemed to sell quickly except the settee until a lady dealer showed interest. She particularly liked it because it would be nice for her dog! I didn't care why she was interested but I needed to sell it as it would take up a lot of room in our tent in the evening and I certainly didn't want to take it back to Sheffield. She wanted to know how much we would take for it, as she was a dealer. I said it was the same piece no matter who bought it. Then she said I will pay you cash. I retorted we only dealt in cash. Finally I said, 'If you pick the settee up yourself I'll knock £25 off.'

She then informed me she was a very good customer of Pat, another Sheffield dealer, whom Philip knew very well. Philip nipped to see Pat and came back to say she was a good customer with plenty of money but always wanted money knocking off before she would buy.

I was adamant that I would only lower the price by £25 if we didn't have to deliver it. She then said she would have the settee and return with a van to collect it later. We were packing up for the evening when she returned to collect the settee with a couple of men and a transit van. The settee only just fitted in the van but the doors wouldn't close and needed tying with rope.

She finally paid but gave me £5 less than I asked for. We argued for a short time but I wasn't going to lose a customer over £5 so I suppose she won but at least it was sold and had been removed.

She then saw the ladies stockings and asked about them. I told her the price and again she thought she could barter, but I certainly wasn't worried about them selling so I just put them back on a table. She again picked up the stockings and again she offered a lower price. I was about to throw them back on to the table when she said she would have them but hadn't got any money left on her. Could she collect them first thing in the morning? I said, 'Okay, we open at 8am.'

I put them in a large box in the tent near the caravan. The next morning there was no sign of her. About 12 o'clock, Anne said there'd been interest in the box and how much was it? Anne sold the large box and asked what to do about the stockings.

I assumed the woman had changed her mind.

'Put them out, they'll sell easily.' Which they did.

Soon after, the lady arrived with her large dog complaining the settee had a small tear in it and asked what I was going to do about it. I looked at her in disbelief.

'It was perfect when it left here. If you damaged it delivering it that's not my problem.' Both Philip and Anne confirmed it was perfect – Anne saying she even thought of keeping it for our home. The lady then asked for her stockings. I pointed to the table that had one or two ordinary boxes.

'That's all we have left.'

'You were saving me boxfuls.'

'Yes, and you told me you would pick them up this morning, I thought you had changed your mind, since it's almost 1 o'clock.'

I never saw her again, but I wasn't sorry, she was a pain in the neck, unlike most of our customers everywhere whom I looked forward to seeing even if we had nothing suitable for them.

Like most people, I like to remember the good times, but there were many that didn't show a profit. I remember moving a flat that belonged to a watch repairer. Among the finds was a gold penknife and a Rolex watch, along with various watch parts.

The watch wasn't working and since there were so many counterfeits I wasn't sure if it was genuine. I had a friend, Peter, who dealt with good quality jewellery and watches. I used to sell him scrap gold and silver, so I decided to show it to him. Unfortunately he couldn't say for sure and needed to go to his shop to get the back off. Yes, it was fake. The watch parts were impossible to sell, so most went to scrap.

The penknife I used in one of my talks, showing it to people at a church group. The event was filmed by my friend Harold Needham. The knife could clearly be seen on the video but when I arrived home it was nowhere to be found. I emptied the bag but it had disappeared.

A lot of people had gathered around the table where I displayed my various props, though I don't remember anyone asking to look at the knife. I went back to the church hall but I have never seen the item since.

34

Toy story

A memorable purchase for me was the contents of a council tower block. Everything had to go, but in the last room I looked in, a strange sight befell me. There before me on homemade tables was a complete train set filling most of the room. I wondered about its value, thinking of the touch I'd had with the German teddy bear.

'The track is secured to the wood. I assure you it isn't worth anything. I know, because I attend model train fairs,' said the executor of the estate. Since I knew nothing about train sets, I took him at his word. 'The price I pay will depend on how long it takes us to move this lot, plus if the caretaker will make the lift available to us to get the goods downstairs, I said. Luckily I found the caretaker who was helpful about closing the lift for our use.

The next job to do was to find out how to dismantle the train set. I decided to leave that till everything was out of the flat. At home I began to worry. Since everything was fixed down, I thought of taking the boards straight to the destructor but this wasn't feasible, as they would not go through the doors. The track had to be removed to get the boards out.

After we had cleared everything except the train set, I remembered I had once met a man socially who specialised in model trains. I rang him and we arranged to meet at the flat. Lo and behold, he said he was interested in the contents of the entire room and how much would I take? He even said he would dismantle and move the stuff himself.

'Well, it's not my field,' I said, 'But I'm open to offers.'

'How about £950 then.'

I don't know how I managed to keep a straight face and of course accepted the offer. I watched as he and one of his men dismantled everything, leaving the room empty. So much for the advice of the man whose hobby it was!

One time I was given the keys to assess the contents of a council bungalow in the Lower Manor area. I was told it was number two, but the keys didn't seem to fit. Eventually I got the door open and walked in to what I thought was an empty flat vacated by the deceased. But in the bedroom I was amazed to see a very old lady in bed. I beat a hasty retreat and drove to the nearest phone box. No, they said. I should have been at number four!

It wasn't the only time that they got their wires crossed. I was asked if I could look at a clearance in covered accommodation in Nether Edge and if possible move the contents that same day.

I was returning from a job with the lads so I didn't have a problem. They could get lunch while I viewed the contents and discussed the price. I asked about the key and was informed it was with the caretaker who was going on holiday that evening, which was why it had to be cleared right away.

The caretaker would show me the flat, so I didn't even need the number though I was told it was number 11. I rang the bell of the caretaker's home, produced a card and said Social Services had sent me. He said he was expecting me and would take me to the flat in question. I duly followed him and he reminded me it had to be moved that day.

There was not a lot of furniture or sundries but it was a long carry to the van. I asked if there was anywhere closer to the flat to park since the flat was on the second floor and we would need to use the lift.

He said the lift wouldn't be necessary, showing me a back door to the lawn where he suggested we park. He then told me to leave any bags of rubbish just inside the front door and he would keep the key because he wouldn't be around after we'd finished. We could use the back door of the flat, which was self-locking, and take the goods across the lawn.

The contents were loaded and went straight to the market the next day. Everything was either sold or scrapped in two days. On the Tuesday morning I received a phone call from Social Services asking which flat had I moved on the Friday. I said, 'The one the caretaker showed me.'

'You moved number seven and it was supposed to be number 11.'

Apparently the person whose flat I moved had been in hospital. He came out to find all his possessions gone! Imagine the shock the poor fellow had.

Later that day I received a further phone call from the housing manager asking for my explanation of the events. I was also asked if I could now move the right flat – number 11 – as soon as possible which we did the next day.

I did ask what had happened to the caretaker and the poor man who had found his flat empty; I can't imagine what went through the man's mind, but I never received a reply to either of my questions but more importantly it didn't spoil my relationship with Social Services.

One unusual clearance was the Sheffield synagogue which was moving to a new building adjacent to the banqueting suite or communal hall. Most of the useful items were either staying with the old building or being moved to the new home. However the Bima[4], from where the Cantor led the service, plus the lecterns, cupboards, a large table, a three-door wardrobe and a large quantity of bentwood chairs were surplus.

The Bima was the big problem since it had been dismantled by the caretaker who dumped everything on the floor in no particular order.

It was a real jigsaw, impossible to reassemble and thus difficult to sell. I did have a photograph of it assembled but most were from weddings.

I decided Newark was the only place it might sell. Moving it was easy but took time because of the number of pieces. The wardrobe split into five sections, which again took time. The large table was nearly impossible to move, since it was in a room adjacent to the ladies' gallery. We managed however to lower it down on ropes over the banister, a little dangerous but successful.

I was also asked to move some 250 large armchairs from the hall adjacent to the new synagogue. These were not up to the fire safety standard since they had upholstered seats and backs and wouldn't stack. They had a place to put books under the seat and the back of each chair had a lift-up shelf to put a prayer book on.

I had to hire a 7.5 ton van to take them to the warehouse. Stacking them proved a nightmare. They took up most of the space and the only time we were able to collect them was a Sunday which meant double time for the lads.

The Bima, wardrobe, large table, plus a small number of the chairs went to Newark along with two marble pillars and the bentwood chairs. I dread to think what the labour cost was in moving everything.

The marble pillars were sold immediately they were unloaded, with more than one customer interested. But again to get them on and off the 7.5 tonner wasn't easy and the lads weren't best pleased. The wardrobe and large boardroom table sold too but it was a case of getting rid quickly.

The perfect bentwoods sold quite quickly but not to one customer. The damaged ones proved harder to sell, the slightest damage meant they were rejected and had to

---

[4] *An area in the centre of the main synagogue which had seats and a reader's desk where the Cantor stood when leading the service.*

be sold later for a much-reduced price. The armchairs, I had a sign made asking for offers for 250, we had taken 15 as a sample, but to little effect. The Bima, we had the photo to show anyone who looked at our large jigsaw puzzle.

Suddenly an Arab, of all people, made an offer which I accepted. He collected it later that day but insisted on taking the photo. Philip did ask what he was going to do with it. In his broken English reply we deciphered, he hoped to sell it when he got back to his home in Tunisia.

We had no enquiries for the chairs on the first day but lunchtime on the second day an Italian dealer had a good look at them and Philip talked him into buying the lot.

I informed him they would have to be collected by a large van and explained we had used a 7.5 tonner to move them. He was going to collect them the following Thursday when we would count them and hopefully get paid.

It was hard to get him to take the 15 with him but he did. He was exporting them to Italy so he said he was worried about the fire regulations. Philip spotted the man who bought the Bima at the next fair and asked how he had gone on with it. He replied he had sold it to a Jewish man for a synagogue in Tunisia.

I was worried he would complain it wasn't all there, but he didn't, so it went to a Jewish home via an Arab. This again wasn't one of my better deals but you can't win them all.

35

Profit in pictures

I received a phone call from a lady in London asking if I would clear her father's house in Ecclesall Road South, Sheffield. I knew the family well and certainly would be interested. I said I would look and report back to her.

Her father had moved to London, to be near his daughter. She informed me that what was left was rubbish and probably needed destroying.

The key was with her father's housekeeper who would meet me at the house. Everything had been put out for me to inspect. The attic had been emptied, plus the kitchen cupboards and drawers. Every spare space in the large detached house had been used to lay out everything – books, crockery, children's toys, clothes, bedding and linen. A quick look and I realised that I could see a picking, plus interesting items and of course plenty of rubbish. I phoned the daughter and said I didn't have a problem clearing the premises but it would be easier if we could have a skip in the drive for the destructor.

This wasn't a problem as the housekeeper could arrange this and pay for it. This was another bonus because skips are not cheap and they usually insisted on cash on delivery, which meant meeting them at the house and waiting for the delivery.

I then asked about the key and was informed the housekeeper would meet me at the premises whenever I wanted. Two of the bedrooms were full of old games, all still in their original boxes. I was worried that pieces would be missing but you could tell by the pictures they were old.

Since the gentleman who had lived there was a very orthodox Jewish man, his office, which I had visited on several occasions, was full of either Jewish prayer books or Judaic subjects. I wasn't certain they would sell. The prayer books I would return to the synagogue, but the rest I was worried would be unsaleable.

Philip usually accompanied me on all the large jobs ensuring I always had a second opinion, plus he could supervise the lads while I sorted goods into the different categories.

Philip suggested the books could all go to Newark, along with the games, clothing and some of the kitchenware. He explained that there were always Hasidic Jews who attended the fair and maybe they would be interested.

Others I sorted for Sheffield and Doncaster, plus plenty for the skips. I was amazed how long it took to move but the housekeeper was always in attendance. The garage housed an old Jaguar, which was immaculate. I inquired about this but was told it had been gifted to the chauffeur-cum-handy man.

At Newark I was again amazed at the interest in the games and the Judaic books. After selling quite a few we had a visit from a Hasidic Jewish man who was annoyed we'd sold some before his arrival. He picked out a lot of books and some of the games that were of Judaic interest.

The bartering took ages but I stood by what Philip had priced them at and managed to get the money in the end.

After he left we received a visit from a book dealer who occasionally bought from us who was also annoyed we hadn't sent for him to look at the books before anyone else had seen them. He had a pitch at Newark and said Judaic books were good sellers.

I was quick to say, 'Well, make us an offer for what's left,' which he did and he took the lot.

I was quite pleased with our takings from the clearance though we had quite a lot of expense for labour, four people working more or less full time for two weeks, clearing every item. After completing the job the housekeeper said she had informed the daughter how efficient we had been.

I received I call from the daughter the next day asking why I hadn't sent a bill for the work in clearing the premises. I had informed her there would be no charge, but she insisted I send a bill for wages for the time involved. I stressed that her father had always been kind and helpful to me over the years in Sheffield. She was still adamant that they would pay the wages for the four of us because we had done such a wonderful job and the house could now be sold.

In the end I sent a bill for the four of us for two weeks work of £485, which was paid by return. This clearance turned out to be very profitable, with both parties satisfied.

The Hasidic man proved a pain afterwards, wanting to know if there were any more games or parts of games that had fallen out of the boxes or more books. Could he come to Sheffield himself to look at the warehouse?

I told him the house we cleared was unusual and probably the only one of its kind in our city. He still came and bought a few more books we had from other sources but insisted I should inform him of our next clearance of a Jewish household.

He then decided to catch the train to London. I took him to the station and Michael had to carry his large case of heavy books. It took longer for us to argue about how much the books were worth than his stay in Sheffield.

I did receive phone calls from him before every Newark fair to enquire if we had anything Judaic. Each time I informed him no and he finally got the message when I retired.

I was asked by John Walsh to look at a house in Huddersfield. The executor, who lived next door, would show us around.

She said, 'There's all these old coins, but I don't know what you can do with them.' I was amazed to see a collection of old English silver coins on the dining room table. Philip and I proceeded upstairs, the lady staying downstairs. He whispered, 'Did you clock the silver coins!'

A bedroom was full of home painted pictures, painted on boards, which I thought were horrible. Philip said, 'Peter will buy the coins, but the paintings need destroying.'

The garage was full of rubbish, but the lady offered to organise a skip − 'but promise me you won't put his paintings on the skip or destroy them. He was an art teacher, you know, and they were his pride and joy.'

We agreed and she allowed me to take some of the coins home for inspection. On our way back to Sheffield I discussed with Philip what we could do with the pictures. He quite rightly said, 'Let's think about it when we look at them as they are loaded on the van.'

I was amazed that the coins had been left for me to take away. Pre-1927 British coins were sterling silver and I soon learned in my call to Peter, the jeweller, that they were fetching ten times their face value, regardless of condition.

At the house I began sorting them into pound lots and suddenly it was well worth the exercise, even if we couldn't get rid of the pictures. We spent one day moving the rubbish into the skip and had a full load to bring back to Sheffield.

While clearing the garage Philip found a toy metal black train still in its box. On arriving back in Sheffield I contacted the model dealer who had bought the last train layout from me.

On the phone he offered £150 for it. I said I would have to consult the owner. Philip had said he would also speak with the toy dealer who bought the German teddy bear. Then we would decide what to do.

Incredibly, Philip phoned to say his man had offered £350 for the train. I can only assume my toy model dealer hadn't done very well with the train layout he had purchased from me and was trying to get some of his money back.

I did phone him back saying my customer believed it was worth at least double his offer. He was very nice and replied, 'You can't win them all.' Needless to say I accepted the toy dealer's offer.

Newark was six weeks later. Philip suggested we take some of the pictures to see if there was any interest. At first all the art dealers ignored them, then one man started examining each one. I had never seen this man before but he was making two piles. Philip was just as quick to spot him and casually said as he passed me, 'Leave him to me.'

This I did until Philip called me over and said, 'He's interested in the lot.'

I replied, 'Good, how much?' Philip gave me a figure which worked out at about £5 each. To me that was fantastic as I didn't expect them to sell in the first place and since the art dealers hadn't given them a second glance. I accepted his offer and added we have maybe three times as many at the warehouse. He asked where we were situated and when he was told Sheffield he said he wasn't that far away and could call the following Friday.

Knowing we were having an art dealer coming, the lads collected every painting we had in one area of the warehouse, including of course the art teacher's work. The expert carefully went through them one by one, picking out all the Huddersfield art and putting the rest aside. Pointing to the teacher's paintings, he said, 'I'm interested in these, how much will you take?'

I replied, 'You're the expert, make me an offer,' which he did. Philip meanwhile had counted the pictures and said, 'They're worth a little more.' I thought about it and picked a figure between the two, which he accepted. The lads loaded them in his car and we were both satisfied.

He did later tell Philip that one of the paintings he'd bought from us fetched £500 but I wasn't bothered. I did relate the story to John, the auctioneer, and he wasn't interested either.

Our business was forced to move again when a new owner of the site got planning permission to build flats. We spent weeks trying to find suitable premises. In the end I acquired a warehouse in Buttermere Road, off Abbeydale Road, near the bottom of Woodseats Road.

It wasn't as large as I would have liked and was considerably more than we'd been paying, plus rates which were included in the old warehouse. Dad had one premises during his working life which spanned 59 years. I occupied six premises in my 41 years in the junk business.

I was still buying quite a number of house clearances but my Wakefield contact slowly dried up. I couldn't work out why, but someone must have taken over this assignment. This left a hole in my work but with my Sheffield contacts intact I was kept busy.

I received a phone call from one of Irvine's friends, Brian, who was moving to a smaller house. His four children were all grown up and had their pick of what he wasn't taking to the smaller house.

The lads began the task of moving items from the garden sheds etc, and then moved into the house.

One item was a dishwasher. I have never managed to actually to sell one, it is impossible to show them working, plus my customers just don't use them. I was then asked if I would like a coffee while the lads disconnected it from the water supply.

As the machine was put on the wheelbarrow to take to the van we heard a rattle from inside. I stopped the lads and asked if they'd put the water pipes inside it but these were tied around the back. I decided to look inside and discovered a number of pots from an expensive dinner service. They were removed and returned to the grateful owner.

My coffee was then brought to me. Yes, a cold black coffee. Since I never drink very hot drinks, especially black coffee, I wasn't particularly bothered but the kettle had never been boiled. Yes, these things happen to me. Brian had been so busy watching what the lads were moving he'd forgotten to switch the kettle on then poured the cold water into the cup.

36

My children's weddings

There are few occasions in life that are so joyful as your child's wedding and that was certainly how we felt on 27th June 1999 when our son Simon tied the knot with Lisa. They had problems finding a venue since the synagogue in Wilson Road was due to close and the new one wouldn't be ready until the end of July.

It was mooted at one stage they go to Israel, but that didn't materialise. Lisa was adamant she didn't want to marry in her home city of Manchester. In the end the Rabbi suggested that the ceremony be held in our garden, which everyone thought was a good idea. A dinner was planned for nearby Kingfield Hall.

Rather like the movie Father of the Bride, this meant our garden was to be transformed into a place fit for a princess, or so Anne and I decided. We bought carpet for the bride to walk down and for the ceremony itself.

Plus we had some 24 stands to use on either side of walkway. They were around two-and-a-half feet high, and already in the warehouse. They were intended to hold candles but the florist used them for sunflowers, the bride's favourite.

Anne decided a rope would look nice to connect the holders, some 25 metres. This alone cost £125, the most expensive rope I've ever purchased and unusable after the wedding.

One of my friends, Ken, gifted old railway sleepers to provide steps to the dais. Luckily over the years I had collected some hundred plastic chairs and I had the lads clean these ready for the big day. They also had to pick up the dais, carpet and canopy[5] under which the ceremony would take place.

Our own gardeners said they couldn't achieve the look we required and suggested a specialist. He certainly wasn't cheap, but by the Friday the garden looked magnificent.

[5] *A Jewish custom called a Chupa*

Most of the out of town guests stayed at the Marriott Hotel, near Kingfield Hall but about ten minutes from our house. My mother-in-law stayed with us, along with Lisa, the bride.

On the Saturday, the day before the wedding, after a service in the synagogue, we had lunch and tea in the garden with people popping in and admiring the work that had been put in. At 11pm I had spent an hour watering the plants and they certainly needed it. We had beautiful sunshine all day.

Alas, on the day of the wedding we awoke to drizzle. Irvine and Philip decided our Newark tents should be erected to provide extra shelter. Neighbours from both sides came to help.

I had arranged that the school car park could be used by our guests, Harold Needham providing notices informing them of this. All the neighbours had been notified what was happening, and nothing was left to chance.

The caterer commandeered the garage to prepare the food and we hired bar staff to serve drinks. We even had a quartet welcome the guests and play during the reception.

Everything was taken care of. Except for the weather. Just after 2pm, the heavens opened. We were only short of Noah and his ark. Millhouses Lane was like a river. Simon arrived from the hotel with his best man and one of his groomsmen, but couldn't go into the house. The old superstition the bridegroom can't see the bride until the wedding was well kept by our Simon.

Some guests had braved the weather and were sitting in the tents with a rendition of 'Singing in the Rain.'

So we took up residence in the garage. I reluctantly agreed the reception be moved to Kingfield Hall. The Rabbi and Cantor arrived and joined us in the garage. Here I kept surplus stock of my own booze, plus boxes of glasses that we had kept for parties. The whiskey took a bashing, I was almost as drunk as on my own wedding day. Everyone but Simon partook, as he, again according to Jewish custom, was fasting until after the wedding ceremony.

Lynda, my sister-in-law, took the flowers to the Wilson Road synagogue which fortunately was still operational because the new building was behind schedule. So instead of the ceremony taking place in what was now our very expensive garden it took place in the synagogue.

The canopy that was to be used in the garden was soaking wet so a large prayer shawl was used with the six groomsmen taking it in turns to hold the four corners. Except for no one realising we hadn't a car to take Anne and myself to the reception everything else went off fine, including the weather. By 5pm it was beautiful and the garden magnificent. Another very expensive mistake.

Simon's wedding day: Part of the gardens at 5 o'clock after the rain had finally stopped

One of the great landmarks in my lifetime was the passing of the millennium and the whole family decided to spend it in Eilat, Israel. Simon came with his wife Lisa and brought Anne's mother.

Unexpectedly Lisa, my daughter, came with her fiancé Nathan. Lisa and Nathan got married in April that year. I certainly wasn't about to repeat Simon and Lisa's expensive exercise, but decided to buy a new canopy for the couple to get married under. I decided while in Israel to have one made there, another expensive mistake.

When it arrived it wasn't fit for use and it was sent back. Luckily we had just time to have one made in Manchester, which is still in use over ten years later.

Our Lisa, as we call my daughter to distinguish her from my daughter-in-law, who is known as Little Lisa, bought a house in Radlett, Hertfordshire with her husband Nathan.

I had been asked to value furniture in my best friend Brian's home since he was getting divorced. The most expensive item I valued was the dining room suite. It consisted of a table, with an extra leaf, eight chairs, a sideboard, a server, plus a cocktail cabinet. This we took to Doncaster and Newark and dealers viewed it in the warehouse, but it didn't sell. I did have an offer for the server and cocktail cabinet but not the rest. I didn't accept this since they would help to sell the rest I thought.

However, an America dealer asked the price of the sideboard. Since they were always hard to dispose of, I decided to sell it. I was surprised to get a reasonable price but the rest seemed impossible.

On visiting our Lisa's home I noticed they were using a wooden garden table in the dining room, a gift from Nathan's parents. I suggested that the walnut suite from

The canopy on Lisa's wedding day

Brian's would look nice. Nathan and Lisa hired a van and collected it along with five wooden chairs we had given them that I had bought some years before.

They still have the suite, although the table has to be supported by two trestles. The garden table, plus the five wooden garden chairs, are still in use and in perfect condition. This meant I didn't make anything on either deal.

Around this time one of the solicitors whom I occasionally did business with was moving out of a large house into a flat and asked if I would move some effects they didn't want.

The best items were some modern prints. These again I gave to our Lisa and they looked very nice in her home. Some months later, the solicitor asked if he could have the prints back, as one of his children wanted them for their new home.

I said I hadn't got them but he was insistent that I was only storing them for him, which I had no recollection of. I certainly didn't want to fall out with him so I had to phone Lisa and ask for them back.

I did feel I had to make it up to Lisa and Nathan at some time. I did see two Gosh prints at Swinderby which weren't cheap, but after discussion with Anne, I bought them to replace the prints Lisa and Nathan had returned.

I did however make up my loss when this solicitor's mother moved into a flat. I was asked to move what his mother, sister and he didn't want. Most that was left needed to go to the destructor except a very nice dining suite that I sold to a dealer without it having to be taken anywhere.

The only problem I had was one of the lads hadn't turned in for work so I had to hire a driver to help Michael because the dining room suite was far too heavy for me to carry and it needed bringing down stairs.

Having had major heart surgery, I now had to have a new knee fitted. I'd been complaining about the pain in my knee for several years but one doctor said it wasn't worth having a knee replacement since I only had ten years left to live. Charming!

Anne wanted to report him but I didn't think it was worth it. Simon said I should take no notice. Nobody could predict anyone's lifespan. Eventually I saw a specialist privately under my health plan. This man treated Sheffield's footballers – not a very good recommendation judging by where the city's two teams were in the league!

I had an unsuccessful operation designed to remove some floating bits from the knee joint and I eventually had a replacement under local anaesthetic. I was awake during the whole operation and didn't feel a thing.

Not long after the 'op' a friend asked me if I could buy and dispose of some furniture from his mother-in-law's home. I wasn't driving and Anne took me, with the van following.

On arriving at the house I attempted to get out of the car but my right leg just wouldn't support me. I feared the worst but after a few minutes I was able to walk.

I had recommended that anything that had value should go to John's auction sale in Wakefield. The two daughters had their pick first, then John received I believe mainly silver, but I left him to look and take whatever he thought he could sell.

I just moved the junk that was left and believe me there was plenty of that, boxes full. I did pick one picture out, an oil painting of a ship, which reminded me of the antique dealer saying, 'Another bloody ship.' I gave this to Lisa and Nathan.

Unfortunately they were not satisfied with the amount I paid them and I believe John had the same belief. The family were quite wealthy but these types are never satisfied. On my return to Sheffield I made an appointment to see the specialist about my knee and I was reassured it was fine and that maybe cramp caused the problem.

37

People require my expertise without payment

Newark was an experience that will remain in my memory for ever. I can't believe what we sold, especially paper. Postcards, magazines, comics, theatre, boxing, cricket programmes, plus bills, receipts, letters, yes most types of paper all created interest and money.

In the late seventies I had sold some Sheffield Wednesday pre-war programmes for £250. I wished I had them at Newark in the nineties!

Old football programmes hold their value. Once in a cupboard in Parsons Cross I found a box full of Sheffield Wednesday programmes, including when they played Manchester United in the first game after the Munich disaster.

Unfortunately, the Manchester team had been filled in with a biro, otherwise it would have been among the most valuable football programme ever. I still did very well out of the box.

When we ourselves moved home, I was about to throw away Simon's more recent Wednesday programmes. Philip and Michael were helping to clear his room which he hadn't used for 16 years. Simon said I was to pick out what I thought he may want and get rid of the rest. I had three piles, one to be sold, one to be destroyed and one to keep for Simon.

Philip looked through the scrapped pile, which included modern Sheffield Wednesday programmes. I'm pleased he did because a customer we had at Newark came from Liverpool to look at them and bought some for £300. I asked Simon if he wanted the money but he said, 'Dad you gave the old ones to me. They're yours and so is the money.'

Some customers stay in your mind for different reasons. One lady employed other young ladies to demonstrate and give away goods in supermarkets. She was the lady who gave me the Outspan paper bags I mentioned in the first chapter.

She asked me if I knew a chemist and giving her an affirmative reply, she said she would bring something to my home. Sure enough a few days later the lady arrived with four cartons of some form of gum that helped people to stop smoking.

I phoned a friend in Nottingham who had chemist shops and he said he would gladly buy them from me. Anne arranged to meet him on the motorway and the goods were transferred. The woman often had goods she promoted and free samples. At the end of the promotion she would be left with goods in her garage which meant that her car was left outside overnight which she didn't like doing as she usually had goods for the next promotion in her car and this would mean emptying the car every night.

I even bought perfume from another source – a chemist's son. His father went on to become managing director of a large group of shops but his son wasn't so savvy. He sold the scent far too cheaply and it sold easily.

Since I sold it to a person who wasn't three miles away I wondered why the person who sold the goods to me didn't do this himself. I did say he just wasn't cut out to be a businessman and this proved my point. He did start a business to sell first aid kits to business premises but I personally didn't see a future in this and I don't believe it lasted very long.

I was constantly asked either to collect goods with the van or to lend people items from the shop or warehouse. The theatres or local dramatic societies were never refused and no charge was made.

I was however, asked if I would loan fridges to acquaintances that were having parties to which I was not invited. This I didn't mind, but it meant two men and the van had to deliver and bring back the items. I was never given or received anything for this. It would have been nice to be asked how much I charged for the favour.

One person asked if he could borrow five tables, plus 50 chairs. I agreed, pointing out they would be plastic tables and chairs used in my garden.

They had to be delivered and collected by our van and lads. Dates were arranged and I was informed that the gardener would be there to receive them. The day arrived but unfortunately my driver didn't turn up for work, so this meant I had to drive. Michael loaded the van and I drove to the bungalow. On arriving we waited for the gardener to appear. Michael unloaded the items onto the tailboard.

The gardener appeared and I told him we had been asked to bring the items, would he help to unload and put them were they had to go?

I was informed that we needed to clean them and then put them in the bungalow. I couldn't believe what I had heard, so I phoned the person who had asked to loan them informing him of the unhelpful gardener. His reply was, 'What do you expect from a Polish man.'

I put the phone down and told Michael to put the tables and chairs on the drive and left. The lads collected the items a few days later but I was never asked how much I was owed. After this episode I always insisted on a donation to charity.

One of my friends asked if I could recommend a possible buyer for his antique table and 12 chairs which were too big for his flat. I said I would look at it and decide if I knew anyone.

The table I had seen before but it was a long time ago and my recollections were vague. The table was obviously too large for the room. I informed the couple that I would phone an auctioneer in Wakefield and see if he would be interested. I rang him while I was there, informing him about the table and chairs, which in my opinion were reproduction. And the table, though it seated 12, was extremely narrow.

John asked if I could send a photograph to help him to decide. I reported my conversation to the couple; the husband said he would send the photograph by email himself. This I believed ended my involvement.

John phoned me and said he had spoken to the husband about the table and chairs but didn't believe they would fetch the money they required to buy a new replacement. I said I wasn't surprised. The table was about a plank wide and not very saleable though the chairs might sell.

Months later my gardener, who did my maintenance, though he had a very large tree felling and pruning business, asked if I ever came across a large table and chairs would I let him know. I never gave the large table and 12 chairs another thought until I bumped into the gentleman who was trying to sell them. I inquired if they were still for sale as I had been asked about a large table that would seat at least ten people. I was informed it was.

I contacted the gardener and told him I knew where there was a large table and 12 chairs and would he like to see them?

He asked me to make an appointment and take him to view them. I went with the gardener and he was interested. I keep out of the way but suddenly I was asked if I believed they were worth the asking price of £3,500. All I could say was, "if you like it and can afford it, if the answer is yes, then it's up to you".

The gardener bought the suite and asked me to deliver it to his home in Dronfield. I gave my stock reply, 'We don't do deliveries, we are not insured for that,' and recommended a removal firm. The gardener then said he would treat the boys and pay me any diesel money. I reluctantly agreed. I was petrified the lads might damage it, so I accompanied them making sure every piece was wrapped.

The table just fitted on the van with chairs placed under and round it.

Getting it out of the flat had not been difficult; it went out through a French window. Getting it in at the other end was different. Luckily the hall itself was large and very open plan displaying two floors. The lads tried every way to get the table into the dining room with little success. I suggested one end should be raised, making sure not to touch the large chandelier, while the other end kept as low as possible almost touching the floor.

It took time, but I was very relieved to see it installed in its new surroundings and it certainly looked nice. The lads had earned their £10 each.

After a few days I was asked how much I wanted for my introduction, and sale of their table and 12 chairs. My answer was nothing, but a week later I received 12 bottles of red and the same of white wine, which was very thoughtful and I was very grateful.

A few years later the gardener informed me he was getting divorced and had furniture he needed to dispose of, would I advise him the best way to go about it. He had an Edwardian bedroom suite and an odd Edwardian robe, plus the dining room suite. I told him I couldn't see him getting his money back for his dining suite but would look at the other items.

After viewing them I realised that the Edwardian furniture would be ideal for Newark, but I wouldn't be interested in his dining suite. I arranged to pick up the furniture in a month and take it directly to Newark. On arriving to collect the furniture they was no one in, but after a phone call the gardener arrived to inform me he had sold the dining suite on the internet to an antique dealer who had also bought the Edwardian furniture. Another wasted journey.

I was often asked by friends and customers to value single items which I was loath to do. Brother Irvine, when he overheard people asking me to undertake this, would say, 'Am I buying or selling?' which were two different valuations. Then there is an insurance valuation, plus a probate one, two more.

The most important one is a sentimental valuation which is impossible to equate. I always think of mother's baby's bootee which was impossible to replace. Maybe the one criterion few take into account, 'is there a willing seller and buyer', without those two, or one of the two, there is no valuation at all.

Yes, where possible, I always declined to do valuations but recommended professional people who would undertake the task and who charged a fee which I wouldn't have been offered.

Some people just want free advice. Other people objected to me making money on any deal involving them, this just wasn't acceptable. All they required were my contacts and expertise without my involvement. I have even been accused of making money out of other people's misfortunes, since I dealt in deceased estates, fire salvages and bankrupt stocks.

After my retirement, I was asked by a friend, if I could recommend anyone who would buy books that were all about India. I was informed there was a large quantity on all forms of Indian culture, people and the country. I first suggested auction, but this wasn't accepted. I said I would be quite willing to look at them myself and then advise the best course of action. I was informed that wouldn't be necessary as they were in London and belonged to a cousin who had died and they were trying to sort out his effects and dispose of them. I suddenly remembered the book dealer who had bought the remaining Judaic books at Newark.

I managed, with Philip's assistance, to find his phone number, since I couldn't remember his name. Philip has an old notebook with everybody's name in it that he had ever met or phoned. I compared these with Anne's business cards she had kept from customers during our time at Doncaster, Swinderby and Newark. By a process of elimination I decided on the book dealer I needed to phone.

On phoning him and after a chat realised I had the right man. I asked if he would be interested in a large quantity of books on India. He said he would be pleased to look at them and if possible buy them. I phoned the people informing them that I had a man who was interested in the books and would be willing to look at them in London. I also added that if I was needed to go with him to introduce them and see the deal was satisfactory I was quite willing to do so, as I could combine this with seeing my daughter, son and their families. I was told this wasn't necessary and if I give them the phone number they would contact him direct. I said I believed he lived near Nottingham but his business often took him to London. I therefore gave the number of the book dealer to the people and left them to it.

Months later I received a phone call from them which asked if I had seen the book dealer recently. Since I no longer went to Newark or indeed worked I hadn't. I did ask why and was told the dealer had moved the books but hadn't paid for them but said they would be placed in an auction sale and he would settle with them after the sale. They hadn't heard from him and the auction room said they couldn't supply them with any details of the sale or the book dealer's details. This to me was strange but I couldn't help either. The phone number I gave them was the only thing I had and this was now unobtainable but I told them I would ask Philip to keep his eye open for him.

To this day I have no idea what happened. In some ways I would have liked to have seen the books myself and the rest of the effects, but in others I am pleased I wasn't involved. I am sure if I'd have been and seen them there would have been a different outcome. Some people always know better and object too anyone else making a living. My father always said, 'You should never begrudge someone else making a profit, providing it's a fair one and you are satisfied with your profit'.

In 2006 my friend Harold Needham died, on 4th July . He had a heart attack and never recovered. His widow Caroline asked me to give the eulogy, something I have never done before or since, but it was an honour.

The weekend before the funeral Anne and I were going to Cornwall to a Masonic Mark Charity Festival. We had also decided to go and visit Michael Haigh who had retired to Devon. We arranged to spend Monday with them in Devon and travel back from there on the Tuesday.

In Cornwall we had been out for a meal with friends and decided to walk back to the hotel. Climbing a hill I had an angina attack for the first time for 20 years. I stood still until the attack was over and then continued back to the hotel.

A couple of days later I took the dog for a walk and had another attack. I decided to go to the doctors and because of my history I was advised to go to hospital to be admitted. I was released four days later since nothing seemed to be wrong. I was pleased to return home but worried because experience told me something brought on the attacks.

I visited my doctor who wasn't satisfied with the report he had received since the people who had examined me were diabetic specialists, not cardiac. I received an appointment to see a registrar at the Hallamshire Hospital who said I didn't have a problem.

I went to see a specialist privately some four hours later. He examined me and thought one of my bypasses had closed up but I would need an angiogram to determine which. The angiogram revealed the problem was a different artery that could be put right with a stent. This was carried out at Nottingham successfully.

However, the medics discovered something showing in my aorta and I would have to see a specialist in that field.

We were due to go to a wedding in America but the specialist confirmed a problem with the aorta and organised a CT scan. I cancelled my trip to Washington and had an operation to isolate the two aneurisms with stents. This needs checking every year.

I was slowly returning to full health assisted by exercise and walking. I started to take the dog out more first with Anne, returning when I had reached my limit, or waiting in the park café while they both completed the walk.

As my confidence and health improved I began to do this walk on my own, slowly, plus the dog each day, but increasing the distance. For a change of scenery I ventured into the woods slowly walking round and then back home. As I reached the edge of the woods I called my dog and put him back on his lead.

I noticed a man on two sticks, plus a lady with a Zimmer frame chatting to each other. Crossing the road, I took the dog off the lead and allowed him to wander about on the path. As we reached the end of it, I put the dog back on his lead. As I stood up the lady said, 'Excuse me sir, but you're the first person I've ever overtaken since I was forced to use this frame.' I was speechless! Returning home, I began to laugh telling Anne of the experience.

Both specialists recommended I give up work. This I decided to do, retiring in January 2007. I hadn't really worked since the first operation in 2006 and I wasn't going to continue after January. Everyone accepted my decision, except the market rent collector who said I had to give them notice. However, one of the other members of the superintendents' office popped down and said it would be all right.

That was it, after almost 50 years association with Sheffield Market and over a 100 years family association.

Holiday memories with my children and grandchildren.
Back row (L-R): Nathan, Simon, Samuel, Rafael, Isaac, Louie, 'Little' Lisa, 'Our' Lisa
Front (L-R): Harry and Max

38

The people I did and didn't meet

I enjoyed my working life, but I do wish I could have met some of the people whose possessions I bought after their death. Impossible, of course, but most I'm sure would have had very interesting lives. I also wish I'd have listened to my own mother and father more, because they knew more about my business, the junk business, than me.

We never have time to listen to our elders and they have more wisdom, experience and knowledge than us. I believe it was George Bernard Shaw who said, 'It's a pity infants don't get as much pleasure out of infancy as adults do out of adultery.'

Retirement allowed me time to do other things, including more talks and increasing my duties with the synagogue and the Freemasons.

I did do one favour out of loyalty to an old contact. Two years after retiring I received a phone call from a lady who used to be the head of the social workers at a Sheffield hospital. She was almost 90 and was moving to be near her nephew.

She asked if I could arrange to dispose of the possessions she was leaving behind since I'd been good in helping the patients in her charge. She must have been retired for more than 25 years, yet she remembered me – a testament, I felt, to the high regard she had for my work.

Since I knew her, and how she had looked after her younger brother who was slightly backward, I said I would take care of everything.

The main items were in the cellar, kitchen and basement, the best being a Globe Wernicke antique bookcase which I was pleased to see as I could find a dealer to buy this, or just move everything for this one item.

To save time I decided to take it to pieces. Each section was separate with its own glass door and stacked on a base with a pelmet on top. The top just fell to pieces, the back being rotted by years of damp. This meant I was extremely careful with the next section that had a glass door.

Unfortunately every section was the same so it took three of us just to dismantle these but we did without breaking any glass. The dealer said he would make new sides and backs but I never found out if he did.

Philip claimed a framed Sheffield print, plus some items for Newark, luggage, tea-trolley etc that would fit in the car. We also found someone to move the scrap iron. Philip fetched Michael and burned the rest in the large garden, almost setting the hedge on fire.

In the September of my years I have slowly moved out of Irvine's shadow. After he was elected to the city council I always seemed to be introduced as 'councillor Patnick's brother.'

Even the Labour leader of the council once rose from his seat next to the Lord Mayor and walked down the chamber to say, 'You must be Irvine's brother. I'm Ron Ironmonger.' Then he returned to his seat.

In 1987 when he was elected to Parliament I became 'Our MP's brother,' and when he was made a Knight of the Realm, 'Sir Irvine's brother.'

I visited Irvine quite often on my frequent visits to London, enjoying lunch on the Commons Terrace with views of the Thames, before going to Mark Grand Lodge. Again, I was greeted with 'you must be Irvine's brother,' by an usher who showed me to Irvine's office. I was introduced to MPs and Cabinet Ministers, many of whom, seeing how I was dressed, asking, 'Which lodge do you belong?'

One of these was Sir Marcus Fox and I took great delight in saying, 'I visited your lodge last week.' His reply was, 'I haven't been for over 20 years.'

Anne and I took our daughter Lisa to a Royal Garden Party and saw the other side of Buckingham Palace, walking through the Palace to the magnificent gardens and seeing most of the Royal family, including Princess Diana who was surrounded by hundreds of people. The rest of the Royals passed round the garden occasionally stopping to speak with guests.

By 2008 people had just about started calling me Edward and at last I was a person in my own right. However in May of that year my son, Simon decided to stand as a candidate for Hertsmere Council.

I was unable to help or attend on the day of the election; as usual I had Masonic duties. That day I attended Supreme Grand Chapter, in London, in the morning and then talked to a Chapter in West Lancashire in the evening. Simon was quite used to me being unavailable.

As I explained earlier, even on the day he was born I was being initiated into freemasonry. However, I caught a train back to London at 6am so I could attend the count on the Friday and see Simon duly elected.

From that day I have always been introduced as 'Councillor Patnick's father.'

In May, 2011, I was honoured to be elected President of the Sheffield Jewish Congregation. A chance for people to then go up to Irvine and say, 'You must be the president's brother' Or to Simon, 'You must be the president's son.'

One bonus of my career is the money I have raised telling people about my life as a junk dealer. I have raised over £23,000 for Tommy's, the baby charity, through the generosity of organisations and people. The charity was chosen because my daughter, Lisa, had a stillborn baby, Isaac, in 2002. Tommy's carry out essential research to try to prevent stillborn children, miscarriages and premature birth.

In recognition of my fundraising, I was invited by Tommy's to a reception at 11 Downing Street, along with Anne, which was hosted by the Chancellor of The Exchequer, George Osborne, who enquired about my involvement.

I explained about my daughter and that in 2004 Simon had run the London Marathon and raised over £6,000 and how I wondered what I could do to help. I certainly couldn't run a marathon but I could speak and this was what I had done for the last eight years.

Rt. Hon George Osborne M.P., Jane Brewer (Tommy's Chief Executive), the author and Anne (almost)

As the Chancellor was about to move on he said, 'You must be Irvine's brother. I wasn't very quick in picking that up, please give him my regards.'

My talks have taken me all over the country and I always ask for donations to Tommy's.

Once, I addressed the Jewish Friendship Club. I thought it would be easy, because all the people present would know me and I wouldn't have to explain any Jewish expressions. When I stated that my great grandfather and grandfather came from Estonia, I was startled that a lady on the front row said, 'Where's that?'

Believing she was deaf, I repeated Estonia three times. Each time the lady asked, 'Where's that?' Each time I said Estonia I repeated it louder. The lady then said, 'I'm not deaf, I wasn't born in Sheffield so I don't know where it is.'

Yes I have met all types even giving talks.

The author and Anne at Number 11 Downing Street after the reception hosted by Tommy's